McDougal Littell

Grammar
for Writing

McDougal Littell
A HOUGHTON MIFFLIN COMPANY

McDougal Littell

Grammar for Writing

- GRAMMAR
- USAGE
- MECHANICS

McDougal Littell

A HOUGHTON MIFFLIN COMPANY

ISBN 13: 978-0-618-56619-8   ISBN 10: 0-618-56619-8

Printed in the United States of America.

Acknowledgments begin on page 363.

   1 2 3 4 5 6 7 8 9—DCI—12 11 10 09 08 07

Contents Overview

Grammar, Usage, and Mechanics

3 Using Phrases   64

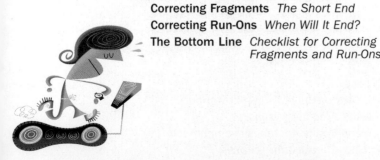

Quick-Fix Editing Machine

Special Features

Real World Grammar

Grammar in Literature

Quick-Fix Editing Machine

Student Resources

Grammar, Usage, and Mechanics

Reaching for the Sky

To achieve your dreams, you need to build them on a firm foundation. The tools of grammar give you the power to make your ideas clear and concise. Once you put your dreams into words, who knows what you can build in your life?

The Parts of Speech

Win tickets to see
JAVA
perform live
this Friday.

In 300 words or less, tell us why you think you should be the winner of the two tickets to see this Grammy-winning band.

Deadline: Tuesday, 12:00 midnight

Winners will be announced Friday morning on WGRE.

Theme: Making Music

Music to the Ears

You want to win tickets to see your favorite band perform, but how do you write an essay that will impress the judges? The first two criteria a judge will look for are originality and creativity. Your essay should stand out from all the other entries. Once you have an original, creative idea, the best way to write a winning essay is to choose nouns, verbs, adjectives, adverbs, and other parts of speech that will make your writing memorable and will dazzle the judges.

Write Away: And the Award Goes to . . .
In a short paragraph, write about your favorite musician or musical group. Explain why this person or group is better than anyone else. Save your paragraph in your ▭ ***Working Portfolio.***

Choose the letter of the term that correctly identifies each numbered item.

An extremely <u>unusual</u> blooper happened at the 100th anniversary
(1)
celebration of <u>The Chicago Symphony Orchestra</u> in 1991. Before the
(2)
concert, a dinner celebration was held <u>for special donors</u> who had paid $500
(3)
or more per person. As a token of <u>its</u> appreciation, the CSO gave the
(4)
sponsors a gift—a lovely desk clock with an alarm. Little did the staff know
that the alarm clocks had not been switched off and were <u>randomly</u> set to
(5)
go off at different times.

After intermission, the constant beeping <u>began</u>. When the disturbances
(6)
reached a peak, the conductor scornfully addressed his audience, but

<u>neither</u> he <u>nor</u> the audience knew that the noise came from the <u>nicely</u>
(7)   (7)   (8)
wrapped gifts instead of personal beepers. A staff <u>member</u> finally figured
(9)
out the problem, and the audience was asked to take the gifts to the lobby.

"<u>Wow</u>, this is one memorable evening," remarked one of the sponsors.
(10)

1. A. adjective
    B. noun
    C. verb
    D. proper noun

2. A. common noun
    B. prepositional phrase
    C. proper noun
    D. adjective

3. A. adverb
    B. noun
    C. interjection
    D. prepositional phrase

4. A. possessive pronoun
    B. preposition
    C. adverb
    D. linking verb

5. A. conjunction
    B. adverb
    C. verb
    D. common noun

6. A. conjunctive adverb
    B. pronoun
    C. verb
    D. preposition

7. A. conjunctions
    B. adverbs
    C. action verbs
    D. linking verbs

8. A. linking verb
    B. indefinite article
    C. pronoun
    D. adverb

9. A. common noun
    B. collective noun
    C. pronoun
    D. conjunction

10. A. conjunction
    B. preposition
    C. interjection
    D. adverb

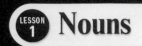

LESSON 1 Nouns

❶ Here's the Idea

▶ *A noun is a word that names a person, place, thing, or idea.*

Persons: George Solti, conductor, audience, musicians

Places: theater, Symphony Center

Things: instruments, chairs, podium, music stands

Ideas: inspiration, joy, cooperation, freedom

A **common noun** is a general name for a person, place, thing, or idea. Common nouns are usually not capitalized.

A **proper noun** is the name of a particular person, place, thing, or idea. A proper noun is always capitalized.

Common	guitarist, museum, lake, month
Proper	B.B. King, Rock and Roll Hall of Fame, Lake Pontchartrain, February

A **concrete noun** names an object that can be seen, heard, smelled, touched, or tasted.

An **abstract noun** names an idea, quality, or state.

Concrete	book, bell, flower, sand, apple
Abstract	independence, curiosity, pride, uncertainty, sadness

Nouns may take either a **singular** or **plural** form, depending on whether they name a single person, place, thing, or idea, or more than one.

Singular	stage, city, foot
Plural	stages, cities, feet

For more about spelling plural forms, see p. 341.

All nouns are either common or proper, concrete or abstract, and singular or plural. For example, *drummer* is a common, concrete, and singular noun. *West Indies* is proper, concrete, and plural.

A **collective noun** refers to a group of people or things. Examples include *audience, family, crowd,* and *staff.* A collective noun is singular in form. It can be used to refer to a group either as a single unit or as a number of individuals.

> **The crew** (unit) **prepares the stage for the concert.**

> **When will the crew** (individual) **test the equipment?**

A **compound noun** is made up of two or more words. It may be written as one word, as separate words, or as a hyphenated word.

Compound Nouns	
One word	airplane, sunlight, keyboard
Separate words	rain forest, parking lot, City Hall, Rocky Mountains
Hyphenated word	mother-in-law, runner-up, fade-out

A **possessive noun** shows ownership or relationship. An apostrophe is used with nouns to show possession.

Ownership	the singer's outfit
Relationship	the singer's aunt

❷ Why It Matters in Writing

Using proper nouns in place of common nouns often makes writing more realistic and specific. A proper noun can help you picture the person, place, or thing that is referred to in writing.

STUDENT MODEL

DRAFT

When I was ten years old, my mother enrolled me in a **piano class.** While I learned to play **songs** by a famous **composer,** my friends were outside enjoying the long, scorching days of our summer vacation.

REVISION

When I was ten years old, my mother enrolled me in **Mrs. Muffet's Piano School.** While I learned to play **Tchaikovsky's "March" from *The Nutcracker,*** my friends were outside enjoying the long, scorching days of our summer vacation.

➌ Practice and Apply

A. CONCEPT CHECK: *Identifying Nouns*

On your paper, write each noun. Identify it as common or proper, concrete or abstract, and singular or plural.

Preserving Rock's Legacy
1. The Rock and Roll Hall of Fame in Cleveland draws visitors from all over the world.
2. This unusual museum honors musicians for their creativity.
3. The building was designed by I. M. Pei, an architect famous for his strikingly modern designs.
4. Fans can spend days satisfying their curiosity by watching videos and listening to recordings.
5. The public can also view fascinating rock and roll artifacts.
6. One exhibit features the collarless jacket that John Lennon wore while performing with the Beatles.
7. Other famous performers whose costumes can be seen include Tina Turner and David Byrne.
8. A crowd usually gathers around the famous guitars.
9. One of these instruments belonged to Elvis Presley.
10. The guitar, a Martin D-18, was supplied by a private collector.

➡ **For a SELF-CHECK and more practice, see the EXERCISE BANK, p. 302.**

B. REVISING: *Using Nouns*

Each of the following sentences contains a common noun. Replace each underlined common noun with a proper noun of your own.

A Star Is Born
1. The public's fascination with the life of <u>the singer</u> continues to grow years after his death.
2. <u>The museum</u> promises to bring satisfaction to all of the fans of the singer.
3. Artifacts and memorabilia from early childhood in <u>the hometown</u> will be on display during the month of June.
4. A replica model of the <u>car</u> the singer drove in the movie *Crossroads* will also be included in the exhibits.
5. <u>A friend</u> thinks that this is the best display of an artist's life because it offers personal reflections from family and friends.

Look at your **Write Away** paragraph on page 4 or another draft in your 🗂 **Working Portfolio** and replace common nouns with proper nouns where necessary.

Personal and Possessive Pronouns

LESSON 2

❶ Here's the Idea

▶ **A pronoun is a word used in place of a noun or another pronoun.**
The word that a pronoun stands for is called its **antecedent**.

STANDS FOR

Ray said he wanted musical talents to audition for the play.
ANTECEDENT   PRONOUN

An antecedent can consist of more than one word, and it may appear in an earlier sentence.

STANDS FOR

Chiyo and I auditioned together. We both got lead parts.
   ANTECEDENT   PRONOUN

The forms of personal pronouns are shown in the chart below.

Personal Pronouns	Singular	Plural
First person	I, me (my, mine)	we, us (our, ours)
Second person	you (your, yours)	you (your, yours)
Third person	he, him, she, her, it (his, her, hers, its)	they, them (their, theirs)

Like possessive nouns, **possessive pronouns** show ownership or relationship. In the chart, possessive pronouns are in parentheses.

Sonia delivered her famous monologue.
   ANTECEDENT   PRONOUN

❷ Why It Matters in Writing

Pronouns replace unnecessary or repetitive nouns.

STUDENT MODEL

During a telephone conversation, the composer

Leonard Bernstein and the choreographer Jerome

Robbins came up with an idea that developed into

their
~~Bernstein's and Robbins's~~ hit musical *West Side Story.*
  ^

> Possessive pronoun helps to avoid repetition.

➌ Practice and Apply

A. CONCEPT CHECK: Personal and Possessive Pronouns

On your paper, write each pronoun and tell whether it is personal or possessive.

A Timeless Love Story

1. Bernstein and Robbins convinced the songwriter Stephen Sondheim and the writer Arthur Laurents to work with them.
2. At first, Laurents intended to follow Shakespeare's plot in *Romeo and Juliet* in every respect, but he later changed his mind.
3. The ending of *West Side Story* is slightly different from the ending of the famous tragedy on which it is based.
4. Like *Romeo and Juliet,* the modern play has a bitter feud and an unlikely romance at the center of its plot.
5. In Shakespeare's play, the foes are two feuding families, and in *West Side Story* they are two feuding street gangs.
6. Like Juliet, Maria in *West Side Story* falls in love with her family's enemy.
7. She remains loyal to him as the feud worsens.
8. Tony, the Romeo figure, tries to make peace between the two gangs, but his efforts backfire.
9. Both versions of the tragic story remain popular in our day.
10. Would you rather perform in a production of *West Side Story* or a production of *Romeo and Juliet?*

➜ **For a SELF-CHECK and more practice, see EXERCISE BANK, p. 302.**

B. REVISING: Using Pronouns

Replace any unnecessary or repetitive nouns with personal or possessive pronouns.

Grease Is the Word

In contrast to *West Side Story,* the musical *Grease* offers a light-hearted look at teenage life in the 1950s. The play's setting is Rydell High School, and the play's main characters are Danny Zuko and Sandy Olsson. Danny and Sandy, who shared a special summer romance, are quite surprised when Danny and Sandy find themselves attending the same school. The main obstacle is that Danny is a rebellious fifties-style "greaser," while Sandy seems hopelessly "square." Will the star-crossed teens find true love, or will the star-crossed teens' differences keep the star-crossed teens apart?

Other Kinds of Pronouns

LESSON 3

❶ Here's the Idea

Pronouns have many forms and serve different purposes in sentences.

Reflexive and Intensive Pronouns

Reflexive and intensive pronouns are formed by adding *-self* or *-selves* to forms of the personal pronouns.

Reflexive and Intensive Pronouns			
	First person	**Second person**	**Third person**
Singular	myself	yourself	himself, herself, itself
Plural	ourselves	yourselves	themselves

A **reflexive pronoun** reflects action back upon the subject and adds information to the sentence.

REFLECTS

Donna **prepared herself for a long day.**
  SUBJECT   PRONOUN

An **intensive pronoun** adds emphasis to a noun or pronoun in the same sentence.

EMPHASIZES

The wait **itself would take hours.**
  NOUN   PRONOUN

WATCH OUT

A reflexive pronoun must have an antecedent. A common error is to use a reflexive pronoun without an antecedent in the sentence.

me
The planning committee appointed Ted and ~~myself.~~

Demonstrative Pronouns

Demonstrative pronouns point out specific persons, places, things, or ideas. They allow you to indicate whether the things you are pointing out are relatively near in time or space or farther away. Demonstrative pronouns are *this, these, that,* and *those.*

The people at the front of the line will get better tickets than those at the end, she thought.

Indefinite Pronouns

An **indefinite pronoun** does not refer to a specific person, place, or thing. An indefinite pronoun usually does not have an antecedent.

Many of the fans had arrived at 6 A.M.

Indefinite Pronouns	
Singular	another, anybody, anything, each, either, everybody, everyone, everything, much, neither, nobody, no one, nothing, one, somebody, someone, something
Plural	both, few, many, several
Singular or plural	all, any, more, most, none, some

Some pronouns can also function as adjectives.

Several people had to wait in the rain. (adjective)

Several of the fans waited anxiously in line. (pronoun)

Interrogative and Relative Pronouns

An interrogative pronoun is used to ask a question.

What is your favorite song?
    ⬆ INTERROGATIVE PRONOUN

A relative pronoun is used to introduce subordinate clauses.

The seats that the students asked for were unavailable.
ANTECEDENT ⬆   ⬆ RELATIVE PRONOUN

Interrogative and Relative Pronouns	
Interrogative	who, whom, whose, which, what
Relative	who, whom, whose, which, that

For more on pronouns, see pp. 180–198.

❷ Why It Matters in Writing

Relative pronouns can be used to combine sentences.

> **STUDENT MODEL**
>
> **DRAFT**
>
>   The girl waited for someone to ask her to dance. She decided to ask a boy if he would like to dance with her.
>
> **REVISION**
>
>   The girl, **who** had been waiting for someone to ask her to dance, asked a boy if he would like to dance with her.

❸ Practice and Apply

A. CONCEPT CHECK: Other Kinds of Pronouns

Write each pronoun and identify its antecedent if it has one.

Tips on Tickets: The Experts' Advice

1. What is the best way to get good seats for a concert?
2. A long wait in line is an experience that concertgoers are likely to recognize.
3. Someone gets up before dawn in order to be first in line.
4. The seats that go with the tickets turn out to be real disappointments, however.
5. A frustrated fan might well ask himself or herself why this happens.
6. The best way to find out is to ask the ticket sellers themselves.
7. All agree that there is no special advantage to getting to the box office early.
8. Ticket agencies usually give out lottery numbers to determine the customers who get to buy tickets first.
9. As a result, people at the end of the line might get better seats than those at the front.
10. Nothing is more important than luck when people are trying to get good seats.

➡ For a SELF-CHECK and more practice, see the EXERCISE BANK, p. 303.

B. REVISING: Relative Pronouns

Combine the following sets of sentences using the relative pronouns in parentheses.

Life on the Road

1. A touring musician's life consists of late nights, fast-food meals, and uneasy rests on tour buses. A musician's life is less romantic than it may seem. (which)
2. Dressing room facilities are often shared by a group of people. Most dressing rooms are not always clean. (which)
3. The audience can vary their response from indifference to ecstasy. The audience's ages range from 16–50. (whose)
4. The music of opening acts may be at odds with your own taste. Some opening acts are unknown to the public. (that)
5. However, there is an energy in music. The music can stir your blood and start your heart pounding. (that)

Verbs

❶ Here's the Idea

▶ **A verb expresses an action, a condition, or a state of being.**
The two main types of verbs are action verbs and linking verbs.

Action Verbs

An **action verb** expresses action. The action may be physical or mental.

The band marches onto the field. (physical)

The audience expects a great performance. (mental)

When an action verb appears with a direct object (that is, a person or thing that receives the action), it is called a **transitive verb.** When an action verb does not have an object, it is called an **intransitive verb.**

Danny plays the trumpet like a professional.
‸TRANSITIVE VERB   ‸OBJECT

He travels around the country with the other musicians.
‸INTRANSITIVE VERB   (NO OBJECT)

Linking Verbs

A **linking verb** links the subject of a sentence to a word in the predicate. There are two groups of linking verbs: forms of *to be,* and verbs that express condition.

The instruments are safe in the bus.
‸LINKING VERB

The students seemed bored during the long trip.
‸LINKING VERB

Forms of *To Be*
is, am, are, was, were, been, being

Verbs that Express Condition
look, smell, feel, sound, taste,
grow, appear, become, seem, remain

Some verbs can be either action or linking verbs.

Verbs	
Action	**Linking**
We felt the seat cushions.	They felt dry.
We tasted the popcorn.	It tasted salty.

If you can substitute *is, are, was,* or *were* for a verb, you know it is a linking verb.

Auxiliary Verbs

Auxiliary verbs, also called **helping verbs**, are combined with verbs to form **verb phrases**. A verb phrase may be used to express a particular tense of a verb (that is, the time referred to) or to indicate that an action is directed at the subject.

The stadium is filled to capacity.
AUXILIARY↗ ↖MAIN

We should save a seat for Jeff.
AUXILIARY↗ ↖MAIN

Common Auxiliary Verbs				
be	have	might	shall	will
can	may	must	should	would

Some of these auxiliary verbs can also be used as main verbs. For example notice how *has* stands alone in the first sentence below and is a helping verb in the second sentence.

Sandra has a pair of Conga drums at home. (main)

She has practiced her drumming all summer. (auxiliary)

➋ Why It Matters in Writing

Action verbs can create a vivid, interesting picture of a scene. Notice how the verbs create a sense of action even as the character is standing still.

> **LITERARY MODEL**
>
> Hana Omiya **stood** at the railing of the small ship that **shuddered** toward America in a turbulent November sea. She **shivered** as she **pulled** the folds of her silk kimono close to her throat and **tightened** the wool shawl about her shoulders.
>
> —Yoshiko Uchida, *Picture Bride*

➌ Practice and Apply

CONCEPT CHECK: Verbs

Write the verbs or verb phrases in each sentence and identify each as an action or a linking verb. Underline any auxiliary verbs. There are 15 in all.

The Big Parade

(1) Every November, bands from across the country visit New York City for the big Thanksgiving Day parade. **(2.)** Even on cold days when strong winds or light rain might scare away spectators, the parade is on schedule. **(3)** The crowd lines the parade route and will stay until the last float has driven out of sight. **(4)** As bands strut down Broadway, drum majors pound their drums, members of color guards rhythmically wave their flags, and baton twirlers toss their batons into the air and catch them as they twirl downward to the ground. **(5)** Meanwhile, giant, colorful cartoon balloons like Betty Boop, Spiderman, and Bart Simpson, and other favorite characters are overhead. **(6)** For young children, the parade remains an eventful experience and becomes a fond memory in their adult lives.

➜ **For a SELF-CHECK and more practice, see the EXERCISE BANK, p. 303.**

Identify the transitive verbs and write the object of each one.

CHAPTER 1

Adjectives

LESSON 5

1 Here's the Idea

An **adjective** modifies or limits the meaning of a noun or pronoun.

MODIFIES   *MODIFIES*

We saw the famous singer at the legendary Carnegie Hall.
ADJECTIVE   **ADJECTIVE**

An adjective tells *what kind, which one, how many,* or *how much.*

Adjectives			
What Kind	**Which One**	**How Many**	**How Much**
famous song	**this** star	**one** dollar	**some** music
squeaky noise	**that** way	**three** tenors	**more** room
green light	**these** words	**several** years	**less** energy

Articles

The most common adjectives are the articles *a, an,* and *the. A* and *an* are **indefinite articles** that refer to one of a general group of people, places, things, or ideas. Use *a* before words beginning with consonant sounds. Use *an* before words beginning with vowel sounds. *The* is the **definite article** that usually refers to a specific person, place, thing, or idea.

Articles	
Indefinite	**Definite**
A student volunteered.	The teacher arrived.
Jessie brought an itinerary.	Phil borrowed the camera from her.

Proper Adjectives

Proper adjectives are formed from proper nouns. They are capitalized and often end in *-n, -an, -ian, -ese,* and *-ish.*

American artists perform in international countries.
Japanese crowds fill Yokohama Stadium.

Proper Nouns	Proper Adjectives
Portugal	Portuguese
Egypt	Egyptian
North America	North American

❷ Why It Matters in Writing

Fresh, original adjectives sharpen your writing where dull, overused adjectives like *good* or *great* leave your reader uninterested. Notice how the writer in the following passage describes a concert scene.

STUDENT MODEL

> The **boisterous** crowd grew anxious as the band played a few **poignant** ballads. Meanwhile, an **obnoxious** fan ran across the stage wearing a corset and wig.

❸ Practice and Apply

A. CONCEPT CHECK: Adjectives

Write each adjective that is not an article in these sentences, along with the word it modifies.

All About Karaoke

1. Karaoke became a major trend in Japan and around the world.
2. The machine is a Japanese invention.
3. The concept is not a new one, however.
4. Years ago, American television featured shows in which people sang along with a chorus.
5. The word *karaoke* means "empty orchestra" in Japanese.
6. Powerful speakers play background music.
7. Meanwhile, the lyrics are displayed on a large screen.
8. Most people enjoy singing along, even those with modest talents.
9. The real purpose is to have fun rather than to give a fabulous performance.
10. In fact, karaoke started in Japan as a way for busy workers to unwind.

➡ **For a SELF-CHECK and more practice, see the EXERCISE BANK, p. 304.**

CHALLENGE Identify the proper adjectives in sentences 1–10.

CHAPTER 1

B. REVISING: Using Strong Adjectives

Replace each underlined adjective with a strong adjective of your own.

Film Music

1. Music has accompanied drama since <u>old</u> times.
2. As a matter of fact, silent films depended on <u>good</u> music to add depth to the visual part of the action.
3. At the time, musical selections were performed live by <u>great</u> pianists who could make smooth transitions within each scene.
4. Silent film music had little, if any, connection to the on-screen action and presented <u>little</u> variation from one scene to the next.
5. The silent film *The Great Train Robbery* is considered a <u>great</u> masterpiece for many reasons, but don't expect the musical selections to resemble the on-screen action.
6. Today music plays a <u>special</u> role in the production of movies.
7. Unlike the <u>small</u> relationship between music and silent films in the past, most movies today depend on music to set the mood.
8. A conductor watches the film closely and cues in music where suspenseful, tragic, dramatic, or <u>funny</u> moments occur in a scene.
9. If you remember Alfred Hitchcock's *Psycho*, then you'll remember the <u>scary</u> music moments before something tragic is about to occur.
10. Can you think of any <u>good</u> movie soundtracks?

C. WRITING: Adding Adjectives

Rewrite the conversation in this cartoon, replacing the words *way cool* in quotations with original adjectives.

9 Chickweed Lane by Brooke McEldowney

Adverbs

LESSON 6

❶ Here's the Idea

▶ **An adverb modifies a verb, an adjective, or another adverb.**

MODIFIES

We instantly recognized Beethoven's Fifth Symphony.
ADVERB   VERB

MODIFIES

The famous notes rang out quite clearly.
ADVERB   ADVERB

MODIFIES

The orchestra waited until the auditorium grew completely quiet.
ADVERB ADJECTIVE

Adverbs	
Where	The student orchestra stopped **here** during a national tour.
When	Will they be returning **soon?**
How	Everyone played **magnificently.**
To what extent	The auditorium was **completely** full.

Many adverbs are formed by adding *-ly* to adjectives. Sometimes the spelling changes because of this addition.

frequent + *-ly* = **frequently**   extreme + *-ly* = **extremely**
true + *-ly* = **truly**   possible + *-ly* = **possibly**

Other Commonly Used Adverbs				
afterward	fast	low	often	today
already	forth	more	slow	tomorrow
also	hard	near	sometimes	too
back	instead	next	still	yet
even	late	not	straight	
far	long	now	then	

An **intensifier** is an adverb that defines the degree of an adjective or another adverb. Intensifiers always precede the adjectives or adverbs they are modifying.

EMPHASIZES   *EMPHASIZES*

We were rather surprised that classical music is very popular.
INTENSIFIER   INTENSIFIER

Intensifiers

extremely	most	quite	so	truly
just	nearly	rather	somewhat	very
more	only	really	too	

❷ Why It Matters in Writing

Adverbs can be used to describe the way things happen.
Notice how the highlighted adverbs in the following passage
provide a time sequence.

STUDENT MODEL

    Recently, many scientists have turned their attention to music
and its possible beneficial effects. In one study, researchers
conducted an experiment with the help of a group of students.
Most students scored significantly higher on an IQ test if they
listened to music by classical composer Wolfgang Amadeus Mozart
immediately before the test, the scientists **subsequently** concluded.

❸ Practice and Apply

A. CONCEPT CHECK: Adverbs

For each sentence below, write each adverb.

Beethoven's Triumph

1. Beethoven tirelessly devoted himself to his music.
2. He often worked late.
3. In fact, his nocturnal piano playing made him very unpopular with his more conventional neighbors.
4. The composer was terribly shocked to realize that he was losing his hearing when he was in his late twenties.
5. His condition gradually worsened.
6. It finally became so severe that Beethoven could not hear his own music.

7. No matter how loudly he pounded on the keyboard of his piano, he still could not hear the notes that it produced.
8. Beethoven stubbornly refused to give up, however.
9. He courageously continued not only to compose but also to conduct performances of his works.
10. Would you be very surprised to learn that he composed his greatest works, including the Ninth Symphony, after he had lost his hearing completely?

→ **For a SELF-CHECK and more practice, see the EXERCISE BANK, p. 304.**

For each adverb above, identify the verb phrase, adjective, or adverb it modifies.

B. REVISING: Using Adverbs

Read the following sentences and replace the words in brackets with an adverb. Write your adverbs on your paper.

Example: [It is surprising] not too many people know that Wolfgang Amadeus Mozart may have been murdered.
Answer: Surprisingly,

The Mozart Murder Mystery
1. [In a rough way] speaking, Beethoven and the great composer Wolfgang Amadeus Mozart were contemporaries.
2. The two crossed paths only [one time] or [two times].
3. This was not because they disliked each other; on the contrary, Beethoven, who was the younger of the two had [at all times] admired Mozart [in a way that is tremendous].
4. [In a way that is tragic] for music lovers, Mozart died at the age of thirty-five.
5. Rumors [in not much time] began to spread that Mozart had [in actual terms] been murdered by a musical rival.
6. [It is alleged], Antonio Salieri, who was a friend of Mozart's and a fellow composer, poisoned the young genius.
7. According to legend, Salieri was [to an extreme degree] jealous of Mozart.
8. Mozart was by all indications one of the most [in a remarkable way] gifted musicians who ever lived.
9. Salieri, by comparison, was only [in a moderate way] talented.
10. The relationship between the two composers is [in a thorough way] explored in a movie called *Amadeus.*

Prepositions

LESSON 7

1 Here's the Idea

▶ **A preposition shows the relationship between a noun or pronoun and another word in a sentence.**

> The sounds **of** a jazz band filled the kitchen.
> The music was coming **from** a radio.

Commonly Used Prepositions

about	before	during	off	toward
above	behind	except	on	under
across	below	for	onto	underneath
after	beneath	from	out	until
against	beside	in	outside	up
along	between	inside	over	upon
among	beyond	into	since	with
around	by	like	through	within
as	despite	near	throughout	without
at	down	of	to	

Prepositions that consist of more than one word are called **compound prepositions**.

> Jazz legend Louis Armstrong sang **in addition to** playing the trumpet.

> When jazz singers perform in a style known as *scatting*, they sing nonsense syllables such as "ba skoodily do" **instead of** words.

Commonly Used Compound Prepositions

according to	by means of	in place of	on account of
aside from	in addition to	in spite of	out of
because of	in front of	instead of	prior to

PARTS OF SPEECH

Prepositional Phrases

A **prepositional phrase** consists of a preposition and its object, and any modifiers of the object. The **object of a preposition** is the noun or pronoun that follows a preposition. Prepositional phrases often express relationships of location (*by, near*), direction (*to, down*), or time (*before, during*).

> Many early jazz bands played in New Orleans. (LOCATION)
> PREPOSITION   OBJECT

> The sounds came from a radio. (LOCATION)
> PREPOSITION   OBJECT

> Musicians traveled to other large cities. (DIRECTION)
> PREPOSITION   OBJECT

> During the 1920s, jazz swept the country. (TIME)
> PREPOSITION   OBJECT

A sentence may contain more than one prepositional phrase. Each preposition has its own object.

> We listened to a solo by Louis Armstrong.

❷ Why It Matters in Writing

Prepositional phrases give specific details and often describe a scene or action. Read the following passage without the prepositional phrases, and then read it with the phrases. Notice how the prepositional phrases add importance to the words they describe or relate to.

LITERARY MODEL

How sweet the moonlight sleeps **upon this bank!**

Here will we sit and let the sounds **of music**

Creep **in our ears:** soft stillness and the night

Become the touches **of sweet harmony.**

—William Shakespeare, *The Merchant of Venice*

❸ Practice and Apply

A. CONCEPT CHECK: Prepositions

For each sentence below, write each prepositional phrase and underline the preposition. Then circle the object of the preposition.

The Birth of Jazz

1. Jazz is a modern form of music.
2. Many musical styles contributed to its birth.
3. Among these influences are gospel and the blues.
4. Rhythms from West Africa are also part of jazz's heritage.
5. In New Orleans, jazz was often played at funerals.
6. During the early years of the 20th century, jazz became popular as entertainment.
7. People loved the new music because of its bold and innovative sound.
8. Jazz is unique in its use of syncopation and improvisation.
9. Syncopation means the shifting of rhythmic accents within a song or composition.
10. In an improvisation, a musician plays notes of his or her own invention.

➜ **For a SELF-CHECK and more practice, see the EXERCISE BANK, p. 304.**

PARTS OF SPEECH

B: WRITING: Using Prepositions

Write five sentences that describe the scene below. Use at least one prepositional phrase in each sentence.

Conjunctions

❶ Here's the Idea

▶ **A conjunction connects words or groups of words.** There are three kinds of conjunctions: coordinating, correlative, and subordinating. Conjunctive adverbs are adverbs that function somewhat like conjunctions.

Coordinating Conjunctions

Coordinating conjunctions connect words or groups of words of equal importance in a sentence.

Sonia and her friends watched the new music video.

The action started out on a beach, but the scene changed quickly.

Coordinating Conjunctions						
and	but	for	nor	or	so	yet

Correlative Conjunctions

Correlative conjunctions are word pairs that serve to join words or groups of words.

You will not only hear your favorite song but also see the performer.

Either the music or the visual images will grab your attention.

Correlative Conjunctions		
both . . . and	neither . . . nor	whether . . . or
either . . . or	not only . . . but also	

Subordinating Conjunctions

Subordinating conjunctions introduce subordinate clauses—clauses that cannot stand alone—and join them to independent clauses.

SUBORDINATE CLAUSE

The band waited while the director checked the lighting.

CONJUNCTION

CHAPTER 1

SUBORDINATE CLAUSE

Although music videos are short, they are expensive to produce.

↖CONJUNCTION

Subordinating Conjunctions

after	as though	if	so that	when
although	because	in order that	than	where
as	before	provided	unless	whereas
as if	even though	since	until	while

Conjunctive Adverbs

Conjunctive adverbs are used to express relationships between independent clauses.

The invention of the transistor radio contributed to the rise of rock and roll; similarly, the introduction of cable television helped launch music videos.

Conjunctive Adverbs

accordingly	consequently	hence	nevertheless	still
also	finally	however	otherwise	therefore
besides	furthermore	instead	similarly	thus

❷ Why It Matters in Writing

Conjunctions explain the relationship between ideas and are used to combine two or more short sentences.

STUDENT MODEL

    Before music videos were broadcast on cable television, fans had fewer opportunities to see their favorite artists perform. Most people think of music videos as a recent innovation, **but** the concept is not entirely new. The art form can be traced back to the 1920s, **when** a German filmmaker named Oskar Fischinger began making short films to illustrate musical works.

❸ Practice and Apply

A. CONCEPT CHECK: Conjunctions

Write the conjunctions and the conjunctive adverbs. If there are none, write *none*.

> **The Video Revolution**
> 1. The face of the music industry changed when cable television came along and began running music videos twenty-four hours a day.
> 2. At first, many people predicted that the idea would fail.
> 3. Either an all-video station would not attract enough viewers, or the producers would never find enough programming to fill all the airtime, they said.
> 4. These predictions seemed reasonable, but the skeptics turned out to be wrong.
> 5. Singers and bands began to make more and more videos; consequently, viewers tuned in to watch.
> 6. Later, while music videos became a major form of entertainment, some critics began to find fault with them.
> 7. According to critics, performers were creating works that were not only visually but also musically insubstantial.
> 8. There's some truth to the criticism that many videos are slick and unimaginative; however, there are plenty that are truly striking and innovative.
> 9. It's been roughly twenty years since videos first appeared.
> 10. Whether you give them a thumbs-up or a thumbs-down, you must admit that they are here to stay.

➜ For a SELF-CHECK and more practice, see the EXERCISE BANK, p. 305.

B. WRITING: Using Conjunctions

Write the missing conjunctions and conjunctive adverbs.

> **Early Video History**
> During the 1940s, jukebox-like machines known as "soundies" showed short films in which famous singers performed hit songs; _____ the popularity of these machines did not last. Musical images did not disappear; _____ other media took the place of soundies. Television variety shows provided entertainers new opportunities to perform; _____, record companies began making short promotional films for records. At the time, _____ producers _____ artists could possibly imagine how important such music films would become.

LESSON 9 · Interjections

❶ Here's the Idea

▶ **An interjection is a word or a phrase used to express emotion.**
Examples of interjections include *wow, gee, hey, ouch, aha, boy, imagine,* and *unbelievable.* A strong interjection is followed by an exclamation point. A mild interjection is set off by commas.

Yikes! Our project is due tomorrow.

Well, where should we start?

❷ Why It Matters in Writing

Interjections add realism to your writing, particularly in dialogue in short stories or essays. Notice the sense of guilt conveyed below by the interjection.

> **LITERARY MODEL**
>
> "If Jim doesn't kill me," she said to herself, "before he takes a second look at me, he'll say I look like a Coney Island chorus girl. But what could I do—**oh,** what could I do with a dollar and eighty-seven cents!"
>
> —O. Henry, "The Gift of the Magi"

❸ Practice and Apply

CONCEPT CHECK: Understanding Interjections

For each item, choose the better interjection.

It's a Wrap!
1. (Great!/Oh, no!) We're almost finished with our multimedia presentation.
2. (Wow,/Well,) we still have to choose the background music for the introduction.
3. (Hey!/All right,) I forgot about that!
4. (Here,/Ouch,) listen to this.
5. (Alas! Wow!) I think that's perfect.

→ **For a SELF-CHECK and more practice, see the EXERCISE BANK, p. 305.**

Real World Grammar

Music Review

When you write a **music review** for your school newspaper, you express an opinion based on a critical review of a musician's performance and work. For example, if you enjoyed a concert, you will probably praise the musician for his or her rendition. By using various nouns, adjectives, adverbs, and prepositional phrases appropriately, you can express specific details about the performance. Proper nouns can be used in place of common nouns for the artist's name and music. Effective adverbs and adjectives can help support your judgment of the performance.

Times

National Edition

Midwest: Partly cloudy, windy and cooler in the Great Lakes and Ohio Valley. In the Plains, partly to mostly sunny and mild. Weather map and other details appear on page C29.

ONE DOLLAR

Mudd Sisters
Madison Square Garden, New York, NY
6/25/00

The Mudd Sisters gave a **spectacular** performance last night. These rising stars haven't hit the road since their **widely** successful tour more than a year ago, so the evening proved **quite** satisfying for the more than 20,000 overzealous fans.

The performance began with some of the Sisters' **touching, bittersweet ballads** and built up to their more than rocking, high-energy numbers like **"Get Over It,"** and **"Liberty."** The Sisters were here to please their fans and proved so when they ended the concert with their number one title **"After You."** The explosive applause **from the audience** brought the foursome back **for an encore performance** in which they delighted us and sent us home **with our hearts aching for more.**

—*Kendra Cox*

Proper noun states the artists' name.

Strong adjective describes the performance.

Adverbs tell the degrees of success and satisfaction.

Adjectives describe the ballads, giving the reader a sense of the music.

Proper nouns name song titles.

Prepositional phrases describe scene and action.

When you write a music review of a concert, you want to provide details that will give your reader the opportunity to understand how you formed your opinion of the musician's work. Here are some of the ways in which the parts of speech can help.

Music Review Checklist

☑ Use proper nouns to identify musicians and song titles.

☑ Use specific nouns like *bassist, pianist,* and *drummer* to describe band members.

☑ Use strong adjectives to describe music, performers, and fans. For music, use words like *mellow, upbeat, playful.* For performers, use words like *outstanding, energetic, invigorating, solid.* For fans, use words like *cheerful, energetic, critical, devoted, animated.*

☑ Use effective verbs like *roared, delighted, hypnotized, charmed* to show action.

PRACTICE AND APPLY: Writing

Using the tips above, write a music review of an artist's latest CD. You may use the information below or facts about a real-life artist whose music you are familiar with.

Artist: Bill Keyes, guitar player, vocalist, and composer

CD: *Living on the Edge*

Songs: "One Day," "Live for Today," "Strange World"

Grammy Nominations: pop album of the year, song of the year, and album of the year

Duet: Teri Starr

Mixed Review

A. Nouns, Pronouns, Verbs, and Adjectives Read this passage. Then answer the questions below it.

> **LITERARY MODEL**
>
> **(1)** I soon found out why old Chong had retired from teaching piano. **(2)** He was deaf. **(3)** "Like Beethoven!" he shouted to me. **(4)** "We're both listening only in our head!" **(5)** And he would start to conduct his frantic silent sonatas.
>
> **(6)** Our lessons went like this. **(7)** He would open the book and point to different things, explaining their purpose: "Key! Treble! Bass! No sharps or flats! **(8)** So this is C major! **(9)** Listen now and play after me!"
>
> **(10)** And then he would play the C scale a few times, a simple chord, and then, as if inspired by an old, unreachable itch, he gradually added more notes . . . and a pounding bass until the music was really something quite grand.
>
> —Amy Tan, "Two Kinds"

1. What is the proper noun in sentence 1?
2. Is the verb in sentence 2 an action verb or a linking verb?
3. What are the personal pronouns in sentence 3?
4. Is the noun in sentence 4 common or proper?
5. What are the adjectives in sentence 5?
6. What kind of pronoun is *our* in sentence 6?
7. What kind of verb is *would* in sentence 7?
8. Is *this* in sentence 8 a demonstrative or an interrogative pronoun?
9. What are the verbs in sentence 9?
10. What are the adjectives in sentence 10?

B. Adverbs, Prepositions, Conjunctions, and Interjections In the sentences below, identify each underlined word as either an adverb, preposition, conjunction, or interjection.

Shape Up, Einstein

A newspaper column **(1)** <u>from</u> 1945 relates an amusing anecdote **(2)** <u>about</u> Albert Einstein, the great mathematician **(3)** <u>and</u> physicist. Einstein, **(4)** <u>according to</u> the account, played the violin as a hobby. One day, he invited Artur Schnabel, a famous concert pianist, to join him in some informal music-making. **(5)** <u>While</u> the two were playing a **(6)** <u>technically</u> difficult Mozart sonata, Schnabel became **(7)** <u>quite</u> frustrated. Finally, he could **(8)** <u>neither</u> concentrate **(8)** <u>nor</u> control himself. He stopped playing, banged **(9)** <u>angrily</u> on the keyboard, and exclaimed: "No, no, Albert. **(10)** <u>For heaven's sake</u>, can't you count? One, two, three, four. . . ."

Write the letter of the term that correctly identifies each underlined item.

    <u>What</u> do Frank Sinatra and the Beatles have in common? Both "Old
    (1)
Blue Eyes" and the "Fab Four" have performed at <u>Carnegie Hall</u>.
                                               (2)

    Opened in 1891, Carnegie Hall was originally known as the New York
Music Hall. The <u>famous</u> composer Peter Ilich Tchaikovsky was guest
               (3)
conductor <u>during its opening week</u>. Since then the hall, which is <u>widely</u>
           (4)   (5)
acclaimed for its acoustics, has showcased some of the most famous
figures of the 20th century. <u>Not only</u> musicians <u>but also</u> dancers, authors,
                             (6)   (6)
and political activists <u>have appeared</u> at Carnegie Hall. Jazz composer and
                   (7)
bandleader Duke Ellington gave <u>annual</u> concerts there. The writer Mark
                          (8)
Twain and the women's rights crusader Emmeline Pankhurst stirred
audiences <u>with their impassioned speeches</u>. <u>Well</u>, we can only guess who
          (9)   (10)
will be the next star to grace the great stage at Carnegie Hall.

---

1. A. relative pronoun
   B. reflexive pronoun
   C. intensive pronoun
   D. interrogative pronoun

2. A. common noun
   B. proper noun
   C. proper adjective
   D. abstract noun

3. A. adjective
   B. adverb
   C. noun
   D. relative pronoun

4. A. prepositional phrase
   B. compound preposition
   C. adverb
   D. demonstrative pronoun

5. A. subordinating conjunction
   B. coordinating conjunction
   C. conjunctive adverb
   D. adverb

6. A. coordinating conjunction
   B. subordinating conjunction
   C. correlative conjunction
   D. conjunctive adverb

7. A. action verb
   B. linking verb
   C. adverb
   D. prepositional phrase

8. A. adverb
   B. adjective
   C. concrete noun
   D. abstract noun

9. A. demonstrative pronoun
   B. reflexive pronoun
   C. prepositional phrase
   D. correlative conjunction

10. A. subordinating conjunction
    B. correlative conjunction
    C. interjection
    D. intensive pronoun

PARTS OF SPEECH

Student Help Desk

Parts of Speech at a Glance

interjection
pronoun
adverb
verb
adjective
noun
adjective

Well, I almost forgot the upbeat lyrics

conjunction
adjective
noun
preposition
pronoun
adjective
noun

and catchy words of your favorite song.

Kinds of Nouns — Unforgettable Nouns

All nouns are either common or proper, concrete or abstract, singular or plural.

The band wrote a song about gratitude for Claudia and her classmates.

band	common, concrete, singular, collective
song	common, concrete, singular
gratitude	common, abstract, singular
Claudia	proper, concrete, singular
classmates	common, concrete, plural, compound

Some nouns are collective or compound.

Kinds of Verbs
Playful Verbs

All verbs are either linking verbs or action verbs.

The girls remained calm but then screamed when the band played their music.

remained	linking
screamed	action, intransitive
played	action, transitive

All action verbs are either transitive or intransitive.

Kinds of Adjectives
Shrewd Adjectives

What Kind	**thoughtful** words **sincere** reply
Which One	**that** book **this** song
How Many	**five** albums **several** concerts
How Much	**less** energy **more** sound

The Bottom Line

Checklist for Parts of Speech

Have I . . .

____ chosen precise nouns?

____ used pronouns to avoid repeating nouns?

____ selected specific verbs?

____ added adjectives to identify nouns?

____ used adverbs to describe actions?

____ made good use of conjunctions to link ideas?

____ used prepositions to vary sentence rhythms?

____ used interjections to show character in dialogue?

The Sentence and Its Parts

HELP!

THIS IS AN ~~EMERGENCY~~

~~WE~~ STARTED ON A THREE-
HOUR TOUR. THE WEATHER

OUR TINY SHIP, THE MINNOW,

THANKS TO THE
COURAGE OF OUR FEARLESS
CREW

OUR LOCATION IS ROUGHLY

PLEASE BEFORE

IT'S TOO LATE!

Theme: Adventures and Disasters

What's the Message?

The stranded passengers who sent this note were the victims of two disasters: first, a shipwreck, and then—incomplete sentences! Can this note and the passengers still be saved? What information would you add to the message?

Prevent your writing from leading to catastrophe. To communicate your own messages effectively, use **complete sentences**—groups of words that convey complete thoughts.

Write Away: What Else Can Go Wrong?

Disasters aren't always shipwrecks and blizzards. Sometimes a disaster is as simple as a message left on the wrong answering machine or an acne attack before a big date. Write a paragraph about one of your own personal disasters. Save the paragraph in your **Working Portfolio.**

Choose the letter of the term that correctly identifies each underlined section.

Have you ever participated in a bicycle race? How fast did you pedal?

Hopefully, you <u>weren't clocked at a speed of 190 mph</u>. In professional
(1)

motorcycle road racing, however, <u>riders</u> actually reach this astonishing
(2)

speed.

<u>Helmets and leather body suits</u> are worn for this sport. <u>Regular
(3)   (4)

motorcycles are purchased and then modified by mechanics.</u> From these

<u>modifications emerge lighter and faster bikes.</u> These special bikes are also
(5)

durable. <u>They have to be to endure the 60-mile course!</u>
(6)   (7)

Racers use a <u>technique</u> called drafting to pass their opponents. As the
(8)

lead racer pushes against the air, the next rider gets as close as possible.

With less wind resistance between the two bikes, the racer on the trailing

bike flies right by. The slightest mistake could be a <u>disaster</u>. To avoid
(9)

accidents, riders attend a special <u>school</u>.
(10)

---

1. A. simple subject
   B. complete subject
   C. simple predicate
   D. complete predicate

2. A. simple subject
   B. simple predicate
   C. compound subject
   D. compound verb

3. A. simple subject
   B. simple predicate
   C. compound subject
   D. compound verb

4. A. interrogative sentence
   B. imperative sentence
   C. declarative sentence
   D. exclamatory sentence

5. A. inverted sentence
   B. imperative sentence
   C. interrogative sentence
   D. exclamatory sentence

6. A. direct object
   B. indirect object
   C. predicate nominative
   D. predicate adjective

7. A. declarative sentence
   B. imperative sentence
   C. interrogative sentence
   D. exclamatory sentence

8. A. direct object
   B. indirect object
   C. predicate nominative
   D. predicate adjective

9. A. direct object
   B. indirect object
   C. predicate nominative
   D. predicate adjective

10. A. predicate adjective
    B. predicate nominative
    C. direct object
    D. indirect object

Simple Subjects and Predicates

❶ Here's the Idea

▶ **Every sentence has two basic parts: a subject and a predicate.**

The **subject** tells whom or what the sentence is about.
The **predicate** tells what the subject is or does or what happens to the subject.

Huge cresting waves	pound the sailboat.
SUBJECT	PREDICATE

Hurricane-force winds tear the sails off the mast.
The fragile sailboat is thrown on its side.

Both parts are usually necessary for the meaning of a group of words to be clear. When a subject or a predicate is missing, the group of words is a **sentence fragment.**

For more on fragments, see p. 116–119.

▶ **The basic elements of a sentence are the simple subject and the simple predicate.**

The **simple subject** is the key word or words in the subject.
The **simple predicate** is the verb or verb phrase that tells something about the subject.

Here's How Finding Simple Subjects and Predicates

The violent storm battered the sailboat.

Simple subjects and simple predicates do not include any modifying words, phrases, or clauses.

Simple subject Ask who or what is or does something.	**Simple predicate** Ask what the subject is or does or what happens to it.
What battered the sailboat? **storm**	What did the storm do? battered

The violent storm battered **the sailboat.**

❷ Why It Matters in Writing

If you can't find a simple subject and a simple predicate (verb or verb phrase) in your "sentence," you've created a fragment. The fragment is missing important information. Check your writing to make sure that each sentence expresses a complete thought.

> **STUDENT MODEL**
>
> **Teen Rescues Sailboat Crew!**
>   Terri Alvarez showed uncommon courage in the face of nature's fury. The Capland sophomore *had* only a small motorboat to rescue a stranded sailboat crew. Battled 20-foot waves and gale-force winds. *He*

The missing verb makes this a sentence fragment.

Who battled? The missing subject would confuse the reader.

SENTENCE PARTS

❸ Practice and Apply

A. CONCEPT CHECK: Simple Subjects and Predicates

Write the simple subject and the simple predicate of each sentence.

Example: The bright Florida sky turned black.
Answer: sky; turned.

> **Deadly Hurricane Slams into Florida!**
> **1.** Hurricane Andrew struck southern Florida in August 1992.
> **2.** This ferocious storm destroyed several communities.
> **3.** The high winds also tore a county zoo apart.
> **4.** Many animals, afraid of the wind, cowered in their cages.
> **5.** Over 150,000 people lost their homes or businesses.
> **6.** Many residents had no water, electricity, or shelter.
> **7.** Relief workers distributed food, clothing, and medicine.
> **8.** Midwesterners sent bottled water to the area.
> **9.** Many Florida residents will remember this storm for the rest of their lives!
> **10.** The hurricane caused $25.5 billion in damages in southern Florida.

➡ **For a SELF-CHECK and more practice, see the EXERCISE BANK, p. 306.**

B. EDITING: Spotting Incomplete Sentences

On a separate sheet of paper, identify each item as a complete sentence (CS) or a fragment (F). For each fragment, tell whether it is missing a subject or a predicate.

Example: The captain and his crew one last trip.
Answer: F; missing a predicate

Courage and Survival at Sea
1. In January 1988, a hurricane struck the Costa Rican coast.
2. Blew a boat with five fishermen out into the Pacific Ocean.
3. Over the next five months, survived by working together.
4. Sharks around the boat all the time.
5. The men watched several ships come close and then sail away.
6. Collected rainwater in canvas bags and old metal containers.
7. Without navigation equipment sailed 4,500 miles.
8. Finally, a Japanese ship rescued the weary crew.
9. Costa Rica a parade and celebration for the men's homecoming.
10. The men had survived an incredible 142 days at sea!

CHALLENGE For each fragment above, add a subject or predicate to make a complete sentence.

Look at your **Write Away** paragraph or another draft from your **Working Portfolio.** Fix any incomplete sentences.

C. WRITING: Creating Disaster Headlines

Simple subjects and simple predicates are used in many headlines ("Warehouse Burns!"). Identify the simple subjects and predicates in Calvin's headlines. Then, with a partner, create three disaster headlines about events in your own lives.

Example: I really messed up my speech.
Answer: SPEECH BOMBS!

Calvin and Hobbes by Bill Watterson

Complete Subjects and Predicates

❶ Here's the Idea

▶ The complete subject includes the simple subject and all the words that modify, or tell more about, it.

▶ The complete predicate includes the verb and all the words that modify, or tell more about, it.

> **Here's How** Finding Complete Subjects and Predicates
>
> **Disaster movies fascinate nearly everyone.**
>
> | **Complete subject** Ask who or what is or does something. What fascinates? | **Complete Predicate** Ask what the subject is or does or what happens to it. What do disaster movies do? |
> |---|---|
> | **Disaster movies** | **fascinate nearly everyone.** |
>
> **Disaster movies** fascinate nearly everyone.

HOT TIP

Notice that every word in a sentence is part of either the complete subject or the complete predicate.

❷ Why It Matters in Writing

Adding details to simple subjects and predicates can help you convey your ideas more clearly to the reader.

> **STUDENT MODEL**
>
> **DRAFT**
>
> Many of the *Titanic's* lifeboats were only half full. The crew was worried about the weight. It might break the winch ropes, spilling passengers into the sea.
>
> > Were the boats in the water at this point? What about the weight? What is the connection between the first two sentences?
>
> **REVISION**
>
> Many of the *Titanic's* lifeboats were **lowered into the water** only half full. The crew was worried about the weight **of full lifeboats**. **The extra weight** could break the winch ropes, spilling passengers into the sea.
>
> > Added details clarify meaning and logic.

❸ Practice and Apply

A. CONCEPT CHECK: Complete Subjects and Predicates

On a separate sheet of paper, write the complete subjects of sentences 1–5. Write the complete predicates of sentences 6–10.

Making the Movie *Titanic*
1. James Cameron had been fascinated by the *Titanic* for years.
2. The filmmaker interviewed several survivors of the tragedy.
3. The special-effects crew created tiny models of the ship.
4. The art director copied the *Titanic*'s original furnishings.
5. The real challenge was the re-creation of the death of the ship.
6. The *Titanic*'s final moments were simulated with a computer.
7. Computer-generated "people" fell against computer-generated "propellers" into a computer-generated "sea."
8. Experts on the disaster were fooled by these scenes.
9. Critics asked Cameron about the Blue Heart necklace.
10. Cameron invented the necklace as part of the love story.

➡ **For a SELF-CHECK and more practice, see the EXERCISE BANK, p. 306.**

On your paper, circle the simple subjects of sentences 1–5 and the simple predicates of sentences 6–10.

B. WRITING: Adding Details

Combine the simple subjects and simple predicates below to form sentences. Add details to each sentence to describe the plot of a disaster movie.

Exchange papers with a partner. Circle the complete subjects and underline the complete predicates on your partner's paper.

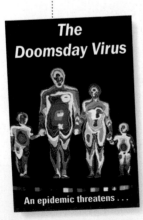

The Doomsday Virus

An epidemic threatens . . .

New Disaster Movie

Simple subjects	Simple predicates
Virus	appears
People	are contaminated
Epidemic	threatens
Scientist/hero	discovers
Girlfriend/boyfriend	doubts
Truth	is uncovered
Scientist/hero	triumphs
Virus	is killed
People	recover
Enemies	are defeated

Compound Subjects and Verbs

LESSON 3

❶ Here's the Idea

▶ **A sentence can have more than one subject or verb.**

A sentence part with more than one of these elements is a compound part.

A **compound subject** is made up of two or more subjects that share a verb. The subjects are joined by a conjunction, or connecting word, such as *and, or*, or *but*.

CONJUNCTION

Divers and climbers share a love of adventure.

COMPOUND SUBJECT   VERB

> Notice that the subjects can be simple or complete.

Extreme danger and exciting challenges are **important.**

COMPOUND SUBJECT

A **compound verb** is made up of two or more verbs or verb phrases that are joined by a conjunction and have the same subject.

The exhausted diver ached **and** moaned.

COMPOUND VERB

A **compound predicate** is made up of a compound verb and all the words that go with each verb.

Both groups must be in top physical condition
and must be ready for any emergency.◀ COMPOUND PREDICATE

❷ Why It Matters in Writing

Using compound parts can help make your writing more concise and help show relationships between ideas.

STUDENT MODEL

Climbing Mount Fuji was turning into
a struggle. ~~I was~~ *Shawn and I were* having trouble breathing
the thinner air. ~~So was Shawn.~~ One of the
women gave us a canister of oxygen∨ *and*
~~She~~ went on ahead.

> Compound subject condenses two sentences into one.

> Compound predicate shows the relationship between two ideas.

❸ Practice and Apply

A. CONCEPT CHECK: Compound Subjects and Verbs

Write the compound subject or predicate in each sentence below. Underline the subjects once and the verbs twice.

Example: The brain and heart function differently at high altitudes.

Answer: <u>brain</u> and <u>heart</u>

Your Brain Underwater and at High Altitudes

1. Children and adults can survive frigid water for a long time.
2. Cold water signals the brain and triggers a "diving reflex."
3. The brain slows and needs only half the normal level of oxygen.
4. Electrical activity and chemical actions in the brain keep the body alive.
5. The heart and brain can survive 40 or 50 minutes in this state.
6. Climbers face a different challenge and must adapt to high altitudes.
7. The brain and heart receive up to 30 percent less oxygen.
8. Sometimes fluid accumulates and causes the brain to swell.
9. Climbers can't think or make good decisions.
10. They must get to lower altitudes right away or risk death.

➡ **For a SELF-CHECK and more practice, see the EXERCISE BANK, p. 307.**

B. REVISING: Improving a Paragraph

Revise the paragraph below, using compound subjects and verbs to combine sentences with similar ideas.

STUDENT MODEL

Hold Your Breath!

 Swimmers know ways to stay underwater longer. Divers also know these tricks. You can learn these techniques too. You start out by taking several quick, deep breaths. Your lungs fill with oxygen. Your lungs transport the gas to your bloodstream. Your body tissues absorb oxygen from your blood. They use it to produce the energy they need. Your muscles need a lot of oxygen. You should relax. You should move only as much as necessary. With these techniques you can train yourself to stay underwater for up to four minutes.

Choose a draft from your 🗀 **Working Portfolio.** How can it be improved by combining sentences?

Kinds of Sentences

LESSON 4

① Here's the Idea

▶ **A sentence can be used to make a statement, ask a question, give a command, or show strong feelings.**

Four Kinds of Sentences

Declarative We've never swum out this far before.

This kind of sentence expresses a fact, wish, intent, or feeling. It always ends with a period.

Interrogative Is that a shark following us?

This kind of sentence asks a question and always ends with a question mark.

Imperative Hide until it leaves. Now swim for shore!

This kind of sentence expresses a command, request, or direction. It usually ends with a period. If the command or request is strong, it may end with an exclamation point.

Exclamatory We almost didn't make it!

This kind of sentence expresses strong feeling. It always ends with an exclamation point.

② Why It Matters in Writing

Using the four different kinds of sentences can help you

- add variety and interest to your writing
- create realistic dialogue

Notice how natural the use of the four kinds of sentences sounds in this dialogue from the play *The Miracle Worker*.

LITERARY MODEL

Keller. Katie? What's wrong?   INTERROGATIVE

Kate. Look.   IMPERATIVE
(*She makes a pass with her hand in the crib, at the baby's eyes.*)
Keller. What, Katie? She's well; she needs only time to—

Kate. She can't see. Look at her eyes.   DECLARATIVE
(*She takes the lamp from him, moves it before the child's face.*)
She can't *see!*   EXCLAMATORY

—William Gibson, *The Miracle Worker*

SENTENCE PARTS

The Sentence and Its Parts **45**

❸ Practice and Apply

A. CONCEPT CHECK: Kinds of Sentences

Identify each of the following sentences as declarative, imperative, interrogative, or exclamatory.

Change sentences 6–10 according to the instructions in parentheses.

> **The Truth About Sharks**
> 1. Did you know that most shark attacks are cases of mistaken identity?
> 2. Sharks think humans are seals or other prey.
> 3. Don't dangle your arms and legs over the side of a boat.
> 4. You can often prevent a shark attack by being aggressive.
> 5. One diver drove a shark off by punching it in the nose!
> 6. People once believed that sharks were frenzied killers. (Change to a question.)
> 7. Are they really just incredibly skilled predators? (Change to an exclamatory sentence.)
> 8. Keep out of shark waters if you have an open wound. (Change to a declarative sentence.)
> 9. These hunters can smell even small traces of blood up to a mile away! (Change to a question.)
> 10. Will they eat exotic items like license plates and inner tubes? (Change to an exclamatory sentence.)

➡ **For a SELF-CHECK and more practice, see the EXERCISE BANK, p. 307.**

B. WRITING: Dialogue

Read the caption of the cartoon and identify the imperative sentence in it. Then write Dewey's response, in which he argues why he *should* play. Use all four types of sentences.

IN THE BLEACHERS   By Steve Moore

JdsmooRe@aol.com   © 1996 Universal Press Syndicate

"Don't let Dewey play. He hasn't metamorphosed yet."

Subjects in Unusual Positions

❶ Here's the Idea

In most sentences subjects come before verbs. However, on some occasions subjects appear in unusual positions—after verbs or inside verb phrases.

Inverted Sentences

▶ **In an inverted sentence the subject comes after the verb or part of the verb phrase.** An inverted sentence can be used for emphasis or variety.

Usual Order

| The savage storm | came down on the Spanish galleon. |

Inverted Order

| Down came | the savage storm | on the Spanish galleon. |

Usual Order

The sea swept across the deck of the hopeless ship.

Inverted Order

Across the deck of the hopeless ship swept **the sea.**

Sentences Beginning with *Here* or *There*

▶ **Though *here* or *there* may begin a sentence, these words are rarely subjects.** In fact, the subject of a sentence that begins with one of these words usually follows the verb.

Here is **the massive anchor of the galleon.**
There lies **the great ship, far beneath the ocean.**

Agreement can be tricky in sentences where the subject follows the verb. Identify the subject before choosing the verb form. Singular subjects take singular verbs, and plural subjects take plural verbs.

AGREES WITH

Here is **the massive anchor of the galleon.**

AGREES WITH

Here are **the massive anchors of the galleon.**

For more on subject-verb agreement, see pp. 158–169.

SENTENCE PARTS

Questions

▶ **In a question the subject usually comes after the verb or inside the verb phrase.**

Subject After Verb

> Was the cargo of the galleon valuable?

Subject Inside Verb Phrase

> Did the great ship survive the storm?

Here's How Finding the Subject

Was the cargo of the galleon valuable?

1. First change the question into a statement.
   The cargo of the galleon was valuable.

2. Then find the verb and ask *who* or *what.*
   verb: was   What was? **cargo** = subject

In some questions, words such as *who* or *what* are the subjects and come before the verbs.

> Who was aboard the galleon? What happened to the people?

Imperative Sentences

▶ **In an imperative sentence the subject is usually *you*.** In most cases, *you* is not stated; it is understood.

> Request: (You) Please read the ancient tale of the galleon.
> Command: (You) Beware the wild sea.

❷ Why It Matters in Writing

Inverting word order allows you to add variety and to change the emphases in your sentences. In this model, it allows the writer to set the scene before presenting a character.

LITERARY MODEL

In front of the house in a squeaky rocking chair sat Miss Lottie's son, John Burke. . . .

—Eugenia Collier, "Marigolds"

❸ Practice and Apply

A. CONCEPT CHECK: Subjects in Unusual Positions

On a separate sheet of paper, write the simple subject and the verb of each sentence below. Be sure to include all parts of each verb phrase.

Example: Have you heard of the destruction of the *Atocha?*
Answer: you; have heard

The Tragedy of the *Atocha*—September 6, 1622

1. There were 28 Spanish ships, including the *Atocha,* on the voyage to Spain.
2. Out of nowhere sprang a fierce storm.
3. From every ship in the fleet came pitiful cries for help.
4. Would the sailors survive this powerful storm?
5. Never doubt the men's skill and bravery.
6. Into the Gulf of Mexico sailed the Spanish vessels.
7. Yet upon a reef crashed the treasure galleon.
8. Who witnessed its destruction and the loss of 260 lives?
9. Here is an important lesson about the power of nature.
10. Remember the misfortune of the great ship and its crew.

➡ **For a SELF-CHECK and more practice, see the EXERCISE BANK, p. 308.**

Rewrite sentences 2, 3, 6 and 7 by putting the subjects before the verbs. How do the revisions change the sentences' effects?

B. WRITING: Revising Word Order

Follow the directions in parentheses to change the word order in each sentence.

The Recovery of the *Atocha*'s Treasure—July 20, 1985

1. The skeleton of the *Atocha* sat on the ocean floor. (Invert sentence order.)
2. The galleon and its precious cargo would be discovered. (Make into a question.)
3. The spectacular treasure was found off Florida's Marquesas Keys. (Invert sentence order.)
4. The treasure lay beneath masses of heavy sand. (Begin sentence with *There.*)
5. People should not forget the remarkable recovery of the *Atocha*'s cargo. (Make into a command.)

Subject Complements

LESSON 6

❶ Here's the Idea

▶ **Complements are words that complete the meaning or action of verbs.** There are two general kinds of complements: subject complements and objects of verbs.

A **subject complement** is a word that follows a linking verb and identifies or describes the subject. Subject complements may be predicate adjectives or predicate nominatives.
Remember linking verbs? If not, see pp. 14–16.

Predicate Adjectives

A **predicate adjective** describes or modifies the subject.

MODIFIES

The climb had been **difficult.**

MODIFIES

The explorers felt extremely **miserable.**

Predicate Nominatives

A **predicate nominative** is a noun or pronoun. It identifies, renames, or defines the subject.

SAME AS

Mount Everest was their **destination.**

SAME AS

The trip became their worst **nightmare.**

❷ Why It Matters in Writing

Well-chosen predicate adjectives and predicate nominatives can help you create vivid descriptions and clear definitions. Notice the subject complements in this model.

PROFESSIONAL MODEL

From the valleys of Nepal and Tibet, Mount Everest appears a stormy **giant.** Its soaring ridges look so **powerful** that observers feel **humble.** The mountain is at once **beautiful** and **dreadful.**

—Laura Cheveriat

❸ Practice and Apply

A. CONCEPT CHECK: Subject Complements

On a sheet of paper, write the subject complement in each sentence, and identify it as a predicate adjective (PA) or a predicate nominative (PN).

Example: The Himalayas are incredibly magnificent.
Answer: magnificent, PA

The Perils of Mount Everest
1. Everest is the highest mountain in the world.
2. Its slopes look risky, even to world-class climbers.
3. Oxygen grows thin beyond the mountain's base.
4. Climbers often become immobile without extra oxygen.
5. Frequently, frostbite becomes a real problem.
6. In such cases the skin appears swollen.
7. Glaciers are great sources of danger.
8. Their surfaces stay slippery because of the constant cold.
9. On the icy ridges, winds become daggers.
10. Mount Everest remains a true test for most climbers.

➜ For a SELF-CHECK and more practice, see the EXERCISE BANK, p. 308.

B. REVISING: Replacing Subject Complements

Rewrite each sentence, replacing the subject complement with a more precise word.

Example: The icy trails look bad.
Answer: The icy trails look **dangerous.**

Extreme Experiences
1. With a peak 29,028 feet above sea level, Mount Everest is tall.
2. The climbers feel good during the day.
3. At nightfall, however, they are cold.
4. Snowdrifts become funny shapes.
5. The trails are hard to climb.
6. Winds sound strange to the climbers.
7. Tents feel thin in the weather.
8. Climbers appear different after their experiences.
9. Climbers are happy upon their return.
10. Mount Everest is a strange place.

Objects of Verbs

LESSON 7

CHAPTER 2

❶ Here's the Idea

▶ **Action verbs often require complements called direct objects and indirect objects to complete their meaning.**

Direct Objects

A **direct object** is a word or a group of words that receives the action of an action verb. It answers the question *what* or *whom*.

The climber caught. (Caught *what?* or *whom?*)

The climber caught the nylon rope.

Indirect Objects

An **indirect object** tells to what, to whom, for what, or for whom an action is done. Verbs that often take indirect objects include *bring, give, hand, lend, make, send, show, teach, tell,* and *write*.

The rescue team gives hot food. (Gives food *to* or *for whom?*)

The rescue team gives (to) the survivors hot food.

> The indirect object is usually between the verb and the direct object.

Here's How Finding Direct and Indirect Objects

The survivors told me their dramatic story.

1. Find the action verb in the sentence. *told*
2. To find the direct object, ask *told what.* told the *story*
3. To find the indirect object, ask *told the story to* or *for whom.* told (to) *me* the story

If the word *to* or *for* appears in the sentence, the word that follows is **not** an indirect object. *Me* is not an indirect object in this sentence: *The survivors told their story to me.*

❷ Why It Matters in Writing

Especially when you are writing dialogue, you need to use objects to convey information and to add important details. Notice the objects in this model.

LITERARY MODEL

"Let's go! Give me the full bottle of oxygen and let's go." But he said, "No, I'm not giving you this bottle."

—Anatoli Boukreev and G. Weston DeWalt, *The Climb*

INDIRECT OBJECT

DIRECT OBJECT

❸ Practice and Apply

A. CONCEPT CHECK: Objects of Verbs

Each sentence below contains at least one complement. Write each complement and identify it as a direct object (DO) or an indirect object (IO).

Mount Everest Expeditions
1. British surveyors calculated the height of Peak XV.
2. In 1865 geographers gave Mount Everest its current name.
3. Irvine lent Mallory a hand in their 1924 expedition.
4. Unfortunately, a sudden ice storm overcame the explorers.
5. In 1953, Hillary and Tenzing showed the world their talents.
6. They conquered the summit of Mount Everest.
7. In 1963, Hornbein and Unsoeld scaled the West Ridge.
8. Their feat earned them praise from professional climbers.
9. On a 1996 expedition fierce blizzards killed 8 climbers.
10. Mount Everest still offers climbers a true challenge.

➜ For a SELF-CHECK and more practice, see the EXERCISE BANK, p. 308.

B. WRITING: Filling in Objects

Write each sentence skeleton five times. Add objects as indicated to create different sentences. Add modifiers as needed.
1. One explorer gave __(indirect object)__ a __(direct object)__ .
2. Rescuers brought __(indirect object)__ some __(direct object)__ .

LESSON 8 · Sentence Diagramming

Here's the Idea

Diagramming is a way of visually representing the structure of a sentence. It can help you understand how the sentence works by showing how each word functions. Once you understand how diagrams work, you may find yourself diagramming for the fun of it!

Watch me for diagramming tips!

Simple Subjects and Verbs

The simple subject and the verb are written on one line and are separated by a vertical line that crosses the main line.

Windows exploded.

Windows | exploded

Compound Subjects and Verbs

For a compound subject or verb, split the main line.

Compound Subject
Windows and clocks exploded.

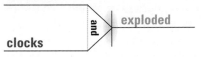

Because there are two subjects, the left side of the main line is split into two parts.

Compound Verb
Windows shattered and exploded.

Because there are two verbs, the right side of the main line is split into two parts.

Compound Subject and Verb
Windows and clocks **shattered and exploded.**

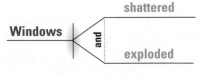

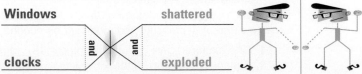

A. CONCEPT CHECK: Subjects and Verbs

Diagram these sentences, using what you have learned.
1. Trees toppled.
2. Trees toppled and fell.
3. Houses and trees swayed and crashed.

Adjectives and Adverbs

Because adjectives and adverbs **modify**, or tell more about, other words in a sentence, they are written on slanted lines below the words they modify.

The atmospheric pressure was falling very rapidly.

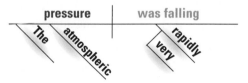

B. CONCEPT CHECK: Adjectives and Adverbs

Diagram these sentences, using what you have learned.
1. The wicked wind whistled wildly.
2. A tornado and a violent rainstorm finally arrived.
3. Roof shingles and tree branches scattered everywhere.

Subject Complements: Predicate Nominatives and Predicate Adjectives

Write a predicate nominative or a predicate adjective on the main line after the verb. Separate the subject complement from the verb with a slanted line that does not cross the main line.

The wind was our enemy.   **All residents felt anxious.**

The slanted line separating a subject complement from a verb does not cross the main line.

Direct Objects

A direct object follows the verb on the same line.

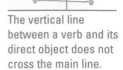

The tornado destroyed **homes.**

The vertical line between a verb and its direct object does not cross the main line.

Sometimes a sentence has a compound direct object. To diagram this kind of sentence, split the main line and write the parts of the direct object on parallel lines.

The tornado destroyed **homes and businesses.**

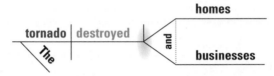

When you have a compound predicate (two verbs, each with its own object), split the line and show the compound parts on parallel lines.

The tornado destroyed **homes and** changed **the landscape.**

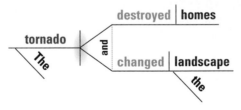

Indirect Objects

An indirect object is written on a horizontal line connected to the verb with a slanted line.

The storm gave townspeople **a terrible night.**

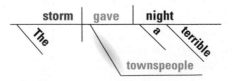

CHAPTER 2

C. CONCEPT CHECK: Subject Complements and Objects of Verbs

Diagram these sentences, using what you have learned.

1. Hurricanes sometimes hit the Gulf Coast and the Atlantic Coast.
2. Most natural disasters are not predictable.
3. Hurricanes give people warning.
4. Floods are often the worst effects.
5. Floods cause homeowners enormous problems.

D. MIXED REVIEW: Diagramming

Diagram the following sentences. Look for all types of complements.

1. Some diseases become international disasters.
2. The 1918 influenza epidemic killed millions.
3. Soldiers and civilians died everywhere.
4. World War I spread the disease.
5. The flu strain was extremely contagious.
6. Soldiers unknowingly gave their buddies the flu virus.
7. Civilians also gave their families the influenza germ.
8. Old people and children caught the disease and died.
9. This global epidemic was universally destructive.
10. Modern scientists still fight such quiet killer diseases.

Don't race madly around in circles when a sentence confuses you. Remembering these two simple diagramming patterns can help you get the drift.

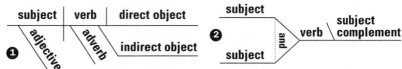

Mother Goose & Grimm by Mike Peters

Real World Grammar

Summer-Job Application

Grammar is not just for school. Suppose you find the ultimate summer job. All you have to do is fill out the application and send it in—you and about 500 other applicants!

Other than by your qualifications, how can you stand out? One way is by using your grammar skills to help you present yourself in the best light. Here's one student's first try. She asked her English teacher to comment on her draft.

Adventure Bound!

WANTED:
Day Camp Leaders
Ages 15-18
$300 per month

APPLY NOW!

APPLICATION

Name Avril Brenner   **Age** 15
Address 11 South Circle Dr., Marshall, CO
Phone 303-555-4893
Parent or Guardian Patrice and David Brenner

In a paragraph, describe your qualifications.

I believe I am uniquely qualified to be an Adventure Bound! day camp leader. I have taught nature crafts to YMCA kids for three years. During that time, I also led YMCA groups on backpacking and camping trips. I have also worked two summers at Wilderness Trek. At this camp, the kids were taught outdoor skills by the counselors to build self-confidence. We were taught to act as a big sister or brother, and cheerleader, to the kids. I know firsthand what a difference a good leader can make. I believe I can make a real contribution to the lives of children at Adventure Bound!

Combine these skills into one strong sentence.

Say more. What is Wilderness Trek? What was your position?

Show your leadership. Change to action verbs.

Again, say more. Difference to whom?

A good leader communicates well. Let your writing show this quality!

Using Grammar in Writing	
Compound parts	Use **compound parts** to combine sentences and present information more concisely. Combining related ideas into one sentence increases their impact on the reader.
Complete subjects and predicates	Use **complete subjects and predicates** to give more information and help your reader understand your meaning. The reader should be able to see clearly why you mention something.
Action verbs	Use **action verbs with their objects** to help you eliminate the passive voice that takes you out of the picture. In an application, you want to state clearly who you are, what you did, and for whom you did it.

REVISED APPLICATION

I believe I am uniquely qualified to be an Adventure Bound! day camp leader. For three years I have taught YMCA kids nature crafts and led them on backpacking and camping trips. For the past two summers I have worked as a camp counselor at Wilderness Trek, an adventure camp for disabled children. As a counselor, I taught the kids outdoor skills to build their self-confidence. I learned how to be a big sister and cheerleader all in one. I know firsthand what a difference a good leader can make in a child's life. I believe I can make a real contribution to the lives of children at Adventure Bound!

Much better! Send it off—Good luck!

SENTENCE PARTS

PRACTICE AND APPLY: Revising

A friend of yours is running for class president and has written the paragraph below for the school newspaper. Your friend asks you to look it over. Use the three writing tips above to revise the paragraph.

Rough Draft

I believe I have the experience to do the best job of serving as class president. Last year, I was treasurer of the student council. I was also captain of the debate team. Student government needs reform. For example, students can't vote on any student council resolutions. Students can't choose their own class projects. A plan for reform was developed by me and my campaign group. Elect someone who will take action!

A. Subjects, Predicates, and Kinds of Sentences Read the story. Then write the answers to the questions below it.

(1) Luisa took her usual homework break and ambled to her favorite room in the house. **(2)** The overhead light in the kitchen revealed at least 100 mosquitoes on the ceiling. **(3)** Luisa quickly grabbed a weapon and faced the enemy.

(4) "Retreat or die, bugs!"

(5) For nearly three hours, Luisa and her trusty fly swatter slapped mosquitoes and shooed them out an open window. **(6)** The pesky insects feasted on her at every opportunity. **(7)** On and on raged the terrible battle. **(8)** Was there no end to this mosquito invasion? **(9)** Finally, by midnight, there were no more mosquitoes. **(10)** An exhausted Luisa forgot about her essay and wearily crawled into bed.

1. What is the compound verb in sentence 1?
2. What is the simple predicate in sentence 2?
3. What are the simple subject and the verb in sentence 3?
4. What kind of sentence is sentence 4?
5. What are the compound parts in sentence 5?
6. What is the complete subject in sentence 6?
7. What is the complete subject in sentence 7?
8. What kind of sentence is sentence 8?
9. What is the simple subject in sentence 9?
10. What kind of sentence is sentence 10?

B. Subject Complements and Objects of Verbs Identify each underlined word in the following passage as a direct object, an indirect object, a predicate nominative, or a predicate adjective.

PROFESSIONAL MODEL

A solution to a problem isn't always a complete **(1)** success. At one high school in California, many students left the **(2)** campus during school hours. To discourage the practice, administrators installed a **(3)** gate in the student parking lot.

On the first day of school, some officials were understandably **(4)** anxious. They stood by to make sure the system worked smoothly. After several cars passed through the gate, a girl jumped out and handed the **(5)** principal her keys. "Great!" she said. "We finally have valet parking."

—Adapted from "Tales Out of School"
by Julia Park, *Reader's Digest,* May 1998

CHAPTER 2

Choose the letter of the term that correctly identifies each underlined section.

"Rogue waves" are a terrifying <u>hazard</u> at sea. <u>They spring up out of</u>
                              (1)   (2)

<u>nowhere and destroy everything in their path.</u> These massive <u>waves</u> can
                                                      (3)

tower over 100 feet high. People <u>often don't know that a wave is coming</u>.
                                                (4)

If they are lucky, another ship may radio <u>them</u> a warning.
                                            (5)

A rogue wave <u>can flip</u> a <u>boat</u> end over end. <u>Small ships and huge</u>
                 (6)   (7)   (8)

<u>tankers</u> are equally helpless in the face of these monsters. <u>Don't think</u>
                                                  (9)

<u>these waves can be outrun</u>. Some travel hundreds of miles an hour.

<u>If you're ever hit by a rogue wave, you're in for a terrifying ride!</u>
                                   (10)

---

1. A. predicate nominative
   B. predicate adjective
   C. direct object
   D. indirect object

2. A. declarative sentence
   B. interrogative sentence
   C. imperative sentence
   D. exclamatory sentence

3. A. direct object
   B. simple subject
   C. predicate nominative
   D. simple predicate

4. A. complete subject
   B. predicate nominative
   C. direct object
   D. complete predicate

5. A. direct object
   B. indirect object
   C. predicate nominative
   D. predicate adjective

6. A. simple subject
   B. predicate nominative
   C. simple predicate
   D. complete predicate

7. A. indirect object
   B. simple predicate
   C. direct object
   D. simple subject

8. A. compound object
   B. compound subject
   C. simple predicate
   D. compound complement

9. A. interrogative sentence
   B. inverted sentence
   C. exclamatory sentence
   D. imperative sentence

10. A. exclamatory sentence
    B. declarative sentence
    C. interrogative sentence
    D. imperative sentence

Student Help Desk

The Sentence at a Glance

**A sentence has two parts, a subject and a predicate.
You should remember that a sentence . . .**

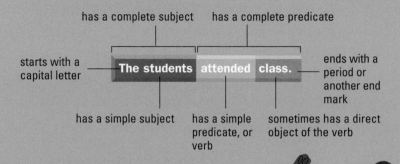

has a complete subject   has a complete predicate

starts with a capital letter ——— **The students** attended **class.** —— ends with a period or another end mark

has a simple subject   has a simple predicate, or verb   sometimes has a direct object of the verb

CHAPTER 2

Subjects and Predicates

The Simple Truth

Term or Concept	Example	Tips and Techniques
Simple subject	Every **sentence** has a subject.	Ask who or what is or does something.
Simple predicate	Every sentence also **has** a verb.	Ask what the subject is or does or what happens to it.

Complements   Objection Overruled

Term or Concept	Example	Tips and Techniques
Predicate nominative	This is **grammar.**	Renames the subject
Predicate adjective	It isn't **boring.**	Describes the subject
Direct object	You can use **it.**	Receives the verb's action. Ask, Uses what?
Indirect object	Give **me** a break.	Tells to or for whom the action is done. Ask, Gives what?

Kinds of Sentences

LIFE SENTENCE

Term or Concept	Example	Tips and Techniques
Declarative sentence	This is a declarative sentence**.**	Ends with a period
Interrogative sentence	Is this an interrogative sentence**?**	Ends with a question mark
Imperative sentence	**[You]** Write an imperative sentence now**.**	Ends with a period or exclamation point. Subject (usually *you*) is generally unstated.
Exclamatory sentence	I won't**!**	Ends with an exclamation point
Subjects in inverted sentences	There **goes** my **grade**.	Locate the predicate and ask who or what does that? *Here* and *there* are usually not subjects.

SENTENCE PARTS

The Bottom Line

Checklist for Editing Sentences
Can I improve my writing by . . .

____ correcting any sentence fragments?

____ using compound subjects or predicates to combine sentences with similar ideas?

____ changing a statement into a question or exclamation?

____ changing the position of a subject to emphasize an important point?

____ replacing a complement with a more specific or exciting word?

____ using action verbs and objects to eliminate the passive voice?

Chapter 3

Using Phrases

Brothers Reunited After 21 Years in Bowling Alley

Coaches' Criticism of Referees Getting Ugly

Missing Last-Second Shot, Championship Trophy Is Lost

Theme: The Will to Compete

Rephrase It!

Can you see how the headlines above could cause confusion? In each, a phrase is misused or put in the wrong place. A **phrase** is a group of related words that acts as a single part of speech. By using phrases effectively and placing them properly, you can make your writing clearer and more descriptive.

Write Away: Headlining Your Life
Write headlines about three different competitions you have participated in—for example, sports, academic competitions, or music auditions. The headlines should focus on the results of the competitions. Save the headlines in your
📁 **Working Portfolio.**

Choose the letter that identifies the purpose of each underlined group of words.

Common sense shows that sports, especially professional sports, have a big effect <u>on the American economy</u>. The question is, How big? One way to
(1)
answer is to look at the impact that one sports star has had.

The basketball superstar <u>Michael Jordan</u> made millions by playing. He
(2)
enriched his team, the Chicago Bulls, by boosting attendance at home games. He also helped send National Basketball Association (NBA) revenues soaring. <u>Greatly increased</u> ticket sales at all of the arenas where
(3)
the Bulls played were part of the story. NBA television revenues and merchandise sales surged too.

Playing spectacular basketball helped Jordan become one of the most famous persons in the world. He has boosted profits of various companies by <u>endorsing products</u>. <u>To measure his economic impact</u>, we must also
(4)   (5)
consider sales of sports videos, books, and more. The greatest basketball player in history added billions to the economy.

PHRASES

1. A. acts as a direct object of the verb *have*
   B. acts as a verb
   C. modifies the noun *effect*
   D. modifies the noun *sports*

2. A. acts as a verb
   B. identifies the noun *superstar*
   C. modifies the noun *basketball*
   D. all of the above

3. A. acts as the subject of the verb *were*
   B. modifies the verb *were*
   C. acts as a predicate nominative
   D. modifies the noun *sales*

4. A. acts as the object of the preposition *by*
   B. modifies the noun *companies*
   C. modifies the adjective *various*
   D. none of the above

5. A. acts as a direct object of the verb *must consider*
   B. modifies the verb *must consider*
   C. modifies the noun *sales*
   D. acts as a verb

Prepositional Phrases

❶ Here's the Idea

▶ **A prepositional phrase consists of a preposition, its object, and any modifiers of the object.**

There are many kinds of sports.
              PREPOSITION ⟋

Some people take a sport to its extreme.
                PREPOSITION ⟋

In the following excerpt from a well-known story, the author uses prepositional phrases to add details. Notice that a prepositional phrase can function either as an adverb or as an adjective.

LITERARY MODEL

"I've always thought," said Rainsford, "that the Cape buffalo is the most dangerous of all big game." For a moment the general did not reply; he was smiling his curious red-lipped smile. Then he said slowly: "No. You are wrong, sir. The Cape buffalo is not the most dangerous big game. . . . Here in my preserve on this island," he said, in the same slow tone, "I hunt more dangerous game."

ADVERB PHRASES

ADJECTIVE PHRASE

—Richard Connell, "The Most Dangerous Game"

Adverb Phrases

Like an adverb, an adverb prepositional phrase modifies a verb, an adjective, or another adverb.

MODIFIES ADJECTIVE
"The Cape buffalo is the most dangerous of all big game."

MODIFIES VERB
. . . he said, in the same slow tone . . .

Adjective Phrases

An adjective prepositional phrase modifies a noun or a pronoun.

MODIFIES NOUN

"Here in my preserve on this island," he said . . .

As you can see in the example above, sometimes an adjective phrase modifies a noun that is part of a different prepositional phrase.

Stringing together too many prepositional phrases can make writing difficult to understand. If you write a sentence that has too many prepositional phrases, check to see if there are any unnecessary details that can be deleted.

Rainsford had fallen off a ship headed from the United States through the Caribbean Sea to the Brazilian city of Rio de Janeiro.

❷ Why It Matters in Writing

Inexperienced writers sometimes confuse readers by putting prepositional phrases in the wrong places in their sentences. Think about how the placement of the prepositional phrase affects the meaning of the following sentences.

Brockton Kennels sells retriever puppies to loving families with vaccinations.
(Is it the families who are vaccinated?)

MODIFIES

Brockton Kennels sells retriever puppies with vaccinations to loving families.

By placing prepositional phrases closer to what they modify, you can avoid confusing your reader.

Golden retrievers are valued for their eagerness to work by hunters.
(Will a retriever work only when it is next to a hunter?)

MODIFIES

Golden retrievers are valued by hunters for their eagerness to work.

❸ Practice and Apply

A. CONCEPT CHECK: Prepositional Phrases

Write each prepositional phrase, along with the word it modifies.

The Challenge of Orienteering
1. Orienteering is a popular type of outdoor competition.
2. People who participate in this sport are called orienteers.
3. Orienteers follow a course that leads through a forest or another natural area.
4. Finishing the course in the fastest time is the goal.
5. Using maps and compasses, orienteers find marked points along the course.
6. At each point, they punch a card.
7. The shortest route between points is often not the fastest.
8. When they finish, orienteers return to a timer's table.
9. People with good navigation skills often do well.
10. Many events have courses for both beginners and experts.

➡ **For a SELF-CHECK and more practice, see the EXERCISE BANK, p. 309.**

B. REVISING: Fixing Misplaced Prepositional Phrases

Rewrite these sentences, changing the position of prepositional phrases so that the sentences are no longer confusing. If a sentence is clear already, write *Correct.*

Hunting Dogs
1. Sporting dogs and hounds are the types of dogs for hunting with the most talent.
2. Sporting dogs are mainly used for hunting birds, and hounds are mainly used for hunting rabbits and foxes.
3. The stamina of a Chesapeake Bay retriever allows it to swim when retrieving ducks for a long time.
4. With its water-resistant fur, a hunter is glad to have a Labrador retriever to swim out and bring back ducks.
5. A pointer holds up a front leg at the scent of a quail with the paw pointed down.
6. Irish water spaniels are funny-looking dogs with tufts over their faces of curly hair.
7. People in Hungary used dogs called vizslas for hunting for centuries with falcons.
8. Beagles were faithful pets of people in ancient Rome.
9. Hunters with English foxhounds on horseback track foxes.
10. With their noses close to the ground, rabbits leave a scent that basset hounds are good at tracking.

❶ Here's the Idea

▶ **An appositive is a noun or pronoun that identifies or renames another noun or pronoun.** An **appositive phrase** is made up of an appositive plus its modifiers.

The appositive phrase in the sentence below identifies a person.

APPOSITIVE PHRASE
Gail Devers, a champion sprinter, was born in Seattle in 1966.
APPOSITIVE

The appositive phrase in the next sentence identifies a place.

Barcelona, a large city in Spain, hosted the Olympics in 1992.

Essential and Nonessential Appositives

An **essential appositive** is an appositive that provides information that is needed to identify the preceding noun or pronoun. It is sometimes called a restrictive appositive.

ESSENTIAL APPOSITIVE
The American sprinter Gail Devers won an Olympic gold medal in the 100-meter dash in 1992.

Notice that no commas are used with an essential appositive.

A **nonessential appositive** adds information about a noun or pronoun in a sentence in which the meaning is already clear. It is also called a nonrestrictive appositive.

NONESSENTIAL APPOSITIVE PHRASE
Devers, a survivor of Graves' disease, overcame many obstacles to achieve athletic success.

As you can see in the sentence above, a nonessential appositive is set off with commas.

❷ Why It Matters in Writing

Using appositives and appositive phrases offers a concise way of explaining how a person or thing is special or unique.

Devers, also a brilliant hurdler, won the gold medal in the 100-meter dash in 1996.

PHRASES

❸ Practice and Apply

A. CONCEPT CHECK: Appositives and Appositive Phrases

Write the appositives and appositive phrases in these sentences, along with the words they rename or identify.

Wilma Rudolph, a True Champion
1. Wilma Rudolph, another champion sprinter, also overcame a disability.
2. As a child, Rudolph contracted the disease polio.
3. Her mother, Blanche Rudolph, helped her recover.
4. Rudolph, a determined child, ignored doctors' predictions about never being able to walk again.
5. A basketball star at age 13, she was known for her speed.
6. The coach Edward Temple invited her to a track camp.
7. In 1956, Rudolph, only a 16-year-old, made the U.S. Olympic team.
8. She and three other women, members of the women's 400-meter relay team, won a bronze medal.
9. Four years later, Rudolph achieved her greatest personal triumph, three gold medals in a single Olympics.
10. Rudolph's hometown in Tennessee, Clarksville, honored her with a big parade after the 1960 Olympic Games.

➡ For a SELF-CHECK and more practice, see the EXERCISE BANK, p. 309.

B. REVISING: Adding Details

Rewrite each sentence, adding the appositive or appositive phrase shown in parentheses. Include commas if necessary.

The Man Who Won Ten Gold Medals
1. The Olympic athlete also overcame polio. (Ray Ewry)
2. Ewry participated in four Olympics. (A specialist in jumping events)
3. Ewry competed in the standing high jump, the standing long jump, and the standing triple jump. (events not part of today's Olympic Games)
4. Ewry never lost an Olympic event he entered. (the only man to win ten gold medals)
5. He had an advantage over today's athletes: when he competed, four Olympics were held during the nine-year period. (1900–1908)

LESSON 3 · Verbals: Participial Phrases

A **verbal** is a verb form that acts as a noun, an adjective, or an adverb. There are three types of verbals: participles, gerunds, and infinitives.

❶ Here's the Idea

▶ **A participle is a verb form that acts as an adjective. It modifies a noun or a pronoun.** A **participial phrase** consists of a participle plus its modifiers and complements.

PARTICIPLE

Played for more than 100 years, high school football has a rich tradition.

Large crowds attend games featuring rival schools.

PARTICIPLE

There are two kinds of participles: past participles (*played*) and present participles (*featuring*).

Writers use participles to describe nouns, as in the following excerpt.

LITERARY MODEL

The coach looked like an old gangster: broken nose, a scar on his cheek like a stitched shoestring.

—Robert Cormier, *The Chocolate War*

PARTICIPLES

Broken modifies *nose; stitched* modifies *shoestring.*

In the next excerpt, notice how Robert Cormier used participial phrases to add details to a description of an injured football player on an autumn afternoon.

LITERARY MODEL

Inhaling the sweet sharp apple air through his nostrils—he was afraid to open his mouth wide, wary of any movement that was not absolutely essential—**he** walked tentatively toward the sidelines, listening to the **coach** barking at the other guys.

—*The Chocolate War*

PARTICIPIAL PHRASES

The first two phrases modify *he;* the third modifies *coach.*

Notice that *coach* is part of a participial phrase and is modified by another participial phrase.

PHRASES

❷ Why It Matters in Writing

Many writers have trouble placing participial phrases in sentences. Putting words in the wrong place can result in a misplaced or dangling phrase that will confuse the reader.

A **misplaced participial phrase** is closer to some other noun than it is to the noun it actually modifies.

STUDENT MODEL

DRAFT

Beginning in the 1890s, Thanksgiving Day was when top high school football teams from different regions paired off in major games.

This sentence makes it sound as if the first Thanksgiving holiday occurred in the 1890s.

REVISION

Beginning in the 1890s, top high school football teams from different regions paired off in major games on Thanksgiving Day.

A participial phrase that begins a sentence should be followed immediately by what it modifies.

A **dangling participial phrase** is one that does not logically modify any of the words in the sentence in which it appears.

STUDENT MODEL

DRAFT

Responding to changes in the rules of football, the forward pass was used more often in high school games in the 1920s.

A forward pass cannot do anything except get caught or hit the ground!

REVISION

Responding to changes in the rules of football, high school coaches began using the forward pass more often in the 1920s.

The coaches were the ones who responded to the rule changes.

Shoe by Jeff MacNelly

© 1998 Tribune Media Services Inc.

❸ Practice and Apply

A. CONCEPT CHECK: Participial Phrases

Write the participial phrase in each sentence. Then write the noun modified by the phrase.

A Sport in Decline?

1. In many parts of the country, steadily declining interest has damaged high school football.
2. Preferring soccer or basketball, many students do not sign up for football.
3. Parents concerned about football injuries suggest other sports.
4. Reacting to a lack of interest, school officials have cut football funds.
5. Remaining popular in many urban areas, however, high school football won't be dying out anytime soon.

➡ For a SELF-CHECK and more practice, see the EXERCISE BANK, p. 310.

CHALLENGE Write a sentence that expresses your opinion about the value of high school football. Include a participial phrase in the sentence.

B. REVISING: Fixing Dangling and Misplaced Participial Phrases

Read the following paragraph. Rewrite the sentences that contain dangling or misplaced participial phrases, adding or rearranging words to eliminate the errors.

A Star in Two Ways

A high school in Colorado had a homecoming queen who played football. There was a special ceremony at halftime of the homecoming game. Queen Katie smiled for the photographers taking off her helmet. Accepting a white rose, the crowd loudly cheered. Katie enjoyed the ceremony, but she was prouder of her performance on the field. With the game on the line, a field goal sailed through the goal posts kicked by Katie. During her four years on the team, Katie played well without receiving any special treatment. She was tackled by large opposing players kicking extra points. Katie was not ready to give up the game after high school. Determined to play college football, Katie's mother gave her full support.

PHRASES

Verbals: Gerund Phrases

❶ Here's the Idea

▶ **A gerund is a verb form that ends in *ing* and acts as a noun.**
A **gerund phrase** consists of a gerund plus its modifiers
and complements.

GERUND
He loves swimming.

GERUND PHRASE
He loves swimming in the ocean.

LITERARY MODEL

Next morning, when it was time for the routine of
swimming and **sunbathing**, his mother said, "Are you
tired of the usual beach, Jerry? Would you like to go
somewhere else?"

—Doris Lessing, "Through the Tunnel"

Like nouns, gerunds and gerund phrases can act as subjects,
objects of prepositions, direct objects, indirect objects, and
predicate nominatives.

Functions of Gerund Phrases	
Function	Example
Subject	**Swimming competitively** requires lots of practice.
Object of a preposition	Jeff got in shape by **swimming at the YMCA**.
Direct object	Mr. Lopez coaches **high school swimming**.
Indirect object	Tameka gave competitive **swimming** a try.
Predicate nominative	Tameka's specialty is **swimming the backstroke**.

❷ Why It Matters in Writing

Gerunds can help you make your writing more concise. Sometimes a
gerund can replace an entire group of words, as in the student
model on the next page.

> *Swimming*
> A person who swims across the English Channel makes an *is*
> awesome accomplishment. A swimmer must travel at least 21
> miles through strong currents. Even the fastest swimmers spend
> more than seven hours to make the trip across the Channel. *in crossing*

❸ Practice and Apply

CONCEPT CHECK: Gerund Phrases

Write the gerund phrase in each sentence. Then indicate whether the phrase functions as a subject (S), an object of a preposition (OP), a direct object (DO), an indirect object (IO), or a predicate nominative (PN).

Pablo Morales, the Swimmer Who Wouldn't Give Up

1. Pablo Morales became known as the comeback kid of Olympic swimming.
2. One of the goals of Morales's mother was having her children learn to swim at an early age.
3. Morales learned quickly, and soon he started winning junior championships.
4. As a student at Stanford University, he attracted attention by winning 11 NCAA championships.
5. Competing in the 1984 Olympics brought him one gold medal and two silver medals.
6. Morales surprised everybody by failing to qualify for the 1988 Olympics.
7. After that, his new goal was earning a law degree.
8. When his mother died in 1991, Morales gave competitive swimming another chance.
9. Having only seven months to prepare made it difficult for him to qualify for the 1992 Olympics, but he did.
10. He touched people's hearts by winning a gold medal in the 100-meter butterfly.

➡ **For a SELF-CHECK and more practice, see the EXERCISE BANK, p. 310.**

Verbals: Infinitive Phrases

❶ Here's the Idea

▶ **An infinitive is a verb form, usually beginning with the word** *to*, **that can act as a noun, an adjective, or an adverb.** An **infinitive phrase** consists of an infinitive plus its modifiers and complements.

INFINITIVE

More and more women are learning to golf.

INFINITIVE PHRASE

To make a living as a golfer **is no easy task.**

The following chart shows examples of the different ways in which infinitive phrases can be used in sentences.

Uses of Infinitive Phrases	
Noun	**To win tournaments on the Ladies Professional Golf Association (LPGA) tour** is the goal of top women golfers. (used as subject)
Adjective	In 1998, Se Ri Pak became the youngest player **to win the U.S. Women's Open golf championship.** (modifies *player*)
Adverb	**To become a champion golfer,** Pak spent many hours practicing in her native land of South Korea. (modifies *spent*)

❷ Why It Matters in Writing

Using infinitive phrases, you can combine sentences in a way that eliminates unnecessary words and sharpens the relationship between ideas.

STUDENT MODEL

DRAFT
Golfers use many different types of clubs during a tournament. Different clubs are needed to hit good shots.

REVISION
Golfers use many different types of clubs **to hit good shots** during a tournament.

❸ Practice and Apply

➡ **For a SELF-CHECK and more practice, see the EXERCISE BANK, p. 311.**

A. CONCEPT CHECK: Infinitive Phrases

Write each infinitive or infinitive phrase, indicating whether it acts as an adjective, an adverb, or a noun.

Tiger's Good Works

1. It is a shame that so few sports stars are willing to help people in need.
2. To give something back to society is important to Tiger Woods.
3. Woods was the first person of African-American descent to win a major tournament in men's professional golf.
4. To overcome golf's history of discrimination was no easy task.
5. Woods is determined to help other persons of color become golf stars.
6. To turn his dreams into reality, he founded a charitable organization, the Tiger Woods Foundation, in 1997.
7. It is one of the few golf organizations to work with disadvantaged children.
8. The foundation sponsors clinics to help children learn golf.
9. At the clinics, Woods likes to work with individual kids.
10. His foundation is also working to create new, affordable golf practice facilities around the country.

➡ **For a SELF-CHECK and more practice, see the EXERCISE BANK, p. 311.**

B. REVISING: Combining Sentences

Use an infinitive phrase to combine each pair of sentences.

Example: Hale Irwin has displayed incredible skill. He has won the U.S. Open three times.

Answer: Hale Irwin has displayed incredible skill to win the U.S. Open three times.

A Golfer Who Keeps Winning

1. Hale Irwin must have amazing physical endurance. He has won tournaments for 30 years.
2. He had weeks of outstanding play on the Senior Tour. He earned nearly $3 million in one year.
3. He possesses extraordinary talent. He has dominated a professional sport for so many years.

PHRASES

Placement of Phrases

LESSON 6

❶ Here's the Idea

A common mistake that writers make is putting phrases in the wrong positions in sentences. This mistake usually involves phrases used as adjectives or adverbs.

Misplaced Phrases

A **misplaced phrase** is a phrase that is placed so far away from the word it modifies that the meaning of the sentence is unclear or incorrect. The types of phrases that are most often misplaced are prepositional phrases and participial phrases.

> **DRAFT**
> MISPLACED PREPOSITIONAL PHRASE
> **The U.S. team in men's indoor volleyball won the most Olympic gold medals during the 1980s.**

The sentence above says that the U.S. men's indoor volleyball team won more Olympic gold medals than any other team in any sport. This is not true.

> **REVISION**
> **The U.S. team won the most Olympic gold medals in men's indoor volleyball during the 1980s.**

Dangling Phrases

When the word or words that a phrase should modify are missing from a sentence, the phrase is called a **dangling phrase.** Most dangling phrases are participial phrases or infinitive phrases.

> **DRAFT**
> DANGLING PARTICIPIAL PHRASE
> **Failing to win a gold medal in the 1900s, the Olympic women's indoor volleyball competition has been disappointing.**

The sentence above says that a competition won a gold medal.

> **REVISION**   WORDS MODIFIED
> **Failing to win a gold medal in the 1900s, the U.S. women's indoor volleyball team was disappointing at the Olympics.**

CHAPTER 3

❷ Why It Matters in Writing

Sentences with phrases that are not placed properly can confuse readers. Such a sentence can end up sounding silly.

To keep their grades up, homework assignments need to take priority over students' athletic activities. (When did homework assignments develop a mind of their own?)

❸ Practice and Apply

CONCEPT CHECK: Placement of Phrases

Rewrite these sentences to fix misplaced and dangling phrases. If a sentence has no error, write *Correct.*

Outstanding American Volleyball Players

1. Mike Lambert is one of the top indoor volleyball players in the United States.
2. To become an outstanding all-around player like Lambert, many hours of training are required.
3. Competing for Stanford University, the most-valuable-player trophy at the 1997 NCAA championship was awarded to Lambert.
4. Growing up in Hawaii, soccer was a favorite sport besides volleyball.
5. Lambert joined a professional team after graduating from Stanford in Greece.
6. Holly McPeak is one of the world's best players in women's beach volleyball.
7. Raised in Manhattan Beach, California, few activities were more enjoyable than volleyball.
8. Having won more than $200,000 during her career, her performances include victories in over 20 tournaments.
9. To have success in two-on-two beach volleyball, the right partner must be found.
10. McPeak is especially well-known for her outstanding defensive play by fans.

➡ **For a SELF-CHECK and more practice, see the EXERCISE BANK, p. 311.**

Give two possible answers for items 2 and 8.

Sentence Diagramming

Mad Mapper

Here's the Idea

Learning how to diagram sentences that contain phrases can help you understand the roles that phrases play in writing.

Watch me for diagramming tips!

Prepositional Phrases

- Write the preposition on a slanted line below the word the prepositional phrase modifies.
- Write the object of the preposition on a horizontal line attached to the slanted line and parallel to the main line.
- Write words that modify the object of the preposition on slanted lines below the object.

Adjective Phrase

Many designers of computer software study artificial intelligence.

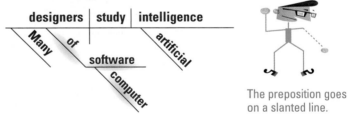

The preposition goes on a slanted line.

Adverb Phrase

These designers program intelligence into computers.

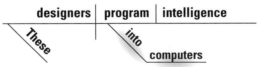

A. CONCEPT CHECK: Prepositional Phrases

Diagram these sentences, using what you have learned.

1. Some computers can play checkers against human opponents.
2. A research team at a Canadian university developed one famous program.

Appositive Phrases

Appositive attitude!

Write an appositive in parentheses after the word it identifies or renames. Attach words that modify the appositive to it in the usual way.

Marion Tinsley, the world champion, played a checkers match against Chinook.

B. CONCEPT CHECK: Appositive Phrases

Diagram the following sentence, using what you have learned.

Tinsley, the best player of all time, beat Chinook in 1992.

Participial Phrases

- The participle curves over an angled line below the word it modifies.
- Diagram an object or a subject complement on the horizontal part of the angled line in the usual way.
- Write modifiers on slanted lines below the words they modify.

Beating other top players brilliantly, Chinook was the new checkers champion.

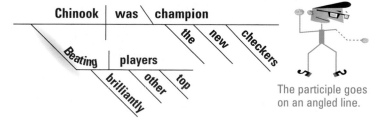

The participle goes on an angled line.

C. CONCEPT CHECK: Participial Phrases

Diagram the following sentence, using what you have learned.

Programmed properly, computers can also play chess expertly.

PHRASES

Gerund Phrases

- The gerund curves over an angled line that looks like a step.
- With a vertical forked line, connect the step to the part of the diagram that corresponds to the role of the gerund phrase in the sentence.
- Complements and modifiers are diagrammed in the usual way.

Gerund Phrase as Subject

Playing chess is the specialty of the program Deep Blue.

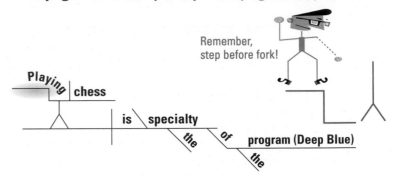

Remember, step before fork!

Gerund Phrase as Object of a Preposition

Careful thought is required for winning a game of chess.

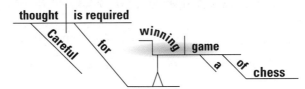

D. CONCEPT CHECK: Gerund Phrases

Diagram these sentences, using what you have learned.

1. For years, researchers worked at refining Deep Blue.
2. Beating the best human player was their goal.

Infinitive Phrases

- Write the infinitive on line, with the word *to* on the slanted part and the verb on the horizontal part.
- If the phrase functions as a noun, use a vertical forked line to connect it to the part of the diagram that corresponds to its role in the sentence.

- If the phrase functions as a modifier, place it below the word it modifies.

Infinitive Phrase as Subject

To defeat top players was the goal of Deep Blue's programmers.

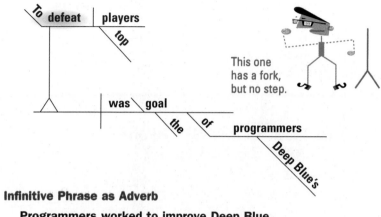

This one has a fork, but no step.

Infinitive Phrase as Adverb

Programmers worked to improve Deep Blue.

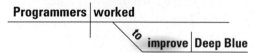

PHRASES

E. CONCEPT CHECK: Infinitive Phrases

Diagram these sentences, using what you have learned.

1. Garry Kasparov agreed to play Deep Blue.
2. To defeat Kasparov was the programmers' dream.

F. MIXED REVIEW: Diagramming

Diagram the following sentences. Look for all the types of phrases you have learned about.

1. IBM Corporation developed the computer program Deep Blue.
2. Playing confidently, Garry Kasparov defeated the first Deep Blue.
3. IBM researchers began a project to improve their program.
4. Kasparov and the second Deep Blue met in 1997.
5. Losing the match embarrassed Kasparov.

Grammar in Literature

Adding Detail with Phrases

Writers often use phrases to provide descriptive details and to show connections between ideas and actions. In the following excerpt, phrases help to create a lively description of a 14-year-old boy trying to fish secretly while canoeing with an older girl he has a crush on. See if you can find phrases other than the ones indicated here.

from THE BASS, THE RIVER, AND SHEILA MANT

W. D. Wetherell

Fish will trail a lure sometimes, trying to make up their mind whether or not to attack, and the slight pause in the plug's speed caused by my adjustment was tantalizing enough to overcome the bass's inhibitions. My rod, safely out of sight at last, bent double. The line, tightly coiled, peeled off the spool with the shrill, tearing zip of a high-speed drill.

> A participial phrase helps describe how fish behave.

> Prepositional phrases vividly describe the manner in which the fishing line is unreeled.

Four things occurred to me at once. One, that it was a bass. Two, that it was a big bass. Three, that it was the biggest bass I had ever hooked. Four, that Sheila Mant must not know.

"What was that?" she said, turning half around.

"Uh, what was what?"

"That buzzing noise."

"Bats."

She shuddered, quickly drew her feet back into the canoe. Every instinct I had told me to pick up the rod and strike back at the bass, but there was no need to—it was already solidly hooked. Downstream, an awesome distance downstream, it jumped clear of the water, landing with a concussion heavy enough to ripple the entire river. For a moment, I thought it was gone, but then the rod was bending again, the tip dancing into the water. Slowly, not making any motion that might alert Sheila, I reached down to tighten the drag.

> Infinitive phrases describe a possible sequence of actions.

> A participial phrase shows how big the bass is.

Ways You Can Use Phrases in Writing	
Prepositional phrases	Use to express relationships of time, location, or manner
Appositive phrases	Use to identify or specify people, places, things, or ideas
Participial phrases	Use to describe people, places, or events and to give a sense of action to your writing
Gerund phrases	Use to make your writing more concise
Infinitive phrases	Use to add details or explain processes

PRACTICE AND APPLY: Adding Detail with Phrases

In each pair of sentences below, one of the sentences adds detail to the other. Use phrases to combine the sentences, following the directions given in parentheses.

Example: Most sports have rules of conduct. These rules discourage participants from unsporting behavior. (Change the second sentence to a participial phrase that begins with *discouraging*.)

Answer: Most sports have rules of conduct discouraging participants from unsporting behavior.

1. For example, football teams whose players taunt opposing players or criticize officials are penalized 15 yards. The penalty is called unsportsmanlike conduct. (Change the second sentence to a prepositional phrase that begins with *for*.)
2. Sometimes a professional basketball player or coach insults a referee. This can cause the referee to call a technical foul and award the other team a free throw. (Change the first sentence to a gerund phrase by replacing the first part of the sentence with "In basketball, insulting . . . ")
3. Arguing with a baseball umpire is a risk. One risks being thrown out of the game. (Change each sentence to an infinitive phrase, and connect the phrases with the verb *is*.)
4. Rules of conduct are especially strict in golf. Golf is a sport with a long tradition of fair play. (Change the second sentence to an appositive phrase.)
5. A tennis player can be penalized points. Two ways this can happen are if the player argues with the umpire or throws a racket. (Change the second sentence to a prepositional phrase that begins with *for* and contains two gerunds.)

Choose a piece of writing in your ⬜ **Working Portfolio** and make it more detailed by adding several types of phrases.

Mixed Review

A. Kinds of Phrases Indicate what type of phrase each of the underlined phrases is.

(1) Centuries ago, Alaska's Eskimo peoples began using dogsleds to travel <u>across the snow</u>. (2) The dogsled, <u>a reliable means of transportation</u>, later carried gold miners and others along Alaska's trails. (3) The invention <u>of the snowmobile</u> changed all that.

(4) Joe Redington, <u>a dedicated dogsledder</u>, wanted to keep dogsledding alive. (5) <u>To spark enthusiasm</u>, he organized the first Iditarod Trail Sled Dog Race in 1973. (6) <u>Competing for $51,000</u>, 34 mushers (sled drivers) and dog teams raced more than 1,100 miles (1,770 kilometers).

(7) <u>Fascinated by the drama</u>, people around the world follow the annual Iditarod. (8) Mushers and dogs must survive subzero temperatures, blizzards, and moose attacks if they hope <u>to win the race</u>. (9) Some sled dogs have died, even though most of the dog owners are committed to <u>providing excellent care</u>. (10) For this reason, campaigns <u>to end the Iditarod</u> have been launched.

B. Misplaced and Dangling Phrases Proofread the following paragraph for dangling and misplaced phrases. Rewrite the four sentences that contain errors, correcting them.

The 1998 Winter Olympics included a sport that no previous Olympics had included. At that Olympics, medals were awarded for snowboarding for the first time. Snowboarding has come a long way from its beginnings. Once banned at most ski resorts, Americans have made snowboarding the nation's fastest growing winter sport. Two events for men and women, the giant slalom and the halfpipe, were held at the Olympics. In the giant slalom, contestants raced downhill, swerving through gates. To win the halfpipe, spectacular moves had to be made by competitors traveling through a chute of snow. Unfortunately, the U.S. team did not do as well as predicted. Winning only two bronze medals, the 1998 Olympics was a disappointment for the U.S. snowboarders.

Choose the letter that identifies the purpose of each underlined phrase.

> Soccer as we know it gained worldwide popularity <u>in the late 1800s</u>.
>
(1)
> <u>Embraced by Americans</u>, the game was played at schools and colleges.
>
(2)
> Soccer clubs were formed for adults wanting to join the fun. By 1900,
>
> however, Americans had become more interested in <u>playing football</u>.
>
(3)
> Soccer, <u>the world's favorite sport</u>, followed a roller-coaster path in the
>
(4)
> United States after 1900. The Brazilian soccer star Pelé sparked
>
> Americans' interest in the game by playing for a U.S. professional team
>
> during the 1970s. <u>To become truly successful</u>, professional soccer needs a
>
(5)
> larger TV audience. Soccer is most popular among young people. Today
>
> millions of American students are happy to spend time on the soccer field.

1. A. acts as a verb
   B. acts as the subject of the verb *gained*
   C. modifies the noun *popularity*
   D. modifies the verb *gained*

2. A. modifies the noun *game*
   B. identifies the noun *schools*
   C. modifies the verb *was played*
   D. all of the above

3. A. acts as the object of the preposition *in*
   B. modifies the noun *Americans*
   C. acts as a predicate nominative
   D. acts as the subject of the verb *had become*

4. A. modifies the verb *followed*
   B. acts as a direct object of the verb *followed*
   C. modifies the noun *path*
   D. none of the above

5. A. acts as the subject of the verb *needs*
   B. modifies the verb *needs*
   C. modifies the noun *audience*
   D. acts as a verb

PHRASES

Student Help Desk

Phrases at a Glance

Kind of Phrase	Functions as	Example
Prepositional phrase	Adjective	The skates on the floor are Elena's.
	Adverb	Elena skated around the rink.
Appositive phrase	Noun	Mr. Gorski, the coach, is here.
Participial phrase	Adjective	Hockey fans wearing jerseys waited patiently.
Gerund phrase	Noun	Rollerblading in the park is fun.
Infinitive phrase	Noun	Armand loves to bowl.
	Adjective	Dropping the ball is something to avoid.
	Adverb	Chiang races to the finish line.

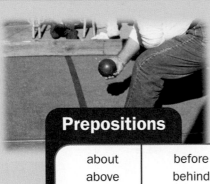

Prepositions

Over the line
Through the hoop

about	before	inside	to
above	behind	into	toward
across	below	near	under
after	beside	of	underneath
against	between	off	until
along	by	on	up
among	down	onto	upon
around	for	out	with
as	from	over	without
at	in	through	

Phrases to Avoid *Modifier Mixups*

What It's Called	What's Wrong with It
Misplaced modifier	**It appears to modify something that it doesn't.** **Example:** We sell gasoline to people in plastic jugs.
Dangling modifier	**What it should modify is missing from the sentence.** **Example:** Walking past the kitchen, the fish smelled delicious.

Comma Do's and Don'ts An Appositive Approach

DO	**Example**
Use commas with nonessential appositives.	Pedro Martinez, a native of the Dominican Republic, is a pitcher for the New York Mets and one of the best players in baseball.
DON'T	**Example**
Do not use commas with essential appositives.	The New York Mets pitcher Pedro Martinez is one of the best players in baseball.

The Bottom Line

Checklist for Phrases
Have I . . .

____ used phrases to add details and clarity to my writing?

____ used commas with nonessential appositives?

____ placed phrases that act as adverbs or adjectives close to what they modify?

____ avoided stringing together too many prepositional phrases?

Clauses and Sentence Structure

Theme: Families

It's All in the Family!

Tennis stars Venus and Serena Williams are two of the most famous sisters in sports. If they were your sisters, how would you describe them to someone else? Chances are you'd say something like, "My sisters, *who are really competitive,* love playing against each other." Or *"How they got started in tennis* is a great story."

You've used clauses to add details and to show relationships between ideas. You can use these sentence parts to do the same things in your writing. Although some clauses can stand on their own, many depend on other parts of a sentence for their meaning.

Write Away: Lean on Me

When the going gets tough, whom do you depend on? Write a paragraph about a family member or friend who lends you moral support. Save your paragraph in your 🗀 **Working Portfolio.**

Choose the letter of the term that identifies each numbered part of this passage.

> Ursula K. Le Guin, <u>who is one of the world's best science fiction</u>
> <u>writers</u>, creates alien characters and societies <u>that are completely</u>
>   (1)   (2)
> <u>believable</u>. <u>As people read her stories</u>, they are often amazed at these
>   (3)
> complex worlds, <u>which she describes in great detail</u>. <u>Where her ideas come</u>
>   (4)   (5)
> <u>from</u> might be explained by her family history. Her father was an
>
> anthropologist, a scientist <u>who studies human cultures</u>. <u>When</u>
>   (6)   (7)
> <u>Le Guin was young</u>, she learned about the great variety of customs,
>   (7)
> languages, and family structures of the world's people. <u>Le Guin's mother,</u>
>   (8)
> <u>Theodora Kroeber, wrote a famous book about a man called Ishi</u>. He was
>
> the last member of his tribe. <u>When Le Guin wanted to create alien people</u>
>   (9)
> <u>and places</u>, she could draw from such material. <u>Le Guin has continued the</u>
>
> <u>family tradition of writing about the exotic, and her novels and stories</u>
>   (10)
> <u>captivate people of all generations.</u>

CLAUSES

1. A. independent clause
   B. subordinate clause
   C. adverb clause
   D. noun clause as subject

2. A. noun clause as direct object
   B. adjective clause
   C. independent clause
   D. nonessential clause

3. A. independent clause
   B. noun clause as direct object
   C. adverb clause
   D. adjective clause

4. A. noun clause as subject
   B. essential clause
   C. nonessential clause
   D. adverb clause

5. A. noun clause as subject
   B. independent clause
   C. simple sentence
   D. adverb clause

6. A. essential clause
   B. independent clause
   C. nonessential clause
   D. noun clause as direct object

7. A. noun clause
   B. essential clause
   C. nonessential clause
   D. adverb clause

8. A. compound sentence
   B. complex sentence
   C. simple sentence
   D. compound-complex sentence

9. A. independent clause
   B. adjective clause
   C. noun clause as subject
   D. adverb clause

10. A. simple sentence
    B. compound sentence
    C. complex sentence
    D. compound-complex sentence

Kinds of Clauses

❶ Here's the Idea

▶ **A clause is a group of words that contains a subject and a verb.**

Your <u>genes</u> <u>carry</u> your family's genetic history.
SUBJECT ⬆   ⬆VERB

Independent Clauses

An **independent (**or **main) clause** expresses a complete thought. It can stand alone as a sentence.

| Genes contain the code for your physical appearance. |
INDEPENDENT CLAUSE

Subordinate Clauses

A **subordinate (**or **dependent) clause** contains a subject and a verb but does not express a complete thought. It cannot stand alone. Subordinate clauses may be introduced by words like *if, because, even though, how, what, why, that, while, when,* and *since.*

| that determines your height |
SUBORDINATE CLAUSE

| because inherited traits often skip a generation |
SUBORDINATE CLAUSE

Creating Complete Sentences

To express a complete thought, a subordinate clause must be combined with, or be part of, an independent clause.

| Genes contain the code | that determines your height. |
INDEPENDENT CLAUSE   SUBORDINATE CLAUSE

SUBORDINATE CLAUSE
| Because inherited traits often skip a generation, | you may |
| resemble your grandparents more than your parents. |
INDEPENDENT CLAUSE

WATCH OUT

Do not confuse a subordinate clause with a verbal phrase. Unlike a clause, a verbal phrase has no subject.

Verbal Phrase: Driving over the bridge, she sneezed.

Clause: As she was driving over the bridge, she sneezed.

❷ Why It Matters in Writing

Many fragments are actually subordinate clauses. To fix these fragments, join them with independent clauses.

STUDENT MODEL

Clasp your hands together. ~~As~~ the
picture shows. Which thumb is on
top? If you clasp your hands to
position the other thumb on top. *it feels wrong.*
This odd little trait is inherited.

❸ Practice and Apply

CONCEPT CHECK: Kinds of Clauses

Identify the underlined clauses as subordinate or independent.

Your Personality—Is It Inherited?

1. Although you inherit your looks, <u>the origin of your personality is more mysterious</u>.
2. Research on identical twins has fueled <u>what scientists call the "heredity versus environment" debate</u>.
3. The debate focuses on one question—<u>whether personality is mainly inherited or mainly shaped by family and other people</u>.
4. Identical twins raised in separate families showed amazing similarities <u>even though the families were very different</u>.
5. Not only did many of the twins have similar IQs, <u>their body language was also remarkably the same</u>.
6. One set of twins tugged at their hair <u>while they read a book</u>.
7. Although they were raised miles apart, <u>they liked the same school subjects and wore the same kinds of clothes</u>.
8. <u>When separated twins had illnesses</u>, they often had identical illnesses at roughly the same time.
9. <u>Another set of twins really amazed researchers</u> because both once had dogs named Toy and had wives named Betty.
10. <u>Because these similarities are so unlikely to happen by chance</u>, heredity probably plays a role in shaping personality.

➡ **For a SELF-CHECK and more practice, see the EXERCISE BANK, p. 312.**

Adjective and Adverb Clauses

LESSON 2

❶ Here's the Idea

Subordinate clauses can function as adjectives and adverbs.

Adjective Clauses

▶ **An adjective clause is a subordinate clause that is used as an adjective to modify a noun or pronoun.** It usually follows the word(s) it modifies. Like adjectives, these clauses answer the questions *which one, what kind, how much,* or *how many.*

MODIFIES

A family is more than a group of people who are related.
                                              NOUN ↑   ADJECTIVE CLAUSE

MODIFIES

It was she who started our family tree.
PRONOUN ↑   ADJECTIVE CLAUSE

An adjective clause is introduced by a **relative pronoun** or by a **relative adverb.** These words are called relative because they *relate* adjective clauses to the words they modify.

Words That Introduce Adjective Clauses	
Relative pronouns	who, whom, whose, that, which
Relative adverbs	when, where, why

Families may also include foster children and people who are adopted.

Some people still live in a hunter-gatherer society, where a "family" may have 20 to 200 members.

Essential and Nonessential Adjective Clauses

An **essential** adjective clause provides information that is essential, or necessary, to identify the preceding noun or pronoun.

Someone who is your first cousin is the child of your uncle or aunt.

A **nonessential** adjective clause adds information about a noun or pronoun in a sentence in which the meaning is already clear. The clause can be dropped without changing the sentence's meaning.

Irene, who is your first cousin, was married last fall.

Irene was married last fall. (meaning is still clear)

Notice that a nonessential clause is set off by commas. The commas separate nonessential information from the main idea of the sentence.

That and Which Writers are often not sure whether to use *that* or *which* to introduce essential or nonessential clauses. Follow these guidelines to use these words correctly.

That is used to introduce an essential clause.

The reception was held at a hotel that looks like a castle.

Which is used to introduce a nonessential clause.

The Clarmont Hotel, which looks like a castle, is 100 years old.

CLAUSES

Adverb Clauses

▶ **An adverb clause is a subordinate clause that modifies a verb, an adjective, or an adverb.** It may come before or after the word(s) it modifies. Like adverbs, the clauses tell *where, why, how, when,* or *to what degree* something was done.

MODIFIES

Most children leave home when the time is right.
VERB ↗   ADVERB CLAUSE

MODIFIES

Many young adults think a career is important because it helps them to become independent.   ADJECTIVE ↗   ADVERB CLAUSE

MODIFIES

Many are marrying later in life than their parents did.
ADVERB ↗   ADVERB CLAUSE

Words That Introduce Adverb Clauses

An adverb clause is usually introduced by a subordinating conjunction. A **subordinating conjunction** relates the adverb clause to the word(s) it modifies. The following is a list of the most common subordinating conjunctions.

Commonly Used Subordinating Conjunctions

after	as though	so that	whenever
although	because	than	where
as	before	though	wherever
as if	even though	unless	while
as long as	if	until	
as soon as	since	when	

When you marry, your spouse's family becomes part of your family "in law."

You gain a second mother and father **even though you are not related by blood.**

Notice that an adverb clause is set off by a comma when it comes *before* the independent clause. When it comes *after* the independent clause, often no comma is needed.

② Why It Matters in Writing

Use adjective and adverb clauses to add details, to clarify relationships between your ideas, and to avoid repetition.

STUDENT MODEL

DRAFT

    Young adults finish college. Some choose to live with their parents again. These young people are called boomerangers. Boomerangers keep returning home.

REVISION

    After they finish college, some young adults choose to live with their parents again. These young people are called boomerangers **because they keep returning home.**

A. CONCEPT CHECK: Adjective and Adverb Clauses

Write the adjective and adverb clauses in the following sentences. After each clause, write the word or words that it modifies.

> **Genealogy for Dummies**
> 1. Humans aren't the only ones who have family trees.
> 2. The crash-test dummy family line started in 1949 when the U.S. Army Air Force bought the first Sierra Sam.
> 3. Sam was used in ejection seat tests that the army ran.
> 4. The Sams had sensors so their crashes could be recorded.
> 5. These dummies were used to test anything that humans could ride, like cars, roller coasters, airplanes, and tanks.
> 6. When testers needed more models, Sam's family expanded to include Stan, Saul, Sue, Susie, and Sammy.
> 7. The later Hybrid II dummy worked better than Sierra Sam because it had more flexibility.
> 8. Crash dummies Larry and Vince, whose TV ads promoted seat belt safety, were probably Hybrid II descendants.
> 9. The 1976 Hybrid III line was developed because the auto industry needed more accurate crash-test results.
> 10. Recent additions to the family tree include infant and child dummies that are used to test problems with airbags.

➜ **For a SELF-CHECK and more practice, see the EXERCISE BANK, p. 313.**

B. REVISING: Adding Details

Combine each pair of sentences by changing the italicized one into an adjective or adverb clause. Use the introductory words given.

Example: Childhood can last a lifetime. *Historical records show.* (as)
Answer: Childhood can last a lifetime, as historical records show.

> **Children or Adults?**
> 1. In old Europe, people had different ideas about parent-child relationships. *The ideas might seem harsh today.* (that)
> 2. Children couldn't marry or work without permission from their fathers. *Their fathers had authority over their lives.* (who)
> 3. *Young people married.* (until) They were considered "youths"— not quite children but not adults.
> 4. *These ideas created two extremes.* (because) You could learn an adult trade at age 7 but still be a "child" at age 30.
> 5. In some countries, even marriage didn't make a son independent. *He and his family lived with his father.* (if)

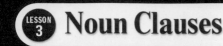

Noun Clauses

LESSON 3

❶ Here's the Idea

▶ **A noun clause is a subordinate clause used as a noun.** A noun clause can serve the same function as a noun in a sentence.

> That my brothers and sisters influence me is obvious.
> SUBJECT

> They know exactly what drives me crazy.
> DIRECT OBJECT

> My parents tell whoever is loudest to quiet down.
> INDIRECT OBJECT

> My sister's or brother's praise is also what inspires me.
> PREDICATE NOMINATIVE

> We encourage each other in whatever ways we can.
> OBJECT OF A PREPOSITION

If you can substitute the word *someone* or *something* for a clause in a sentence, it is a noun clause. (They know *what drives me crazy.* They know *something.*)

Words That Introduce Noun Clauses

A noun clause can be introduced by a **subordinating conjunction** or by a **pronoun.** The chart below lists the most common words that introduce noun clauses.

Words Used to Introduce Noun Clauses	
Subordinating conjunctions	that, how, when, where, whether, why
Pronouns	what, whatever, who, whom, whoever, whomever, which, whichever

> How much brothers and sisters argue depends on their ages.

> You usually argue most with whoever is closest to your age.

Sometimes the introductory word in a noun clause is omitted. However, you can still substitute *someone* or *something* for the clause to determine whether it is a noun clause.

> **Most experts say (that) many brothers and sisters become close later in life.**

> **Most experts say something.**

CHAPTER 4

❷ Why It Matters in Writing

Sometimes a one-word noun won't do. You may need a noun clause to explain something. Notice the difference in the following two paragraphs.

DRAFT

How children have been raised may depend on the **year**. In the late 1920s, Dr. John B. Watson, a famous psychologist, advised **people** to withhold affection from their children. **This** didn't work. The reason is obvious. Parents found it too hard to follow.

REVISION

How children have been raised may depend on **when they were born**. In the late 1920s, Dr. John B. Watson, a famous psychologist, advised **whichever parents would listen** to withhold affection from their children. **Why this advice didn't work** is obvious. Parents found it too hard to follow.

CLAUSES

❸ Practice and Apply

A. CONCEPT CHECK: Noun Clauses

Write the noun clause in each sentence. Then indicate whether it functions as a subject (S), direct object (DO), indirect object (IO), predicate nominative (PN), or object of a preposition (OP).

Are You the Oldest, Middle, or Youngest Child?
1. That birth order influences personality is an intriguing idea.
2. Some evidence shows that first-born children tend to be more conservative and traditional.
3. Yet this fact doesn't explain why many of the greatest inventors are first-born children.
4. Whichever child is born in the middle may become a good negotiator.
5. These negotiating skills could be useful in whatever career the person chooses later.
6. Why the youngest ones are usually risk takers is not hard to understand.
7. Parents may give whoever is the youngest more freedom.

8. Therefore, how parents treat each child also strongly influences personality.

9. People's self-images should not be defined by what some experts say about birth order.

10. Regardless of birth order, people can be whoever they want to be.

➡ **For a SELF-CHECK and more practice, see the EXERCISE BANK, p. 313.**

B. REVISING: Using Noun Clauses

Replace the underlined word in each sentence in the first column with an appropriate noun clause from the second column.

Are You an Only Child?

1. Recent studies show <u>something.</u>

2. For example, <u>someone</u> has his or her parents' undivided love and attention.

3. Also, they don't have to defend their possessions against siblings, so they often discover <u>something</u>.

4. They may have a larger vocabulary depending on <u>something</u>.

5. <u>Someone</u> may dispel the myth that an only child is spoiled.

a. that it's easier to share with others

b. whichever expert you read

c. how much they talk with adults

d. that being an only child has its advantages

e. whoever is an only child

C. WRITING

Have you ever felt like Jason in the cartoon? Write a paragraph about a time when you did something to be accepted by a relative or friend. Use noun clauses in two of your sentences.

Example: *What I did* embarrasses me now. I was convinced *that my parents liked Jeff better.* I decided *that if I learned magic tricks,* I would get their attention.

Foxtrot by Bill Amend

Sentence Structure

❶ Here's the Idea

The structure of a sentence is determined by the number and kind of clauses it contains. Sentences are classified as simple, compound, complex, and compound-complex.

Simple Sentences

▶ **A simple sentence consists of one independent clause and no subordinate clauses.**

Most TV family shows idealize family life.

A simple sentence may contain a compound subject, a compound verb, and one or more phrases.

COMPOUND SUBJECT

***Leave It to Beaver* and *Father Knows Best* were examples of the "ideal" American family.**

PHRASE

According to TV, parents could understand and solve almost any problem. SUBJECT COMPOUND VERB

Compound Sentences

▶ **A compound sentence consists of two or more independent clauses joined together.**

INDEPENDENT CLAUSE INDEPENDENT CLAUSE

The TV father worked, and the TV mother stayed at home with the TV children.

Independent clauses can be joined with a comma and coordinating conjunction, a semicolon, or a semicolon and a comma with a conjunctive adverb.

TV families often owned dogs, but you rarely saw a cat.

Housekeepers were family too; they often gave wise advice.

In 1968, viewers saw their first African-American family (*Julia*) on TV; however, the stories were like those on *Father Knows Best*.

For more on coordinating conjunctions and conjunctive adverbs, see pp. 26–27.

WATCH OUT

Don't use a comma to join two independent clauses. This error— a comma splice—creates a run-on sentence.

CLAUSES

Complex Sentences

A **complex sentence** consists of one independent clause and one or more subordinate clauses.

INDEPENDENT CLAUSE

A 1970s sitcom called *The Brady Bunch* featured a blended family **that consisted of two of the original parents, three girls, and three boys.**   SUBORDINATE CLAUSE

SUBORDINATE CLAUSE

Although it was not as popular as other programs at the time, **the show went on to become an enduring classic.**

INDEPENDENT CLAUSE

Compound-Complex Sentences

A **compound-complex sentence** consists of two or more independent clauses and one or more subordinate clauses.

INDEPENDENT CLAUSE

On January 12, 1971, *All in the Family* appeared on TV, and **audiences saw a show** **that changed the course of TV comedy.**   SUBORDINATE CLAUSE

INDEPENDENT CLAUSE   SUBORDINATE CLAUSE

Each week the show broke new ground, and, **as the actors tackled one sensitive subject after another,** **the show quickly became the number one program on television.**

INDEPENDENT CLAUSE

② Why It Matters in Writing

Using different sentence structures will help you clarify the relationships between your ideas and add variety to your writing.

STUDENT MODEL

DRAFT

Other black characters had been on TV. *The Jeffersons* was the first show about an affluent black family. The show was a spinoff from *All in the Family.* The show lasted nearly ten years.

REVISION

Although other black characters had been on TV, *The Jeffersons* was the first show about an affluent black family. The show, **which was a spinoff from *All in the Family*,** lasted nearly ten years.

❸ Practice and Apply

Identify each sentence as simple (SS), compound (CD), complex (CX), or compound-complex (CC).

Breaking TV Family Taboos

1. Television once had strict codes for family sitcoms.
2. Networks didn't want to offend their viewers, and they had a long list of topics to avoid.
3. *All in the Family* broke most of the TV taboos in its eight years.
4. The show was the first sitcom to deal with topics that previous shows had ignored.
5. For the first time, audiences heard a toilet flush on a sitcom!
6. Archie and Edith Bunker became household names, and the show made stars out of actors Carroll O'Connor and Jean Stapleton.
7. Shows based on minor characters were also hits, which made *All in the Family* even more famous.
8. The show opened doors for other sitcoms; in fact, when *The Simpsons* aired, critics called it a cartoon *All in the Family.*
9. Homer, the father on *The Simpsons,* acts like Archie, but Homer is better at avoiding work.
10. When *The Simpsons* tackles a subject, it spares no one.

➜ For a SELF-CHECK and more practice, see the EXERCISE BANK, p. 314.

B. REVISING: Using Sentence Variety

Rewrite this paragraph by following the directions below it.

The Brady Bunch: From the 1970s to Now

(1) *The Brady Bunch Movie* shows how out of place the Brady family is now. (2) They are stuck in the 1970s. (3) The family has sack races on the lawn. (4) They still wear polyester clothes. (5) Middle sister Jan plots to make older sister Marcia look ugly. (6) Marcia always remains beautiful. (7) The Bradys' neighbor hates them. (8) He tries to force them to move. (9) The Bradys raise enough money to save their home.

1. Combine sentences 1 and 2 to form a complex sentence by turning sentence 2 into a subordinate clause.
2. Combine sentences 3 and 4 to form a compound sentence.
3. Combine sentences 5 and 6 to form a complex sentence by turning sentence 5 into a subordinate clause.
4. Combine sentences 7, 8, 9 to form a compound-complex sentence, turning sentence 7 into a subordinate clause.

CLAUSES

LESSON 5 Sentence Diagramming

Mad Mapper

Here's the Idea

Diagramming is a way to represent visually the parts of a sentence. It can help you understand the sentence structure by showing how the words and clauses in a sentence are related.

Watch me for diagramming tips!

Simple Sentences

Simple sentences are diagrammed on one horizontal line, with a vertical line separating subject and predicate. The horizontal line may be split on either side to show a compound subject or a compound verb.

For more on diagramming simple sentences, see pp. 54–56.

Compound Sentences

- Diagram the independent clauses on parallel horizontal lines.
- Connect the verbs in the two clauses by a broken line with a step.

Most children live in nuclear families, but many have extended families too.

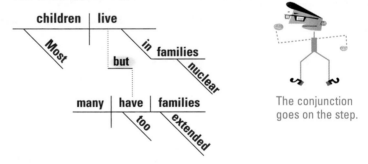

The conjunction goes on the step.

A. CONCEPT CHECK: Simple and Compound Sentences

Diagram these sentences, using what you have learned. For additional help, see pages 54–56.

Family Matters
1. American families have changed over the years.
2. The Census Bureau documents these changes, and it publishes them.
3. The bureau counts a sample population each month, but it tries to count every resident every ten years.

Complex Sentences

Adjective and Adverb Clauses

- Diagram the subordinate clause on its own horizontal line below the main line, as if it were a sentence.
- Use a dotted line to connect the word introducing the clause to the word it modifies.

Adjective Clause Introduced by a Relative Pronoun
The relatives who live with you are your nuclear family.

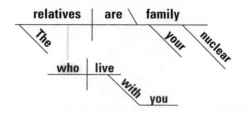

Here, the pronoun introducing the clause is the subject of the clause.

Adjective Clause Introduced by a Relative Adverb
Other relatives may live in the town where you were born.

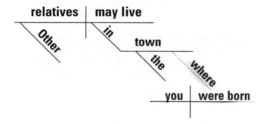

The adverb introducing the clause goes on the dotted line.

Adverb Clause

Because people move so often, families are more scattered.

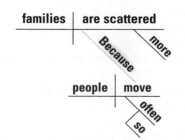

The conjunction goes on the dotted line connecting the verbs in the clauses.

Noun Clauses
- Diagram the subordinate clause on a separate line that is attached to the main line with a forked line.
- Place the forked line in the diagram according to the role of the noun clause in the sentence.
- Diagram the word introducing the noun clause according to its function in the clause.

Noun Clause Used as Subject
What teenagers need is strong family support.

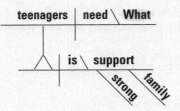

Here, the pronoun introducing the clause functions as a direct object in the clause.

Noun Clause Used as Direct Object
Psychologists report that families handle stress differently.

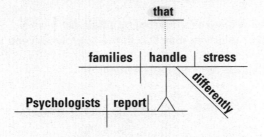

Here, the word introducing the clause is a subordinating conjunction.

B. CONCEPT CHECK: Complex Sentences
Diagram these sentences, using what you have learned.

Wedding Bell Blues
1. The Census Bureau, which compiles many statistics, records people's ages at marriage.
2. The census shows that today both men and women are marrying later.
3. Because marriage is an important responsibility, people shouldn't rush into it.

Compound-Complex Sentences

- Diagram the independent clauses first.
- Attach each subordinate clause to the word it modifies.

Because families are so scattered, many people use e-mail, and grandparents also use computers!

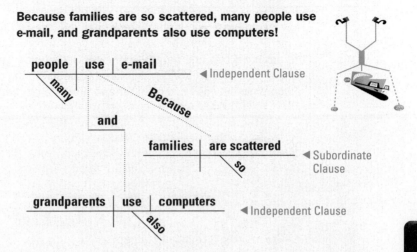

C. CONCEPT CHECK: Compound-Complex Sentences

Diagram these sentences, using what you have learned.

Marry Sooner or Later?

1. Once, a woman married when she was twenty, and she started a family immediately.
2. Attitudes have changed, and today a woman is nearly twenty-five when she first marries.
3. Because they have more choices, many women delay marriage, but most still want a family.

D. MIXED REVIEW: Diagramming

Diagram the following sentences. Look for different types of clauses.

1. Blended families, which include children from each parent's previous marriage, are more common now.
2. When two families merge, the children acquire new siblings.
3. Whether such families are happy depends on how well everyone cooperates.

CLAUSES

Grammar in Literature

Sentence Structure and Vivid Writing

How do you write about someone whom you love and resent at the same time? The narrator in *The Scarlet Ibis* wanted a brother—but not the sickly one he got. In the passage below, James Hurst uses a variety of sentence structures to describe the complex relationship between the narrator and his little brother Doodle.

The Scarlet Ibis

James Hurst

Although Doodle learned to crawl, he showed no signs of walking, but he wasn't idle. He talked so much that we all quit listening to what he said. It was about this time that Daddy built him a go-cart and I had to pull him around. At first I just paraded him up and down the piazza, but then he started crying to be taken into the yard, and it ended up by my having to lug him wherever I went. If I so much as picked up my cap, he'd start crying to go with me, and Mama would call from wherever she was, "Take Doodle with you."

He was a burden in many ways. The doctor had said that he mustn't get too excited, too hot, too cold, or too tired and that he must always be treated gently. A long list of don'ts went with him, all of which I ignored once we got out of the house. To discourage his coming with me, I'd run with him across the ends of the cotton rows and careen him around corners on two wheels. Sometimes I accidentally turned him over, but he never told Mama.

Compound-complex sentence contrasts Doodle's disability with his determination.

Compound-complex sentence with **adverb clause** shows Doodle becoming his brother's burden.

Simple sentence bluntly states the narrator's feelings.

Subordinate clauses explain the "burden" in more detail.

Compound sentence contrasts the narrator's roughness with Doodle's loyalty.

Your sentences do more for your writing if you vary their structure.

Revising to Vary Sentence Structure	
Letting an independent clause stand alone	Use simple sentences to focus on a single idea, describe a series of actions, or create a quick, choppy rhythm.
Combining independent clauses	When you need to connect similar or contrasting ideas of equal importance and create a more fluid rhythm, use compound sentences.
Adding subordinate clauses	When you want to build momentum, add details, or show relationships between ideas, use these clauses to form complex or compound-complex sentences.

PRACTICE AND APPLY: Revising Sentence Structure

The paragraph below consists entirely of simple sentences. To improve its clarity and style, try rewriting it, varying the sentence structures. Follow the directions below. After you finish, you might want to try different ways of revising some of the sentences.

(**1**) Tracing your family tree can be more than just fun. (**2**) It might also help save your life. (**3**) Some serious conditions may be inherited. (**4**) These include diabetes, high blood pressure, cancer, and sickle cell anemia. (**5**) People need to know the facts. (**6**) They may be at risk for these diseases. (**7**) Family documents include medical records. (**8**) These records can show causes of death. (**9**) You know about your family's medical history. (**10**) It can help you safeguard your own health.

1. Combine sentences 1 and 2 to form a compound sentence.
2. Combine sentences 3 and 4 by changing sentence 4 into an adjective clause modifying *conditions*.
3. Combine sentences 5 and 6 by changing sentence 6 into an adverb clause.
4. Combine sentences 7 and 8 by changing sentence 8 into an adjective clause.
5. Combine sentences 9 and 10 by changing sentence 9 into a noun clause.

Choose a draft from your 🗐 **Working Portfolio,** and revise it by combining sentences in at least three of the ways suggested above.

Mixed Review

A. Types of Clauses In the sentences below, identify each underlined subordinate clause as an adjective clause, adverb clause, or noun clause.

(1) People of all ages are learning <u>how they can research their family history</u>. (2) <u>Whoever has Chinese ancestry</u> may have a more difficult time finding family names, however. (3) <u>Because Asian immigration was restricted from 1882 to 1965</u>, many Chinese adopted the names of Chinese families already here. (4) An Internet Web site now helps people search cemetery records <u>that might give their ancestors' true names</u>. (5) One educator, Albert Cheng, <u>who traced his family back 2,800 years</u>, has helped Chinese-American teenagers find their ancestral villages in China.

B. Kinds of Clauses and Sentence Structure Read the passage. Then write the answers to the questions that follow it.

> **LITERARY MODEL**
>
> (1) Here was a flesh and blood man [poet Walt Whitman], belching and laughing and sweating in poems. (2) "Who touches this book touches a man."
>
> (3) That night, at last, I started to write, recklessly, three, five pages, looking up once only to see my father passing by the hall on tiptoe. (4) When I was done, I read over my words, and my eyes filled. (5) I finally sounded like myself in English!
>
> (6) As soon as I had finished that first draft, I called my mother to my room. (7) She listened attentively, as she had to my father's speech, and in the end, her eyes were glistening too. (8) Her face was soft and warm and proud. (9) "That is a beautiful, beautiful speech, Cukita. (10) I want for your father to hear it before he goes to sleep."
>
> —Julia Alvarez, "Daughter of Invention"

1. Is this sentence simple, compound, or complex?
2. What is the function of the noun clause in this sentence?
3. Is this sentence simple, compound, or compound-complex?
4. What verb does the clause "When I was done" modify?
5. Is this sentence simple, compound, or complex?
6. Is this sentence simple, complex, or compound-complex?
7. Is the subordinate clause an adjective, adverb, or noun clause?
8. How would you combine sentence 8 with this sentence: "I looked at my mother's face"?
9. Is this sentence simple, complex, or compound-complex?
10. What is the independent clause in this sentence?

Choose the letter of the term that identifies each numbered part of this passage.

Many people <u>who attend rock concerts</u> in the Los Angeles area are
(1)
amazed by one performer, Eloise Baugh. <u>The 83-year-old grandmother</u>

<u>introduces the main acts by break dancing and singing rap music.</u> She
(2)
looks like the main act <u>when she performs.</u> <u>She spins on the floor to wild</u>
(3)
<u>applause; she springs to her feet and hears the crowd roar.</u> <u>That a woman</u>
(4)   (5)
<u>in her 80s can break dance</u> astounds younger people. She usually gives

<u>whoever sits in the first row</u> a few "Break Dancin' Grannie" T-shirts.
(6)
<u>Eloise also writes many of her own rap lyrics, although her granddaughter</u>
(7)
<u>helps her to select the music.</u> She credits break dancing, <u>which is vigorous</u>
(8)
<u>exercise,</u> for keeping her limber. <u>Whatever else Eloise may do,</u> she has
(9)
proved <u>that "old" doesn't mean "slow."</u>
(10)

1. A. adjective clause
   B. adverb clause
   C. independent clause
   D. noun clause

2. A. simple sentence
   B. compound sentence
   C. complex sentence
   D. compound-complex sentence

3. A. nonessential clause
   B. noun clause
   C. essential clause
   D. adverb clause

4. A. simple sentence
   B. compound sentence
   C. complex sentence
   D. compound-complex sentence

5. A. noun clause as predicate
      nominative
   B. noun clause as subject
   C. noun clause as direct object
   D. noun clause as predicate
      adjective

6. A. noun clause as subject
   B. nonessential clause
   C. noun clause as indirect object
   D. essential clause

7. A. simple sentence
   B. compound sentence
   C. complex sentence
   D. compound-complex sentence

8. A. independent clause
   B. noun clause as subject
   C. nonessential clause
   D. adverb clause

9. A. subordinate clause
   B. nonessential clause
   C. independent clause
   D. essential clause

10. A. adjective clause
    B. adverb clause
    C. noun clause as predicate
       nominative
    D. noun clause as direct object

CLAUSES

Student Help Desk

Clauses and Sentence Structure at a Glance

A clause is a group of words that contains a subject and a verb. Clauses may be either independent or subordinate. An independent clause can stand alone or be combined with other independent and subordinate clauses.

SIMPLE SENTENCE = | independent clause |

COMPOUND SENTENCE = | independent clause | + | independent clause(s) |

COMPLEX SENTENCE = | independent clause | + | subordinate clause(s) |

COMPOUND-COLLEX SENTENCE = | independent clause | + | independent clause(s) |
+ | subordinate clause(s) |

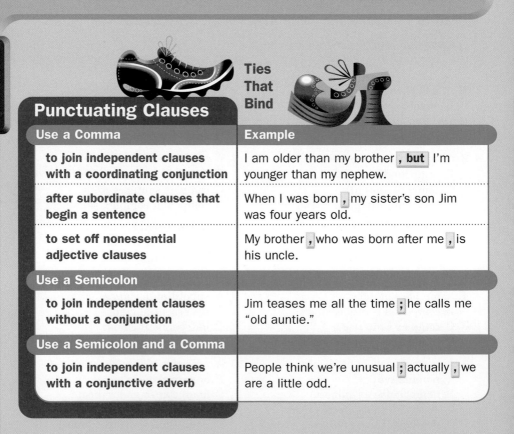

Ties That Bind

Punctuating Clauses

Use a Comma	Example
to join independent clauses with a coordinating conjunction	I am older than my brother **, but** I'm younger than my nephew.
after subordinate clauses that begin a sentence	When I was born **,** my sister's son Jim was four years old.
to set off nonessential adjective clauses	My brother **,** who was born after me **,** is his uncle.

Use a Semicolon	
to join independent clauses without a conjunction	Jim teases me all the time **;** he calls me "old auntie."

Use a Semicolon and a Comma	
to join independent clauses with a conjunctive adverb	People think we're unusual **;** actually **,** we are a little odd.

Subordinate Clauses It's All Relative

Kind of Clause	Function	Example
Adjective clause	Modifies a noun or pronoun	Her family has a coat of arms, **which features a gold lion.**
Adverb clause	Modifies a verb, adjective, or adverb	**When her cousins visited,** she showed it to them.
Noun clause	Acts as a subject, complement, or object of a preposition	She told them **that the lion stands for loyalty.**

Sentence Structure The Variety Show

Kind of Sentence	Structure	Example
Simple sentence	one independent clause	A coat of arms is fascinating.
Compound sentence	two or more independent clauses	It has many symbols, and each one means something.
Complex sentence	one independent clause and one or more subordinate clauses	When a sword appears, it may represent the family's service to the king.
Compound-complex sentence	one or more independent clauses and one or more subordinate clauses	The symbols look complex, but they make sense after you decode them.

CLAUSES

The Bottom Line

Checklist for Clauses and Sentence Structure

Can I improve my writing by . . .

____ making sure that every sentence contains at least one independent clause?

____ using subordinate clauses for details or supporting ideas?

____ combining some simple sentences to avoid repetition or to show relationships between ideas?

____ varying sentence structure?

Writing Complete Sentences

La Cucina Italiana
This restaurant anything but traditional.
Opened in 1996 by Marcelo and Theresa Cellini. Crowds of all ages will enjoy the virtual tour of Italy the tour takes you through
• the romantic city of Venice
• the architecture of Rome
• the busy streets of Florence
After you have walked through the lifelike scenes. Can relax and enjoy an authentic taste of Italian cuisine. Do not pass up any of the pizza creations they offer a taste of Italy you'll want to savor until your next visit. The service excellent in this trendy restaurant ♪♪♪♪

Theme: The Story of Food

Food for Thought

If you were looking for a good place to eat, would this reviewer's notes be helpful? The restaurant sounds great, but if you read closely, you may start to feel confused. Notice how some of the sentences seem to be missing information while others are long and lack coherence.

When you take notes, it's all right to use incomplete sentences or long, rambling sentences. When you write for an audience, however, you should construct sentences that clearly communicate your ideas.

Write Away: Savor the Flavor
Write a paragraph about a combination of foods you've experimented with or would like to create. Save your paragraph in your 🗂 **Writing Portfolio.**

For each numbered item, choose the best way to write the underlined section.

Pizza has a long and colorful history that traces back to ancient Rome.

Surprisingly, tomatoes a regular ingredient only in the late 1800s.
(1)

According to legend. The tomato-based pizza got its start in 1889. Then a
(2)

baker in Naples created a pizza topped with tomatoes, mozzarella cheese,

and basil leaves to present to Italy's Queen Margherita. The red, white,

and green pizza displayed the colors of the Italian flag and was named

Pizza Margherita in honor of the popular monarch.

The first pizza restaurant, or pizzeria, in the United States opened in
(3)

New York City in 1905. The next milestone in the history of pizza

occurred after World War II. Men and women who had acquired a taste for

pizza while they were serving in Europe returned home. They continued
(4)

to eat pizza pizza sales soared. Today pizza is still popular, Americans
(5)

spend more than $31.2 billion dollars on pizza each year.

SENTENCES

1. A. Surprisingly, tomatoes became a regular ingredient. Only in the late 1800s.
   B. Surprisingly, tomatoes a regular ingredient. Only in the late 1800s.
   C. Surprisingly, tomatoes became a regular ingredient only in the late 1800s.
   D. Correct as is

2. A. According to legend, the tomato-based pizza got its start in 1889.
   B. According to legend, the tomato-based pizza its start in 1889.
   C. According to legend, the tomato-based pizza got its start. In 1889.
   D. Correct as is

3. A. The first pizza restaurant, or pizzeria; in the United States opened in New York City in 1905.

   B. The first pizza restaurant, or pizzeria, in the United States in New York City in 1905.
   C. The first pizza restaurant in New York City in 1905.
   D. Correct as is

4. A. They continued to eat pizza sales soared.
   B. They continued to eat pizza. Pizza sales soared.
   C. They continued to eat pizza, pizza sales soared.
   D. Correct as is

5. A. Today pizza is still popular more than $31.2 billion spent.
   B. Today pizza is still popular $31.2 billion is spent on pizza each year.
   C. Today pizza is still popular. Americans spend more than $31.2 billion dollars on pizza each year.
   D. Correct as is

Sentence Fragments

❶ Here's the Idea

▶ **A sentence fragment is part of a sentence that is punctuated as if it were a complete sentence.**

Fragments Caused by Missing Parts

Sometimes a sentence fragment does not express a complete thought because the subject or the verb is left out.

FRAGMENT **In 1853, Native American George Crum served his version of French fries at Moon Lake Lodge. Soon thereafter faced a guest's disapproval.**

> Fragment lacks a subject.

SENTENCE **In 1853, Native American George Crum served his version of French fries at Moon Lake Lodge. Soon thereafter he faced a guest's disapproval.**

FRAGMENT **Chef Crum angered by the rejection. Eventually, he created the potato chip.**

> Fragment lacks a complete verb.

SENTENCE **Chef Crum was angered by the rejection. Eventually, he created the potato chip.**

 Sometimes when writers rush to get several ideas on paper, they not only forget to use subjects or verbs, but they also make punctuation errors that result in sentence fragments. Notice how the writer corrected this error in the following model.

STUDENT MODEL

George Washington Carver created more than 300 products. Which included peanut butter and peanut-butter cookies, from the peanut.

Phrases as Fragments

A **phrase** is a group of words that functions as a part of speech and does not have a subject or a verb. A phrase that stands alone is a fragment.

FRAGMENT **The pretzel has a long and interesting history. Dating back to A.D. 610.**

SENTENCE **The pretzel has a long and interesting history dating back to A.D. 610.**

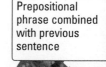
Participial phrase combined with previous sentence

FRAGMENT **Popular folklore suggests that the pretzel was created. By a medieval Italian monk to reward children.**

SENTENCE **Popular folklore suggests that the pretzel was created by a medieval Italian monk to reward children.**

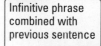
Prepositional phrase combined with previous sentence

FRAGMENT **He shaped the pretzel in the image of children's folded arms in prayer. To motivate them to memorize their prayers.**

SENTENCE **He shaped the pretzel in the image of children's folded arms in prayer to motivate them to memorize their prayers.**

Infinitive phrase combined with previous sentence

Sentence fragments often are used in fiction and in advertisements for emphasis or effect. Don't use fragments in your compositions. Readers might not recognize these fragments as intentional.

For more on phrases, see pp. 66–77.

SENTENCES

Subordinate Clauses as Fragments

A **clause** is a group of words that contains a subject and a verb. A clause that cannot stand alone as a sentence is a subordinate, or dependent, clause. Fragments often occur because a subordinate clause is mistaken for a complete sentence.

FRAGMENT **Earl Charles Grey helped abolish slavery throughout the British Empire. Although he is better known for Earl Grey tea.**

SENTENCE **Earl Charles Grey helped abolish slavery throughout the British Empire, although he is better known for Earl Grey tea.**

> Clause is combined with the previous sentence.

FRAGMENT **After a British diplomat saved the life of a Chinese government official. The earl received the recipe for the tea as a gift.**

SENTENCE **After a British diplomat saved the life of a Chinese government official, the earl received the recipe for the tea as a gift.**

> Subordinate clause is combined with the independent clause.

For more on subordinate clauses, see pp. 92–93.

❷ Why It Matters in Writing

If you use a sentence fragment when you speak, your gestures and facial expressions can help convey its meaning. When you write, the reader can't ask you to provide more details, so every sentence has to express a complete thought.

STUDENT MODEL

One of the world's most well-known gluttons. Diamond Jim Brady sometimes would eat four or five meals a day. Breakfast included a gallon of orange juice, three eggs, half a loaf of bread. Grits and bacon, muffins, and a stack of hotcakes.

> An appositive phrase as a fragment will not make sense.

> Misplaced punctuation in a series of items makes the meaning unclear.

❸ Practice and Apply

A. CONCEPT CHECK: Sentence Fragments

Rewrite the numbered fragments as complete sentences. You may add words to the fragments or combine them with sentences.

Rising to Any Occasion

(1) Have been baking bread since prehistoric times. About 4,600 years ago, bakers in Egypt learned how to use yeast. **(2) To make bread rise.** Before that, people made various kinds of breads. **(3) By baking mixtures of water and ground grain on heated stones. (4) Because breads contained no leavening agents.** They did not rise. Today most cultures have their own traditional breads. **(5) Examples of flatbreads from around the world the Mexican tortilla, the Indian chapati, and the Ethiopian injera.** Many cultures serve yeast-risen bread. **(6) Including the Russian black bread and the Danish sourdough bread.** French bakeries make and sell baguettes. **(7) Which are long, thin loaves of white bread with crisp brown crusts.** In Mexico, bakers make a special bread called fiesta bread. **(8) And hide small ornaments within it.** Be sure to check out the selection of breads. **(9) If you find yourself at a large international food market. (10) Won't regret it!**

➡ For a SELF-CHECK and more practice, see the EXERCISE BANK, p. 315.

B. REVISING: Fixing Incomplete Sentences

Rewrite the five fragments in the paragraph below as complete sentences by adding words or combining the fragments with sentences.

A Tasty History

Like corn, the potato, and the tomato. Chocolate originated in the Americas and went on to have a tremendous impact on other parts of the world. Is made from the bean of the cacao tree. The Aztecs used the beans as currency and also roasted and ground them. To make a rich, frothy drink. After the Spanish conquered the Aztec empire in the early 1500s. Chocolate eventually became hugely popular in Europe. The modern chocolate industry was born in 1828. When a Dutch invention revolutionized the processing of cacao beans. People tasted the rich, dark candy, and their craving for chocolate continued to grow! Today, of course, the production of chocolate is a huge international industry.

Run-On Sentences

❶ Here's the Idea

▶ **A run-on sentence is two or more sentences written as though they were one sentence.**

The Comma Splice

A **comma splice,** or comma fault, occurs when the writer mistakenly uses a comma instead of a semicolon or period.

> **STUDENT MODEL**
>
> For generations, people have enjoyed the ever-popular ice cream as a dessert, historical records show that ice cream was invented by the Chinese around 2000 B.C.

Missing Punctuation or Conjunction

Joining two sentences together without a comma and a conjunction, or without a semicolon, can confuse the reader.

> **STUDENT MODEL**
>
> Historians believe that the Chinese included overcooked rice, milk, and spices in their recipe no one is sure how the recipe spread to Europe.

Separate independent clauses with a period or a semicolon.

❷ Why It Matters in Writing

Run-on sentences can cause confusion—and a headache. Your reader can't tell where one idea ends and another begins.

> **STUDENT MODEL**
>
> One popular myth credits Marco Polo with the discovery of this heavenly dessert ∨yet another tells how a Tuscan confectioner introduced Italians to ice milk and fruit ice.

❸ Practice and Apply

A. CONCEPT CHECK: Run-On Sentences

Correct the run-ons below. There may be more than one way to fix each run-on. If a sentence is not a run-on, write *Correct.*

Famous Names in Food

1. Julia Child originally had not prepared for a career in the food industry, in fact, she majored in history in college.

2. During World War II, Child served with a secret intelligence agency her assignments took her around the world.

3. After the war, she took courses at a cooking school in Paris there she met two chefs with whom she wrote the book *Mastering the Art of French Cooking.*

4. The book paved the way for Child's television series *The French Chef* eventually Child became a star in the world of cooking.

5. On her show Julia Child shared recipes, demonstrated cooking techniques, and offered good-humored advice.

6. Paul Newman became famous as a movie actor now he is also known for a line of food products.

7. Newman's food company is somewhat unusual, its after-tax profits are donated to educational and charitable causes.

8. The company began on a small scale Newman and writer A. E. Hotchner decided to market the actor's homemade salad dressing.

9. At first they sold the dressing only locally soon orders were pouring in from all over the country.

10. The company so far has donated more than $100 million to the American Red Cross and many other not-for-profit organizations.

➔ **For a SELF-CHECK and more practice, see the EXERCISE BANK, p. 315.**

B. EDITING: Spotting Incorrect Sentences

Reread the reviewer's notes on page 114. Then locate and revise the six fragment and run-on errors. The first one is done for you here.

Fragment: This restaurant anything but traditional.

Revision: This restaurant is anything but traditional.

Real World Grammar

Science Report

Sometimes when you write a paper from notes you have made, you may accidentally use sentence fragments. Whenever you translate notes into more formal writing, remember to check your work for possible fragments.

This edible dish is prepared with fried grasshoppers.

Niabe Gunther
Science 104
2nd Period

Insects as Food for the Future

If you lived in a land where meat was rare, would you eat a fat, juicy spider instead? Many people in Eastern Europe, Asia, Africa, and Latin America wouldn't think twice about it. In these protein-poor regions, insects are a regular part of a daily diet. Only in the Western world do people shudder at the idea of eating insects. bugs as nasty pests. Insects, however, may well become the food of the future. And for good reasons.

Fix these fragments.

Insects are not only among the most plentiful forms of life on earth, they are some of the most nutritious as well in fact, nature's "perfect food." As the table below shows, some popular insect snacks are high in protein, calcium, and iron and lower in fat than lean red meat.

This is really confusing! Fix run-on.

Nutritional Value of Various Insects (per 100 grams)

Insect	Protein (g)	Fat (g)	Carbs (g)	Calcium (mg)	Iron (mg)
Giant Water Beetle	19.8	8.3	2.1	43.5	13.6
Cricket	12.9	5.5	5.1	75.8	9.5
Small Grasshopper	20.6	6.1	3.9	35.2	5.0
Beef (86% lean ground)	25.3	14.0	NA	NA	2.3

Source: *The Food Insects Newsletter,* July 1996 (Vol. 9, No. 2, ed. by Florence V. Dunkel, Montana State University); *Bugs in the System,* by May Berenbaum; and *USDA Handbook,* 8–13, 1990.

REVISED MODEL

If you lived in a land where meat was rare, would you eat a fat, juicy spider instead? Many people in Eastern Europe, Asia, Africa, and Latin America wouldn't think twice about it. In these protein-poor regions, insects are a regular part of a daily diet. Only in the Western world do people shudder at the idea of eating insects, because here bugs are regarded as nasty pests. Insects, however, may well become the food of the future and for good reasons.

Insects are not only among the most plentiful forms of life on earth, they are some of the most nutritious as well. In fact, they are considered nature's "perfect food."

Now that it contains mealworms, this candied apple treat is packed with protein.

PRACTICE AND APPLY

Suppose you had to correct this passage of Niabe's science report. Use the previous lessons in this chapter to help "debug" her sentences.

STUDENT MODEL

Dry-roasted insects can be used in many ways. For instance, crickets can be substituted. For nuts in cookies, breads, brownies, or crispy treats. Usually, live crickets are stored in the refrigerator for a day or two. Because this slows them down and makes them easier to handle. Then the insects are washed and spread on a baking sheet they are baked at 200° F for one to two hours. Usually the legs, wings, and egg sacs are removed after dry roasting, the insects are then crushed and used in a recipe. Like the popular Chocolate Chirpy Chip Cookies.

Mixed Review

A. Fragments and Run-ons Identify each numbered item as a complete sentence, a fragment, or a run-on. Then revise each incorrect item.

Reading *The Dictionary of American Food and Drink* may bring a few laughs or an upset stomach. **(1) Depending on your mood.** Although it may not be surprising, some food names had comic beginnings. **(2) While others happened by accident. (3) Still others originated from religious, artistic, or geographical terms. (4) For example, Buffalo wings have nothing to do with the buffalo, as a matter of fact, they are deep-fried chicken wings served with a side order of hot sauce and blue-cheese dressing.** In 1964 in Buffalo, New York, Teressa Bellisimmo invented this savory snack. **(5) For her son and his visiting friends. (6) Another example, perhaps one that is enjoyed as a mishap, is the origin of German chocolate cake the original recipe appeared in a Texas newspaper in 1957. (7) The recipe called for Baker's German's Sweet Chocolate, the name *Baker* refers to Dr. James Baker, who helped to finance the first chocolate factory in the United States.** The word *German* had nothing to do with the country. **(8) Because it actually refers to the creator of sweet chocolate, Samuel German. (9) Incidentally, French fries probably aren't French either. (10) They have been traced to Belgium in the 19th century, authorities believe they spread to France some time later.**

B. Editing and Revising Read the e-mail message below. Identify and correct any fragments or run-on sentences.

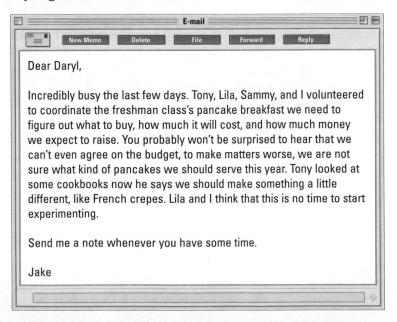

> **E-mail**
>
> New Memo   Delete   File   Forward   Reply
>
> Dear Daryl,
>
> Incredibly busy the last few days. Tony, Lila, Sammy, and I volunteered to coordinate the freshman class's pancake breakfast we need to figure out what to buy, how much it will cost, and how much money we expect to raise. You probably won't be surprised to hear that we can't even agree on the budget, to make matters worse, we are not sure what kind of pancakes we should serve this year. Tony looked at some cookbooks now he says we should make something a little different, like French crepes. Lila and I think that this is no time to start experimenting.
>
> Send me a note whenever you have some time.
>
> Jake

Look at your paragraph from page 114, or another draft from your 🗂 **Working Portfolio.** Fix any fragments or run-on sentences.

For each numbered item, choose the best way to write the underlined section.

> For centuries, people produced their own sausages and named them after their places of origin. <u>For example, the wiener sausage originated in Vienna, the frankfurter came from Frankfurt.</u> (1) <u>Sometimes, use these names today as alternatives for *hot dog.*</u> (2)
>
> <u>The hot dog can claim Coney Island, New York. As its home.</u> (3) In the early 1890s, Charles Feltman introduced frankfurters, or hot dogs, at this seaside resort. His customers later included Eddie Cantor, a singing waiter, and Jimmy Durante, a piano player. <u>The musicians urged Feltman's delivery boy, Nathan Handwerker. To open his own hot dog stand.</u> (4) His lower-priced, five-cent hot dogs won out over Feltman's. Meanwhile, Cantor and Durante left Coney Island. <u>Both ended up in Hollywood, they became movie stars.</u> (5)

1. A. For example, the wiener sausage originated in Vienna the frankfurter came from Frankfurt.
   B. For example, the wiener sausage originated in Vienna; the frankfurter came from Frankfurt.
   C. For example, the wiener sausage originated. In Vienna, the frankfurter came from Frankfurt.
   D. Correct as is

2. A. Sometimes, people use these names today. As alternatives for *hot dog.*
   B. Sometimes, people use these names today as alternatives for *hot dog.*
   C. Sometimes, people use these names. For the *hot dog.*
   D. Correct as is

3. A. The hot dog can claim. Coney Island, New York, as its home.
   B. The hot dog Coney Island, New York, as its home.
   C. The hot dog can claim Coney Island, New York, as its home.
   D. Correct as is

4. A. The musicians urged Feltman's delivery boy. to open his own hot dog stand.
   B. The musicians urged Feltman's delivery boy. To open his own hot dog stand.
   C. The musicians urged Feltman's delivery boy, Nathan Handwerker, to open his own hot dog stand.
   D. Correct as is

5. A. Both ended up in Hollywood, and they became movie stars.
   B. Both ended up in Hollywood; and became movie stars.
   C. In Hollywood became movie stars.
   D. Correct as is

SENTENCES

Student Help Desk

Fragments and Run-Ons at a Glance

Fragment A part of a sentence that is punctuated as if it were a complete sentence. It cannot stand alone.

Run-On Two or more sentences written as though they were one sentence

THE SHORT END

Correcting Fragments

Fragment Type	Example	Quick Fix
Missing Subject	Serves more than 15,000 lunches a day.	**The Pentagon** serves more than 15,000 lunches a day.
Missing Verb	A waffle topped with ice cream my favorite breakfast meal.	A waffle topped with ice cream **is** my favorite breakfast meal.
Misplaced Punctuation	For lunch, I can eat two slices of pizza, fries, a hamburger. And a diet soda.	For lunch, I can eat two slices of pizza, fries, a hamburger**, and** a diet soda.
Phrase	It is not healthy to eat. In the middle of the night.	It is not healthy to eat **in** the middle of the night.
Subordinate Clause	If you eat an orange every day. You may avoid getting a cold.	If you eat an orange every day**, you** may avoid getting a cold. **or** You eat an orange every day.

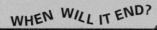

WHEN WILL IT END?

Correcting Run-Ons

Concept	Example	Quick Fix
Comma Splice	Thanksgiving Day meals can include turkey, dressing, potatoes, yams, and pumpkin pie, I usually ask for more.	REPLACE COMMA WITH PERIOD Thanksgiving Day meals can include turkey, dressing, potatoes, yams, and pumpkin pie**.** I usually ask for more.
Missing Conjunction and Punctuation	I dislike most leafy, green vegetables I will eat lettuce.	INSERT COMMA AND CONJUNCTION I dislike most leafy, green vegetables**, but** I will eat lettuce. INSERT SEMICOLON AND CONJUNCTION I dislike most leafy, green vegetables**; however,** I will eat lettuce.

SENTENCES

The Bottom Line

Checklist for Correcting Fragments and Run-Ons

Does each sentence . . .

____ have a subject?

____ have a verb?

____ express a complete thought?

Have I . . .

____ avoided a run-on sentence by adding a conjunction and a comma or a semicolon or a period?

____ corrected any comma splices with a semicolon or a period?

Using Verbs

June 18, 1867

We are six weeks into our journey and have traveled nearly 700 miles. Our wagons are on the south side of the Platte River. Until the last couple of days, we had not experienced any heavy rain.

Thunderstorms are now causing the river to rise. We are not sure how to get our cattle and horses across the river. We will not have much hope for survival if we become trapped in the mountains.

Theme: Travels Across Time and Place

A Ride Back in Time

This journal entry describes a situation during a migration along the Oregon Trail in the 1800s. Look at the verbs in the entry, and think about the effect they create.

The present-tense verbs in the journal entry act as a time machine that makes you feel as if you are at the river crossing with the pioneers. The past-tense and future-tense verbs help you understand the sequence of events. You can use verb forms in your own writing to help express relationships among events.

Write Away: A Voice from the Past

Imagine that you are present at an important historical event. Write two or three paragraphs about what is happening. Use different verb tenses in your account. Put your writing in your **Working Portfolio.**

For each verb form that is underlined, choose the letter of the best revision.

When Marta and her family <u>taked</u> a vacation in Australia, they <u>are</u>
(1)   (2)
surprised at how the time changed during their airline flights across the
Pacific Ocean. When they <u>flied</u> from Los Angeles to Sydney, Australia,
(3)
they arrived at a time that was nearly 32 hours later than the time when
they left. Coming back to Los Angeles, however, they <u>were arriving</u> at a
(4)
time three and one-half hours *earlier* than when they left Sydney. Did
Marta's family <u>fly</u> in a time machine on the way back from Sydney?
(5)
The arrival times were so different because the airplanes <u>cross</u> the
(6)
International Date Line during the flights. The world <u>divides</u> into 24 time
(7)
zones so that the sun is high in the sky at noon almost everywhere on
earth. The International Date Line <u>lays</u> between two time zones in the
(8)
Pacific Ocean. The time in the first time zone east of the date line is 23
hours earlier than the time in the first time zone to the west. Suppose a
person travels around the world and <u>adjusted</u> a watch each time he or she
(9)
enters a new time zone. If there <u>were</u> no date line, he or she would arrive
(10)
home with a watch whose date is a day off from everyone else's.

---

1. A. taken
   B. tooked
   C. took
   D. Correct as is

2. A. will be
   B. were
   C. would be
   D. was

3. A. flown
   B. fly
   C. will fly
   D. flew

4. A. arrived
   B. have been arriving
   C. are arriving
   D. will arrive

5. A. be flying
   B. have flew
   C. have flown
   D. Correct as is

6. A. crossed
   B. will cross
   C. are crossing
   D. was crossing

7. A. divided
   B. is divided
   C. is being divided
   D. has divided

8. A. is laying
   B. lay
   C. lies
   D. Correct as is

9. A. had adjusted
   B. will be adjusted
   C. adjusts
   D. will adjust

10. A. is
    B. was
    C. will be
    D. Correct as is

The Principal Parts of a Verb

① Here's the Idea

▶ **Every verb has four principal parts: the present, the present participle, the past, and the past participle.** You use the principal parts to make all of a verb's tenses and forms.

The Four Principal Parts of a Verb			
Present	**Present Participle**	**Past**	**Past Participle**
look	(is) looking	looked	(has) looked
break	(is) breaking	broke	(has) broken

Here are some examples of how the principal parts are used:

PRESENT
Astronomers use a valuable information collector in space.

PRESENT PARTICIPLE
The Hubbell Space Telescope is providing scientists with new insights about the universe.

PAST
Space agencies decided that a more sophisticated device needed to be sent into orbit.

PAST PARTICIPLE
A number of countries have worked together to build an International Space Station.

When the present participle and the past participle are used to form verbs in sentences, they always take auxiliary verbs.

Regular Verbs

There are two kinds of verbs—regular and irregular. A **regular verb** is a verb that forms its past and past participle by adding -*ed* or -*d* to the present.

PRESENT	PRESENT PARTICIPLE	PAST	PAST PARTICIPLE
look	**(is) look + ing**	**look + ed**	**(has) look + ed**
work	**(is) work + ing**	**work + ed**	**(has) work + ed**

Irregular Verbs

Verbs for which the past and past participle are formed in some other way than by adding *-ed* or *-d* are called **irregular verbs.** The following chart shows you how to form the principal parts of many irregular verbs.

Common Irregular Verbs			
	Present	**Past**	**Past Participle**
Group 1 **The forms of** **the present, the** **past, and the** **past participle** **are the same.**	burst cost cut hit hurt let put set shut	burst cost cut hit hurt let put set shut	(has) burst (has) cost (has) cut (has) hit (has) hurt (has) let (has) put (has) set (has) shut
Group 2 **The forms of** **the past and** **the past** **participle are** **the same.**	bring catch get lay lead lend lose make say sit seek teach	brought caught got laid led lent lost made said sat sought taught	(has) brought (has) caught (has) got *or* gotten (has) laid (has) led (has) lent (has) lost (has) made (has) said (has) sat (has) sought (has) taught
Group 3 **The vowel** **changes from** *i* to *a* to *u.*	begin drink ring shrink sink spring swim	began drank rang shrank sank sprang *or* sprung swam	(has) begun (has) drunk (has) rung (has) shrunk (has) sunk (has) sprung (has) swum

A dictionary entry for an irregular verb shows the correct spelling of the verb's past and past participle.

Common Irregular Verbs

	Present	Past	Past Participle
Group 4 **The past** **participle is** **formed by** **adding -n or** **-en to the past.**	beat break choose lie speak steal tear wear	beat broke chose lay spoke stole tore wore	(has) beaten (has) broken (has) chosen (has) lain (has) spoken (has) stolen (has) torn (has) worn
Group 5 **The past** **participle is** **formed from** **the present—** **frequently by** **adding -n, -en,** **or -ne.**	blow do draw eat give go grow know rise run see take throw write	blew did drew ate gave went grew knew rose ran saw took threw wrote	(has) blown (has) done (has) drawn (has) eaten (has) given (has) gone (has) grown (has) known (has) risen (has) run (has) seen (has) taken (has) thrown (has) written

❷ Why It Matters in Writing

If you use incorrect verb forms, you will leave your readers with a poor impression of your writing. Your errors will distract them from your ideas.

STUDENT MODEL

    The Hubble Space Telescope ~~costed~~ *cost* millions of dollars to

build, and at first it looked as if the telescope would be a big

failure. Then space shuttle astronauts ~~brang~~ *brought* new equipment to

the telescope and put it in during a space walk. People have

~~began~~ *begun* to appreciate the important discoveries that astronomers

have made by using the telescope.

❸ Practice and Apply

Choose the correct form of the verb in parentheses.

A Future Glimpse into the Past

1. The Hubble Space Telescope has (maked, made) astronomers hungry for more information about the universe.
2. They are (seeking, sought) new information about the creation of the universe.
3. NASA has (wanted, want) to send even better telescopes into space.
4. NASA (chose, choosed) four new telescope projects: The Space Infrared Telescope Facility (SIRTF), Space Interferometry Mission (SIM), Next Generation Space Telescope (NGST), and Terrestrial Planet Finder (TPF).
5. By the year 2050, astronomers will have (took, taken) a new look at the universe with the help of the new telescopes.
6. Hubble's replacements will be able to see through the clouds of gas that (gotten, got) in the way before.
7. SIRTF will (detect, detected) infrared light.
8. By the end of its five-year life, SIRTF will have (cut, cutted) through clouds of gases to reveal superplanets and very dim stars called brown dwarfs.
9. SIM will (spot, spotting) individual stars in clusters.
10. Hubble has (brang, brought) us blurry images of clustered stars.

➜ **For a SELF-CHECK and more practice, see the EXERCISE BANK, p. 316.**

B. WRITING: Stellar Events

List the principal parts of the following irregular verbs. Then use any five of the words below to write about an unusual or amazing sky that you have seen in real life or in the movies.

know	set	sink
rise	teach	catch

Look at a recent draft from your 📂 **Working Portfolio.** Proofread the draft to correct any errors in the use of principal parts of irregular verbs.

VERBS

Forming Verb Tenses

❶ Here's the Idea

▶ **A tense is a verb form that shows the time of an action or a condition.** A verb's tenses are formed from its principal parts.

Simple Tenses

The **present tense** shows that an action or a condition

- occurs regularly or is generally true:

  Good stories transport us across time and space.

- is occurring in the present:

  I have the new book by Stephen King.

- occurs regularly:

  Every night, I read several chapters of this chilling tale.

The **past tense** shows that an action or a condition occurred in the past:

King published _Carrie,_ his first novel, in 1974.

The **future tense** shows that an action or a condition will occur in the future:

I will lend you King's new book next week.

Simple Tenses		
Tense	**Singular**	**Plural**
Present		
First person	I travel.	We travel.
Second person	You travel.	You travel.
Third person	He/she/it travels.	They travel.
Past		
First person	I traveled.	We traveled.
Second person	You traveled.	You traveled.
Third person	He/she/it traveled.	They traveled.
Future _will (shall)_ + present		
First person	I will (shall) travel.	We will (shall) travel.
Second person	You will travel.	You will travel.
Third person	He/she/it will travel.	They will travel.

If you want to give special force to a verb, use the emphatic form. You make the emphatic form by adding _do, does,_ or _did_ to a verb.

I did finish my work!

Perfect Tenses

The **present perfect tense** shows that an action or a condition

- was completed at one or more indefinite times in the past:

  King has published several books under the pen name of Richard Bachman.

- began in the past and continues in the present:

  King has written more than 30 novels in the last 30 years.

The **past perfect tense** shows that an action or a condition in the past preceded another past action or condition:

  King had written two novels that were rejected by publishers before he published *Carrie*.

The **future perfect tense** shows that an action or a condition in the future will precede another future action or condition:

  By next summer, I will have read half of King's books.

Perfect Tenses

Tense	Singular	Plural
Present perfect *have/has* + past participle		
First person	I have traveled.	We have traveled.
Second person	You have traveled.	You have traveled.
Third person	He/she/it has traveled.	They have traveled.
Past perfect *had* + past participle		
First person	I had traveled.	We had traveled.
Second person	You had traveled.	You had traveled.
Third person	He/she/it had traveled.	They had traveled.
Future perfect *will (shall) have* + past participle		
First person	I will (shall) have traveled.	We will (shall) have traveled.
Second person	You will have traveled.	You will have traveled.
Third person	He/she/it will have traveled.	They will have traveled.

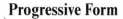

Progressive Form

▶ **The progressive form of a verb expresses an event in progress.**
Each tense has a progressive form, made by using the corresponding tense of the verb *be* with the present participle.

  I am reading this horror story.

  A group of friends were camping in the Maine woods.

  An escaped convict had been hiding in a nearby cabin.

❷ Why It Matters in Writing

Knowing which verb tense to use can help you make it clear when something happened. Notice how Stephen King uses verb tenses in the following screenplay scene in which a gravedigger is talking to a dead novelist who has just been buried.

LITERARY MODEL

(Exterior view of the grave)

(A groundskeeper pats the last sod into place.)   **PRESENT**

Groundskeeper. My wife says she wishes
    you'd written a couple more before you   **PAST PERFECT**
    had your heart attack, mister. (pause) I like   **PAST**
    Westerns, m'self.

(The groundskeeper walks away, whistling.)

      —Stephen King, *Sorry, Right Number*

❸ Practice and Apply

CONCEPT CHECK: Forming Verb Tenses

In each sentence below, the underlined verb is in the incorrect tense or form. Write the verb in the correct tense or form.

Portals to Distant Places

1. Books offer us pleasure and <u>opened</u> doorways to other places and times.
2. Right now, Shay <u>was reading</u> a book.
3. Although she is in the library, her mind <u>had been transported</u> to another time and place.
4. By the end of the day, who knows how far she <u>has traveled</u>.
5. Perhaps Mark Twain <u>invites</u> her on a trip down the Mississippi while she was choosing something to read.
6. As she <u>scanned</u> the shelves, maybe a pioneer family has made room for her on a journey westward.
7. Yesterday she <u>is thinking</u> about ocean voyages.
8. Now she <u>will be following</u> the *Titanic* across the Atlantic.
9. If tomorrow she thinks about circling the globe, undoubtedly she <u>chooses</u> Jules Verne's famous novel.
10. After all, Verne's *Around the World in Eighty Days* <u>had taken</u> many an armchair traveler on an exciting adventure.

➡ **For a SELF-CHECK and more practice, see the EXERCISE BANK, p. 317.**

Using Verb Tenses

LESSON 3

❶ Here's the Idea

You can use different verb tenses to describe single events and ongoing actions that are related. Verb tenses are especially helpful when you are writing a story, because they allow you to show how a series of events are related in time.

Writing About the Present

When you are writing about the present, you can use the

- simple present tense
- present progressive form
- present perfect tense
- present perfect progressive form

A Real-Life Adventure

Verb Tenses

I like to read about real-life adventures. I especially enjoy stories in which people struggle against nature.

> The simple present shows an action or a condition that is continuously true.

I am reading the book *Back from Tuichi* by Yossi Ghinsberg. The suspense is so intense that I am getting goose bumps.

> The present progressive shows action that is now in progress.

So far I have learned that Yossi is a young Israeli man who is on an adventure through the rain forests of Bolivia.

> The present perfect shows an action or a condition that began in the past and continues into the present.

I have been trying to resist the urge to skip ahead in the book.

> The present perfect progressive shows an action that began in the past and is still in progress.

VERBS

Writing About the Past

When you write about the past, verb tenses can help you show the sequence of events. Describing such a sequence can be very complicated because some events are ongoing and overlap other events. By using correct tenses, you can make it easier for your readers to follow the events.

Yossi Struggles Through the Rain Forest

Verb Tenses

Yossi Ghinsberg traveled to Bolivia in the 1980s. He explored the rain forests near the Tuichi River.

The simple past shows actions that were completed in the past.

At first Yossi was traveling with three men. They were searching for a remote Indian village and gold.

The past progressive shows actions that continued over time in the past.

After the men had experienced difficult travel for several weeks, two of them gave up and headed back to civilization on foot.

The past perfect shows an action in the past that came before other actions in the past.

Yossi and the remaining man, Kevin, had been trying to raft down a dangerous river when they became separated.

The past perfect progressive shows an action that was in progress in the past when another action happened.

Writing About the Future

Future tenses allow you to describe what will happen, what will be happening, or what will have happened in the future.

What Will Happen to Yossi?

Verb Tenses

When you get to the part where Yossi has been left alone in the rain forest, you will be eager to find out what happens to him.

The simple future shows a condition that will occur in the future.

Yossi will be trying to make it out of the jungle with the help of only a few supplies.

The future progressive shows an action that will be in progress in the future.

You may wonder if any wild animals will have attacked Yossi before he reaches the nearest village.

The future perfect shows an action in the future that will occur before another action.

Yossi will have been causing you to lose a lot of sleep at night before you get to the end of his book.

The future perfect progressive shows an action in progress in the future when another action will happen.

VERBS

❷ Why It Matters in Writing

By learning when and how to use verb tenses, you can clearly show actions and conditions occurring one right after another.

> **PROFESSIONAL MODEL**
>
> Suddenly I **understood** where I **was**: I **had entered** the canyon and **was being swept** swiftly toward the treacherous Mal Paso San Pedro. The raft **bounced** from wall to wall.
>
> —Yossi Ghinsberg, *Back from Tuichi*

❸ Practice and Apply

CONCEPT CHECK: Using Verb Tenses

In each sentence below, the underlined verb is in the incorrect tense. Write it in the correct tense.

A Question of Survival
1. Often I <u>am wondering</u> if I would have the courage to survive in the wilderness.
2. You never <u>knew</u> what you can do until you are put to the test.
3. Yossi Ghinsberg's story was so engrossing that I <u>feel</u> that I was with him in the jungle.
4. He <u>has been traveling</u> with three other men when his personal tale of survival began.
5. The group split up: two headed back to civilization, but Ghinsberg <u>will continue</u> with Kevin.
6. As the two careened down the river on a handmade raft, they <u>run</u> into rapids, rocks, and whirlpools.
7. During one accident, they became separated, and Ghinsberg <u>will find</u> himself alone on the raft.
8. Kevin <u>shouts,</u> "Hang on tight!" just before Ghinsberg plunged over a waterfall.
9. I <u>am gasping</u> for breath as he described the horrible dance of death in the raging waters.
10. He almost drowned, but he finally <u>struggles</u> to the riverbank, about to face even deadlier challenges.

➡ **For a SELF-CHECK and more practice, see the EXERCISE BANK, p. 317.**

Rewrite sentences 1–5 to show the action in the future.

Mixed Review

A. Proofreading Each pair of sentences in the following paragraph contains one error in verb parts or verb tenses. Write the incorrect verb, and then write the correct part or tense for each of the five.

(1) If you are a science fiction fan like me, you have probably read stories about people traveling backward or forward in time. Science fiction authors have wrote about characters using time machines and vortexes to travel through time. **(2)** A vortex is a whirling mass of water or air that sucks everything near it toward its center.

Scientists had studied whether it might actually be possible to travel through time. **(3)** Most of these scientists have used Einstein's theory of relativity as a basis for their research. According to this theory, people experienced time differently depending on where they are and how fast they are moving. **(4)** Suppose a person leaves earth and traveled in a spaceship for many years at a speed close to the speed of light. When the person returns to earth, she or he will not be much older than when she or he left. **(5)** The spacecraft that we have today, however, do not travel fast enough to make much of a difference in the way astronauts age—especially since most space missions last only days or weeks. The technology for ultrafast space travel is not available anytime in the near future.

B. Writing Look in your 🗀 **Working Portfolio** and find the paragraphs you wrote for the **Write Away** activity on page 128. See if you can use different tenses to make your meaning more precise.

VERBS

Shoe by Jeff MacNelly

CHAPTER 6

❶ Here's the Idea

In most cases, use the same verb tense within a sentence to describe events that happen at approximately the same time.

SIMPLE PAST   SIMPLE PAST

Michiko finished her history assignment and turned on a public television channel.

Some situations require you to shift tenses within a sentence. For example, use a progressive form and a simple tense to describe an ongoing action interrupted by a single event.

PAST PROGRESSIVE

Michiko was watching a nature program about Alaska when she decided to find out more about the state.

SIMPLE PAST

was watching (ONGOING ACTION)

decided (SINGLE EVENT)

When you are describing an event as a point of reference for another event, shift from a perfect tense to a simple tense.

PAST PERFECT   SIMPLE PAST

Michiko had been at the library for an hour when she found a book about Alaska called *Coming into the Country*.

❷ Why It Matters in Writing

Keep verb tenses consistent unless you have a good reason not to. Mixing verb tenses unnecessarily can confuse your readers.

STUDENT MODEL

Long ago a strip of land ~~had~~ connected Alaska with Asia, and
                                                 traveled
Asian peoples ~~are traveling~~ across the strip to settle in Alaska.

❸ Practice and Apply

For each sentence below, choose the correct verb from the pair shown in parentheses.

Example: After John McPhee (had spent, was spending) several months in Alaska in the mid-1970s, he wrote *Coming into the Country,* a book about his experiences there.

Answer: had spent

A Narrow Escape

1. One day John McPhee was flying a helicopter over Alaska, and he (is seeing, saw) an old plane wreck down below.

2. He (was traveling, travels) with officials who were looking for a site for a new state capital.

3. He learned that the plane was a World War II bomber; it (had crashed, will have crashed) during a training flight.

4. The crew of five (will be conducting, was conducting) some tests when some of the plane's controls broke.

5. Three of the crew members (were, have been) able to parachute out after the plane went into a spin.

6. A search team later found the burned remains of the other two crew members in the crashed plane; they (had failed, were failing) to get out in time.

7. Leon Crane piloted the plane; he (had been, was) the only one of the five who survived.

8. After Crane (had waited, waits) eight days for a rescue team, he set off to search for help.

9. Just as Crane (begins, was beginning) to lose his strength, he reached a cabin that was stocked with food.

10. Crane's story is just one part of McPhee's book; *Coming into the Country* (contains, contained) several other accounts of Alaska.

➜ For a SELF-CHECK and more practice, see the EXERCISE BANK, p. 318.

VERBS

Active and Passive Voice

❶ Here's the Idea

▶ **When a verb's subject performs the action expressed by the verb, the verb is in the active voice.**

PERFORMER OF ACTION   VERB

A group of 16 countries | constructed the International Space Station.

▶ **When a verb's subject receives the action expressed by the verb, the verb is in the passive voice.**

RECEIVER OF ACTION   VERB

The International Space Station | was constructed by a group of 16 countries.

Use the passive voice only when you want to emphasize the receiver of the action or when the performer of the action is not known. Otherwise change passive to active voice as follows:

> **Here's How** Changing Passive Voice to Active Voice
>
> **1.** Determine the verb and the performer of the action.
>
> **The space station is being lived in by astronauts.**
>
> **2.** Move the performer of the action before the verb and change the verb to the active voice.
>
> **Astronauts is living in the space station.**
>
> **3.** Make sure the verb agrees in number with the new subject.
>
> **Astronauts are living in the space station.**

❷ Why It Matters in Writing

If you use the passive voice too often, it can make your writing vague and lifeless.

STUDENT MODEL

DRAFT

    Skylab 2, one of the first space stations, was launched in 1973.

REVISION

    The United States launched *Skylab 2,* one of the first space stations, in 1973.

❸ Practice and Apply

CONCEPT CHECK: Active and Passive Voice

Rewrite each sentence to change the verb from the passive voice to the active voice. Change other words as necessary.

Example: The story of the space station *Mir* was followed by people around the world.

Answer: People around the world followed the story of the space station *Mir*.

Danger at 250 Miles Above the Earth

1. In 1986, the first section of the space station *Mir* was launched by Russia.
2. Years later, another space station was created by Gene Roddenberry for *Star Trek: Deep Space Nine*.
3. Undoubtedly, Roddenberry's station would be preferred by anyone who has ever dreamed of living in space.
4. In 1997 alone, many disasters were suffered by *Mir's* crew members.
5. A science lab was severely damaged by fire.
6. In June 1997, *Mir* was rammed by a 65-ton unmanned cargo ship.
7. A hole was punctured in the hull by the strong impact.
8. Also, a solar panel was destroyed by the crash.
9. The space station was also plagued by computer failures.
10. At one point, departure in the escape capsule had been considered by the frightened crew.

➜ **For a SELF-CHECK and more exercises, see the EXERCISE BANK, p. 319.**

With a partner, discuss whether changing all the sentences from passive to active voice was an improvement. Which sentences might you leave in the passive voice?

Choose a recent draft from your 🗂 **Working Portfolio.** Revise your work to eliminate any unnecessary use of the passive voice.

VERBS

The Mood of a Verb

LESSON 6

❶ Here's the Idea

▶ **The mood of a verb conveys the status of the action or condition it describes.** Verbs have three moods: indicative, imperative, and subjunctive.

Indicative Mood

Use the **indicative mood** to make statements and ask questions. The indicative is the most commonly used mood.

My friend Lisa likes to copy the hairstyles of movie stars.

Why is it that so many people are not happy with who they are?

Imperative Mood

Use the **imperative mood** to make a request or give a command. Notice that the subject, *you,* is omitted.

Be independent. Stop worrying about what others think.

Subjunctive Mood

Use the **subjunctive mood** to express a wish or state a condition that is contrary to fact. In this type of subjunctive expression, use *were* instead of *was.*

I wish I were older, and Grandpa wishes he were younger.

The subjunctive mood also is used in sentences that give a command or make a request. When the subjunctive is used this way, it requires the base form of a verb.

The school requires that students be in homeroom by 8 A.M.

❷ Why It Matters in Writing

The subjunctive mood helps writers express things that are different than they seem to be. Notice how the author of the passage on the next page expresses the feelings of a boy who happens to bump into a girl from school while he is on his paper route.

CHAPTER 6

❸ Practice and Apply

CONCEPT CHECK: The Mood of a Verb

For each numbered item, identify the underlined verb as indicative, subjunctive, or imperative mood.

A Note from Ida Knowitall, Advice Columnist

Dear Wishful Thinker,

(1) In your letter, you wrote, "I wish I <u>were</u> older." **(2)** Why <u>are</u> you in a hurry? **(3)** If your wish <u>were</u> granted, you would soon want to be younger. What a waste of time! Each person is born in a certain space and time. **(4)** Nothing he or she does <u>will</u> ever <u>change</u> that. **(5)** <u>Don't waste</u> energy wishing for the impossible. **(6)** <u>Spend</u> the time you do have on learning, growing, and enjoying what life has to offer. **(7)** John Adams once said, "Facts are stubborn things; and whatever <u>may be</u> our wishes, . . . they cannot alter the state of facts." **(8)** The fact <u>is</u> that you are the age you are. **(9)** <u>Take</u> full advantage of that fact, and **(10)** <u>use</u> your precious time more wisely.

→ For a SELF-CHECK and more practice, see the EXERCISE BANK, p. 319.

Write your own response to Wishful Thinker, and use verbs in the indicative, subjunctive, and imperative moods.

Commonly Confused Verbs

LESSON 7

❶ Here's the Idea

Writers often confuse certain pairs of verbs and use one when they should use the other.

lie/lay

The verb *lie* means "to rest in a flat position."

Someday I would like to lie on a beach and watch whales.

The verb *lay* means "to place." It is accompanied by a direct object.

DIRECT OBJECT

Lay your binoculars down here; we'll use them later.

One reason that people often confuse *lie* and *lay* is that the past participle of *lie* is spelled *lay*.

learn/teach

Use the verb *learn* when a person is receiving information. Use *teach* when a person is giving information to someone else.

In biology class we learned about whale migration.

Ms. Rodriguez taught us that whales travel great distances.

raise/rise

Use the verb *raise* when someone or something is lifting someone or something else up. When something is lifting itself up, use *rise*.

A large wave raised the boat high into the air.

Whales must rise up above the water often to breathe.

set/sit

Set means to place something. It requires a direct object. Do not use *set* when you mean *sit*.

DIRECT OBJECT

The captain of the boat set our course for a pod of whales.

We must all sit down in the boat before we can leave.

❷ Why It Matters in Writing

Although some verbs are often used incorrectly as part of slang, they should be used correctly in writing.

> **STUDENT MODEL**
>
> My friend Stan took a boat tour that included whale
> watching. The guide ~~learned~~ *taught* him that when a whale ~~raises~~ *rises*
> completely up out of the water, it is called breaching.

❸ Practice and Apply

CONCEPT CHECK: Commonly Confused Verbs

Choose the correct verb from the pair shown in parentheses.

A Whale of a Time
1. Three boats filled with whale watchers (sit, set) waiting in the still waters of Mexico's San Ignacio Lagoon.
2. A mother gray whale has been (teaching, learning) her newborn calf important whale lessons.
3. The people don't notice that another whale is (laying, lying) in the water behind them.
4. The whale submerges and then (raises, rises) directly in front of them.
5. One woman had (raised, risen) her camera just before the whale's head appeared in the viewfinder.
6. Startled, she (lays, lies) the camera in her lap and strokes the whale affectionately.
7. Sometimes a calf will (rise, raise) from the water on its mother's back.
8. As the gray whales migrate from the Bering Sea to Mexico, whale watchers (set, sit) their sights westward.
9. In San Ignacio Lagoon and elsewhere, whales will sometimes (lie, lay) quietly while humans touch them.
10. No one knows why; maybe someday a scientist will be able to (learn, teach) us.

➡ **For a SELF-CHECK and more exercises, see the EXERCISE BANK, p. 320.**

Grammar in Literature

Using Verb Tenses to Describe Events

When expert writers are describing a series of events, they use different verb tenses to give a clear picture of when events occurred. By indicating which events happened first and which events were ongoing, writers help their readers understand why things happened as they did.

The following passage was written by Beryl Markham, the first person to make a solo nonstop flight from England to North America. As you read her description of the point during her flight when she reached the eastern coast of Canada, notice how she uses verbs as she recounts the key moments of the flight.

FROM

West

WITH THE

Night

BY BERYL MARKHAM

I saw the ship and the daybreak, and then I saw the cliffs of Newfoundland wound in ribbons of fog. I felt the elation I had so long imagined, and I felt the happy guilt of having circumvented the stern authority of the weather and the sea. But mine was a minor triumph; my swift Gull was not so swift as to have escaped unnoticed. The night and the storm had caught her and we had flown blind for nineteen hours.

I was tired now, and cold. Ice began to film the glass of the cabin windows and the fog played a magician's game with the land. But the land was there. I could not see it, but I had seen it. I could not afford to believe that it was any land but the land I wanted. I could not afford to believe that my navigation was at fault, because there was no time for doubt.

South to Cape Race, west to Sydney on Cape Breton Island. With my protractor, my map, and my compass, I set my new course.

> The simple past is used with the past perfect to show how a feeling lasted over time.

> The past perfect tells what happened leading up to this part of the story.

> The past perfect shows that the author remembers the land even though she can't see it now.

Imagine that you are a news writer for a radio station and the year is 1936. You are assigned to write a brief news story about Beryl Markham's historic flight. Your story must be at least 50 words long. You have been provided with a reporter's notes to use for whichever story you choose, but you must put the information into your own words. The information should appear in a logical order.

News story #1 This story will be broadcast the day before Markham takes off on her flight. Include at least two different forms of future-tense verbs in your account.

Beryl Markham is scheduled to take off at 8 P.M. tomorrow, 9/4/36.

She is 33 years old; has worked as a pilot and horse trainer in Kenya.

Born in Leicester, England

Will take off from a military air base in Abingdon, England

She is trying to become the first person to fly solo and nonstop from England to North America.

News story #2 This story will be broadcast as if it were a live account of Markham's takeoff. Use at least two forms of present-tense verbs.

The single-engine Vega Gull plane was built especially for Markham's flight.

The plane has no radio equipment—would add too much weight.

The plane has extra fuel tanks for the long flight across the ocean.

This would be the first solo nonstop flight from England to North America.

As the plane heads down the runway for takeoff, it takes a while for it to lift off the ground—it carries much weight.

But the takeoff is successful, and she is on her way.

News story #3 This story will be broadcast the day after Markham completes her flight. Use at least two forms of past-tense verbs.

Plane crash-landed in a peat bog in the Canadian province of Nova Scotia

Markham suffered minor injuries.

Has become the first person to make a solo nonstop flight from England to North America

Time of flight: 21 hours 25 minutes

Plane did not make it to airport for landing because fuel line froze

Markham to be honored with ticker-tape parade in New York City

VERBS

Mixed Review

A. Revising Incorrect Verb Parts and Tenses For every sentence, write the incorrect verb part or tense, and then write its correct form. If all verbs in a sentence are correct, write *Correct.*

(1) At one time, most people thinked the world was flat. **(2)** To them, the Phoenicians must have been seeming very brave. **(3)** These geniuses of sea travel sailed where no other ancient people had went before. **(4)** No one knows for sure when they begun to make their voyages. **(5)** From their home in Phoenicia, which today was the country of Lebanon, they roamed the seas and established ports. **(6)** For hundreds of years, they lead the world in sea exploration. **(7)** Intrepid Phoenicians sailed around Africa centuries before Vasco da Gama done it. **(8)** Some historians have proposed the theory that the Phoenicians had even sailed to America. **(9)** Imagine an ancient Phoenician voice from beyond the grave saying, "Sorry, Columbus, but we was there first!" **(10)** In fact, the Phoenicians would have beat him by more than 2,000 years.

B. Proofreading for Improper Use of Verb, Voice, or Mood The following passage contains seven errors involving the use of the wrong verb, the unnecessary use of the passive voice, or the use of the wrong mood. Write each error, and then write its correct form.

Do imagine that for some reason you have vanished. Most of your possessions are laying in the hands of your enemies. Because a journal has never been kept by you, there is no record of your daily life, thoughts, and feelings. The only way people can learn about you is by reading what your enemies have written.

In a sense, this is what happened to the Phoenicians. After they were conquered by Alexander the Great, their culture virtually disappeared. Many historians wish they could go back in time and have Phoenicians learn them about Phoenician culture. If a Phoenician was alive today, we could find out if the Phoenicians discovered America. In reality, we can rely only on what was written by the Greeks about the Phoenicians.

C. Writing Write a paragraph describing the events in this time line, using different verb tenses. Write from the point of view of 842 B.C.

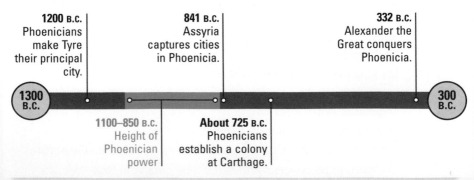

| **1200 B.C.** Phoenicians make Tyre their principal city. | **841 B.C.** Assyria captures cities in Phoenicia. | **332 B.C.** Alexander the Great conquers Phoenicia. |

1300 B.C. ——— 300 B.C.

1100–850 B.C. Height of Phoenician power

About 725 B.C. Phoenicians establish a colony at Carthage.

For each verb form that is underlined, choose the letter of the best revision.

Courage and determination <u>have took</u> Bill Pinkney to places he had
(1)
only read about in his youth. In 1992, Pinkney made his dream come true

by sailing around the world alone. He <u>had become</u> the first African
(2)
American to accomplish that feat. For a man who claims to be a terrible

swimmer, the trip must have been especially challenging. Pinkney

<u>will have said</u>, however, that when a person is 5,000 miles from shore, a
(3)
safety harness <u>was</u> far more important than knowing the backstroke.
(4)

Pinkney <u>gone</u> on another adventure in 1999. That voyage retraced
(5)
the Middle Passage, a route across the Atlantic Ocean that slave ships

<u>have used</u> for hundreds of years. He <u>had saw</u> this voyage as an
(6)   (7)
opportunity to draw attention to a period of history that is too often

ignored. If Pinkney <u>were</u> self-centered, he would have traveled alone, but
(8)
he invited 16 educators to join him. He wanted to <u>learn</u> people about the
(9)
slave route from Africa to the Americas. Who knows what other goals

Pinkney <u>sets</u> for himself in the future?
(10)

---

1. A. take
   B. have taked
   C. have taken
   D. are taking

2. A. becomes
   B. became
   C. was becoming
   D. Correct as is

3. A. will say
   B. is saying
   C. had said
   D. has said

4. A. will be
   B. is
   C. had been
   D. Correct as is

5. A. went
   B. has gone
   C. had been going
   D. is going

6. A. will have used
   B. have been using
   C. use
   D. used

7. A. had seen
   B. will see
   C. seen
   D. Correct as is

8. A. has been
   B. is
   C. was
   D. Correct as is

9. A. be learning
   B. be teaching
   C. teach
   D. Correct as is

10. A. has set
    B. will have been
       setting
    C. will set
    D. Correct as is

VERBS

Student Help Desk

Verbs at a Glance

Parts
Serve as building blocks for tenses

Voice
Shows whether the subject performs or receives an action

Tense
Indicates when something happened and how events or conditions are related in terms of time

Mood
Indicates a statement, a question, a command, or a condition contrary to fact

Cooking with Verbs

Creating Progressive Tenses

Tense or Form	Formula	Example
Present progressive	*am/are/is* + present participle	We are flying.
Past progressive	*was/were* + present participle	You were flying.
Future progressive	*will be* + present participle	They will be flying.
Present perfect progressive	*has/have* + *been* + present participle	I have been flying.
Past perfect progressive	*had* + *been* + present participle	You had been flying.
Future perfect progressive	*will have* + *been* + present participle	They will have been flying.

Combining Tenses

To show related events, use . . .

the past perfect with the simple past.

PAST PERFECT   SIMPLE PAST

I **had left** for summer camp before my cousin **arrived** for a visit.

the simple past progressive with the simple past.

SIMPLE PAST PROGRESSIVE   SIMPLE PAST

I **was starting** to enjoy myself at camp when I **got** a letter from Mom.

the past perfect progressive with the simple past.

PAST PERFECT PROGRESSIVE

Mom **had been warning** my cousin to stay away from my computer before he **destroyed** it.
                      SIMPLE PAST

the simple future progressive with the simple present.

SIMPLE FUTURE PROGRESSIVE

I **will be staying** around the house the next time my cousin **visits.**
            SIMPLE PRESENT

VERBS

The Bottom Line

Checklist for Using Verbs

Have I . . .

_____ used the right past and past participle of irregular verbs?

_____ used the correct tenses?

_____ used progressive forms to show ongoing actions?

_____ avoided switching tenses unnecessarily?

_____ avoided unnecessary use of the passive voice?

Subject-Verb Agreement

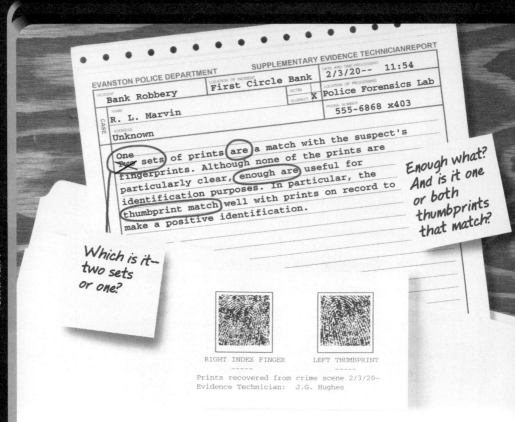

Theme: Mysteries

What's the Crime?

In this case, the first crime is the robbery, but the second "crime" is the writer's carelessness. If you were the district attorney, would you base your case on this report?

Not only does correct subject-verb agreement help your readers understand what you write; it also indicates that you're likely to be careful with your facts.

Write Away: Stop, Thief!
Write a paragraph about a recent crime or trial that fascinated you. What happened, and what was the outcome? Save the paragraph in your 🗁 **Working Portfolio.**

Choose the best way to write each underlined section and mark the letter of your answer. If the underlined section needs no change, mark the choice "Correct as is."

Fingerprints have provided a practical and effective method of
(1)
identification for over a hundred years. Each person's pattern of loops and
(2)
swirls are unique. No one, not even identical twins, have exactly the same
(3)
pattern as anyone else. Juan Vucetich and Edward R. Henry was the first to
(4)
develop efficient methods of classifying fingerprints. Today, the police
compare a suspect's fingerprints with thousands of prints stored in
computer data banks. A computer can find a match in only a few minutes.
From this work comes the facts that prosecutors need for their cases.
(5)

---

1. A. Fingerprints has provided a practical and effective method
   B. Fingerprints has been providing a practical and effective method
   C. Fingerprints was providing a practical and effective method
   D. Correct as is

2. A. Each person's pattern of loops and swirls seem unique.
   B. Each person's pattern of loops and swirls is unique.
   C. Each person's pattern of loops and swirls have looked unique.
   D. Correct as is

3. A. No one, not even identical twins, has exactly the same pattern
   B. No one, not even identical twins, is having exactly the same pattern
   C. No one, not even identical twins, are having exactly the same pattern
   D. Correct as is

4. A. Juan Vucetich and Edward R. Henry is the first to develop efficient methods
   B. Juan Vucetich and Edward R. Henry has been the first to develop efficient methods
   C. Juan Vucetich and Edward R. Henry were the first to develop efficient methods
   D. Correct as is

5. A. From this work has come the facts that prosecutors need for their cases.
   B. From this work is coming the facts that prosecutors need for their cases.
   C. From this work come the facts that prosecutors need for their cases.
   D. Correct as is

LESSON 1 Agreement in Number

❶ Here's the Idea

▶ **A verb must agree with its subject in number.** *Number* refers to whether a word is singular or plural. Singular subjects take singular verbs. Plural subjects take plural verbs.

SINGULAR	PLURAL
One early fictional detective was Di Renjie of China.	**Today's detectives are very similar to Di Renjie.**
This book describes ways to analyze evidence of all kinds.	**These books describe ways to examine physical evidence.**

For the most part, agreement problems occur with verbs in the present tense. (The exceptions include sentences with "to be" verbs.) Therefore, pay special attention to subject-verb agreement when you are writing in the present tense.

▶ **In a verb phrase, it is the first helping verb that must agree with the subject.**

In the play *Trifles,* a neighbor has reported a murder.

The officers have been searching for clues.

❷ Why It Matters in Writing

Errors in subject-verb agreement can occur when you revise your work. If you change a subject from singular to plural or from plural to singular, don't forget to change the verb to match.

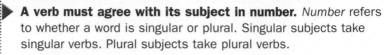

STUDENT MODEL

After a crime, detectives go over the scene inch by inch. Gradually, ~~each clue~~ *the clues* tell̶s̶ the story of the crime.

Clues requires the plural verb *tell.*

CHAPTER 7

❸ Practice and Apply

A. CONCEPT CHECK: Agreement in Number

Rewrite the incorrect sentences so that the verbs agree with their subjects. If a sentence contains no error, write *Correct*.

The *Trifles* Crime Scene

1. The play's setting are a farmhouse in the early 1900s.
2. John Wright has been murdered in his own bed.
3. The local sheriff suspect the victim's wife, Minnie.
4. Her motive remain a mystery, however.
5. Two women collects a few belongings to take to Minnie.
6. They piece together the murder from a few "trifles" in the house.
7. Two important clues surface—a broken birdcage and a dead canary.
8. Gradually, these people discovers Minnie's motive for murder.
9. Their next action have surprised many readers.
10. This drama contain some clever twists and turns in the plot.

➡ **For a SELF-CHECK and more practice, see the EXERCISE BANK, p. 320.**

B. EDITING: Making Subjects and Verbs Agree

Rewrite the following paragraph, changing each singular subject to a plural subject. Be sure to change the verbs to agree with the new subjects.

How to Investigate a Crime

(1) A murder investigation involves several specialists. **(2)** A police officer is usually the first at a crime scene. **(3)** The officer guards the evidence and takes statements from witnesses. **(4)** The homicide squad sends detectives to the scene. **(5)** The medical examiner studies the condition of the body. **(6)** The homicide detective discusses the cause of death with the medical examiner. **(7)** A crime team also arrives at the scene. **(8)** The crime photographer takes pictures of the body and the rest of the crime scene. **(9)** A crime specialist collects physical evidence to study later. **(10)** The homicide detective pieces together all the findings of the various investigators.

LESSON 2 Words Between Subject and Verb

❶ Here's the Idea

▶ **The subject of a verb is never found in a prepositional phrase or an appositive phrase.** Don't be fooled by words that come between the subject and verb. Mentally block out those words. Then it will be easy to tell whether the subject is singular or plural.

Prepositional Phrase

AGREE

The **files** ~~of any computer~~ **are vulnerable to electronic-age thieves.**

> *Files* takes the plural verb *are*.

AGREE

A computer **thief** ~~with the right codes~~ **controls all the data files.**

> *Thief* takes the singular verb *controls*.

Appositive Phrase

AGREE

These **thieves,** ~~people like the hacker Kevin Mitnick,~~ **steal government and industry secrets.**

AGREE

Mitnick, ~~the most cunning of the thieves,~~ **was caught by one of his victims, Tsutomu Shimomura.**

❷ Why It Matters in Writing

By making sure that a verb agrees with its actual subject, you help the reader understand who or what is responsible for an action.

STUDENT MODEL

  Theft by some computer hackers
give honest hackers a bad name. In
fact many hackers help the police
catch computer thieves.

> The subject is *theft*, not *hackers*.

❸ Practice and Apply

A. CONCEPT CHECK: Words Between Subject and Verb

Correct the subject-verb agreement errors in the sentences below by writing the correct verb forms on a separate sheet of paper. If a sentence contains no error, write *Correct.*

To Catch a Cyber Thief
1. One day in 1994, Kevin Mitnick, one of the country's most wanted computer criminals, makes a critical mistake.
2. Mitnick, already under FBI investigation, break into the home computer of Tsutomu Shimomura.
3. Files of a highly sensitive nature is compromised by Mitnick.
4. Shimomura, a computer expert, vow to catch him.
5. Agents from the FBI joins Shimomura to track down Mitnick.
6. A trail of e-mail messages provide vital clues.
7. Calls from two different locations also help the team.
8. Mitnick, a self-taught expert, believe his calls to be untraceable.
9. Shimomura, with his technical skill, pinpoints Mitnick's exact location in North Carolina.
10. Experts on computer security follows such stories with great interest.

➜ For a SELF-CHECK and more practice, see the EXERCISE BANK, p. 321.

B. PROOFREADING: Making Subjects and Verbs Agree

Find the four errors in subject-verb agreement in this paragraph. Change the verbs to agree with their subjects.

Computers on the Case
   Private investigators like Kinsey Millhone often uses computers to help solve their cases. In the story "Full Circle" Kinsey is asked to investigate a young girl's death in a car crash. A young man in a blue truck had shot the girl right before the accident. A news photo of the accident scene show the truck parked nearby. The license plate on the vehicle provide Kinsey with her first clue. Computerized records at the Department of Motor Vehicles helps her find the truck's owner. The owner tells her a friend borrowed the truck the day of the murder, providing Kinsey with another lead.

LESSON 3

Indefinite-Pronoun Subjects

1 Here's the Idea

An **indefinite pronoun** refers to an unspecified person or thing. Some indefinite pronouns are always singular, and some are always plural. Others can be singular or plural, depending on how they're used.

Indefinite Pronouns	
Singular	another, anybody, anyone, anything, each, either, everyone, neither, nobody, no one, one, someone
Plural	both, few, many, several
Singular or plural	all, any, more, most, none, some

▶ **Singular indefinite pronouns take singular verbs.**

Everyone has heard of Sherlock Holmes and Dr. Watson.

Does anyone know about the detective work of their creator?

▶ **Plural indefinite pronouns take plural verbs.**

Few realize that Arthur Conan Doyle solved real-life cases.

Several were difficult even for a man of Doyle's skill.

▶ **Some indefinite pronouns take singular verbs when they refer to one person or thing. They take plural verbs when they refer to two or more people or things.** To determine whether the pronoun takes a singular or plural verb, find the noun it refers to.

Most of the story takes place in England.

Most of the stories take place in England.

2 Why It Matters in Writing

Mistakes in agreement with indefinite-pronoun subjects are common in writing. Watch for these errors when you revise and proofread.

STUDENT MODEL

All of the suspects deny that they killed the victim. Each claim^s to have been elsewhere.

The writer corrects the verb to agree with the subject.

CHAPTER 7

❸ Practice and Apply

A. CONCEPT CHECK: Indefinite-Pronoun Subjects

Correct the subject-verb agreement errors in the sentences below by writing the correct verb forms on a separate sheet of paper. If a sentence contains no error, write *Correct*.

A Case of Night Blindness

1. Many of Arthur Conan Doyle's fans enjoy reading about the real-life cases Doyle solved.
2. One of these cases involve George Edalji, a young man from a small English village.
3. Someone among the villagers are viciously killing animals.
4. Nearly all of the animals are killed at night in open fields.
5. According to the police, most of the evidence point to Edalji.
6. Everyone on the jury find him guilty.
7. Someone writes Doyle, asking him to help Edalji.
8. One of Doyle's tests reveal Edalji's "night blindness."
9. No one with night blindness are able to chase and kill animals in the dark.
10. After hearing Doyle's evidence, all of the commissioners pardons Edalji.

➡ For a SELF-CHECK and more practice, see the EXERCISE BANK, p. 321.

Look at the paragraph you wrote for the **Write Away** on page 156 or another piece in your 🗂 **Working Portfolio.** Make sure that verbs with indefinite-pronoun subjects agree with those subjects.

B. EDITING: Making Verbs Agree with Indefinite Pronouns

Write the correct verb form for each of the following sentences.

Hercule Poirot: The Belgian Sherlock Holmes

(1) Many of Agatha Christie's stories (feature, features) the Belgian detective Hercule Poirot.
(2) Almost everyone (agree, agrees) that he and Sherlock Holmes have much in common. **(3)** Both (has, have) a keen knowledge of human nature. **(4)** Neither of the detectives (tolerate, tolerates) deceit or criminal behavior.
(5) Each (owe, owes) his success to a talent for noticing small details. **(6)** Nobody (fool, fools) these two detectives for long.

Compound Subjects

LESSON 4

❶ Here's the Idea

A **compound subject** consists of two or more parts joined by a conjunction, such as *and, or,* or *nor*. To decide whether a compound subject takes a singular or a plural verb, follow these guidelines.

Subjects Joined by *And*

▶ **A compound subject whose parts are joined by *and* usually requires a plural verb.**

The Hardy Boys and Nancy Drew are **the world's most famous teenage detectives.**

These detectives and their fathers have been solving **crimes since the 1920s.**

 Sometimes a compound subject containing *and* refers to a single thing and takes a singular verb.

Spaghetti and meatballs was my favorite takeout food.

Subjects Joined by *Or* or *Nor*

▶ **When the parts of a compound subject are joined by *or* or *nor,* the verb should agree with the part closest to it.**

AGREE

Neither the Hardy Boys **nor** Nancy is **the stay-at-home type.**

AGREE

Nancy or the Hardy Boys are **always near a crime scene.**

❷ Why It Matters in Writing

It's important to remember the rules about agreement with compound subjects. You can't just rely on how the singular or plural form of a verb sounds with a compound subject, since the differences between sentences may be very minor.

The office managers and the law intern are **guilty.**

Either the office managers or the law intern is **guilty.**

❸ Practice and Apply

A. CONCEPT CHECK: Compound Subjects

Write the verb form that agrees with the subject of each sentence.

What's the Verdict on Teenage Detectives?

1. Nancy Drew and the Hardy Boys (has, have) been around for years.
2. Frank and Joe Hardy first (appear, appears) in the 1920s.
3. Neither the two boys nor Nancy (has, have) aged much.
4. Students and even adult fans (continue, continues) to demand more stories.
5. The brothers or Nancy always (show, shows) courage and quick thinking.
6. Unlike the fans, however, critics and parents often (find, finds) fault with the popular detectives.
7. According to the critics, these books and their characters (show, shows) a lack of reality.
8. The average girl or boy (live, lives) in a far different world from the one in the detective books.
9. Neither Nancy nor the brothers (experience, experiences) problems at home or at school.
10. Nevertheless, the detectives' sharp wits and intelligence (inspire, inspires) their readers.

➜ **For a SELF-CHECK and more practice, see the EXERCISE BANK, p. 322.**

B. PROOFREADING: Making Verbs Agree with Compound Subjects

Write the correct forms of the incorrect verbs in these sentences. If a sentence contains no error, write *Correct.*

Chester Himes: African-American Mystery Writer

(1) Historians and many black writers recognizes Chester Himes as a groundbreaking African-American author.
(2) Neither mystery fans nor the general reader were exposed to black detectives until Himes's novels appeared. **(3)** Grave Digger Jones and Coffin Ed Johnson are his most famous characters. **(4)** Neither Coffin Ed nor Grave Digger have much use for criminals or corrupt politicians. **(5)** In the movie *Cotton Comes to Harlem,* the two detectives and a criminal gang tries to outwit each other.

LESSON 5 · Other Problem Subjects

① Here's the Idea

Some subjects, such as collective nouns, singular nouns ending in s, and titles can be confusing. Singular or plural—how do you decide?

Collective Nouns

Collective nouns refer to groups of people or things. Common collective nouns include the following:

class	committee	flock	crowd
team	family	staff	police
club	herd	jury	majority

▶ **When a collective noun refers to a group as a unit, it takes a singular verb. When it refers to a group acting as individuals, it takes a plural verb.**

In 1911 a robbery team steals the Mona Lisa from the Louvre in France.

> The team acts as one unit—the verb is singular.

The team separate after the theft.

> The team act as individuals—the verb is plural.

The museum staff argue about what to do.

> The staff act as individuals.

Fortunately, the staff alone is not investigating this case.

> The staff is considered as one unit.

Nouns Ending in *S*

Some nouns ending in s appear to be plural but are really singular in meaning. Use singular verbs with these words.

mumps	measles	humanities	news
genetics	physics	molasses	

News about fake Mona Lisas appears every week in the papers.

Eventually, forensics is used to help solve the crime.

Titles, Amounts, and Time

▶ **Titles of works of art, literature, and music are singular. Words and phrases that refer to weights, measures, numbers, and lengths of time are usually treated as singular.**

Titles and Amounts

Titles	Another genuine *Mona Lisa* **has been discovered.**	*The Twelve Chairs* **is** a comic mystery story.
Amounts	**Fifty thousand dollars has been raised** to ransom the missing painting.	Over **two-thirds** of the money **comes** from private donations.
Time	**Twelve years is** a long time for an investigation to continue.	**Fifty years was** the maximum sentence for stealing a masterpiece.

Remember that even a plural title (*Mysteries of Sherlock Holmes, 100 Great Detectives*) takes a singular verb.

② Why It Matters in Writing

Besides occurring in your own writing, these tricky subjects often show up on standardized tests. Knowing the rules of subject-verb agreement can help you choose the right verbs in either situation.

The museum security staff __(1)__ sure that Louvre employees are involved in the *Mona Lisa* theft. Ordinarily, the museum carpenter, Vincenzo Perugia, would be a prime suspect. His right-hand fingerprints are already on record. Forensics __(2)__ little help in this case, however. The police __(3)__ a thumbprint at the crime scene, but it is from Perugia's *left* hand.

1. A. are	2. A. offer	3. A. has found
B. is	B. have offered	B. finds
C. have been	C. offers	C. are finding
D. were	D. is offered	D. find

Answers: 1. B (*Staff* refers to a single unit.) **2.** C (*Forensics* is singular.) **3.** D (*Police* is a plural collective noun.)

❸ Practice and Apply

A. CONCEPT CHECK: Other Problem Subjects

Write the verb form that agrees with the subject of each sentence.

Steal the *Mona Lisa?* Impossible!

1. The usual crowd (begins, begin) to gather at the Louvre Museum on an August day in 1911.
2. The *Mona Lisa* (is, are) not hanging on the wall.
3. The security staff (think, thinks) that the painting is being photographed.
4. Sixty minutes (is, are) all that the robbery and escape took.
5. The robbery team (consists, consist) of a mastermind, a forger, a carpenter, and two accomplices.
6. A million francs (does, do) not even come close to the amount represented by the loss.
7. News of the robbery (break, breaks) slowly.
8. The staff (does, do) not agree about what to tell the press.
9. Forensics (is, are) used to help detect fake *Mona Lisa*s.
10. *The Day They Stole the Mona Lisa* (is, are) a nonfiction book about the robbery and investigation.

➡ For a SELF-CHECK and more practice, see the EXERCISE BANK, p. 322.

B. PROOFREADING: Correcting Agreement Errors

Find the subject-verb agreement errors in the following sentences. Write the correct verbs on a separate sheet of paper.

The Story Continues

1. Three minutes are all it takes to remove the painting from the museum wall.
2. *La Joconde,* as the painting is known in France, remain hidden in a shabby apartment across the city.
3. The robbery team argues about selling forgeries of the real *Mona Lisa.*
4. Nearly two million dollars are what the forgeries earn.
5. The French public demand the return of the painting.

Agreement Problems in Sentences

① Here's the Idea

In some sentences, the placement of the subject and verb makes it hard to choose the right verb form.

Predicate Nominatives

A verb always agrees with its subject, never with a predicate nominative. A predicate nominative is a noun or pronoun that follows a linking verb and names or explains the subject.

AGREE
The robbers' main target is banks.

AGREE
Banks are the target.

Inverted Sentences

A subject can follow a verb or come between parts of a verb phrase in the following types of sentences.

Inverted Sentences	
As questions	Does the **bank** want the robbers punished?
Beginning with *here* or *there*	Here is a **book** about dumb criminals.
Beginning with a phrase	Right by the police speeds the **truck.**

There is an easy way to find the true subjects of these sentences.

Here's How Finding the Subject

Out of the bank (come, comes) the two robbers.

1. Turn the sentence around so that the subject comes before the verb.

   The two robbers (come, comes) out of the bank.
2. Determine whether the subject is singular or plural.

   robbers (plural)
3. Make sure the subject and verb agree.

   The two robbers come out of the bank.

For more about subject-verb agreement problems, see p. 47.

SUBJECT-VERB

❷ Why It Matters in Writing

By knowing how to find subjects, you can make sure that verbs agree with their subjects in questions, in sentences beginning with *here* or *there,* and in other inverted sentences. What are the subjects in the following model?

LITERARY MODEL

Mrs. Peters (*crosses right looking in cupboard*). Why, here's a birdcage. (*Holds it up.*) Did she have a bird, Mrs. Hale?

—Susan Glaspell, *Trifles*

❸ Practice and Apply

A. CONCEPT CHECK: Agreement Problems in Sentences

Write the subject of each sentence. Then write the verb form that agrees with the subject.

Dumb and Dumber Criminals

1. (Has, Have) you ever heard stories about dumb criminals and their crimes?
2. In the book *Crimes and Misdumbmeanors* (appears, appear) several bungling criminals.
3. Here (is, are) one example of a badly botched robbery.
4. To a large sewing shop (dashes, dash) two police officers.
5. Near a basement window (lies, lie) pieces of broken glass.
6. "(Is, Are) anything missing?" one officer asks.
7. There (is, are) clear evidence that a sewing machine has been stolen.
8. Across the floor of the shop (run, runs) a single bright thread, snagged on a rough floorboard.
9. (Has, Have) the robbers left a trail for police to follow?
10. Out the door, across the alley, and up to the thieves' apartment (goes, go) the police officers, following this "thread of evidence."

→ For a SELF-CHECK and more practice, see the EXERCISE BANK, p. 323.

B. EDITING AND PROOFREADING: Correcting Agreement Errors

Rewrite these sentences, correcting errors in subject-verb agreement. If a sentence contains no error, write *Correct*.

Example: On the hairy legs of one robber is sheer nylon stockings.

Answer: On the hairy legs of one robber **are** sheer nylon **stockings.**

Why the Taos Bank Robbery Failed

1. Does some people have bad luck even in crime?
2. Into the Taos bank walks two robbers, one in women's clothes.
3. There is few things more obvious than a poor disguise.
4. The robbers' main problem are curious onlookers.
5. In one robber's hand gleams a pistol in plain sight!
6. Have someone spread the word to the police?
7. Outside the front door gathers people who know about the robbery.
8. There is only one thing for the robbers to do—run!
9. Has the robbers thought of a getaway plan?
10. There are nowhere to hide after the robbery attempt.

Proofread a piece of writing in your 🗒 **Working Portfolio** to make sure that subjects and verbs agree.

Zits by Scott and Borgman

Real World Grammar

Report

Writing is a lot like private-detective work. In both cases you need to know how to operate within the rules. You need to be thorough. And you need to look after your reputation.

Here are two paragraphs from a student's research report. The comments you see at the sides were made by a trusted friend who caught a few subject-verb agreement errors.

Careers in Forensics

Forensics, the science of crime solving, are an important and exciting field. There is more opportunities within this profession for people with varied backgrounds than you might expect.

Movies and television shows always seem to focus on chemists and doctors working in crime labs and morgues. However, specialists in other branches of science, such as geology and botany, also works on cases, analyzing soil, mud, pollen, and other physical evidence at a crime scene. Psychologists and psychiatrists are also called in to help the police capture or evaluate suspects, especially in cases of murder and other serious crimes. A specially trained photographer records information at a crime scene. Anyone who witnesses a crime talk to forensic artists to help them create pictures of the suspects.

"Forensics" is one of those "ics" words that take singular verbs.

The subject is "opportunities," not "there."

This should agree with "specialists."

You need a singular verb here to agree with the indefinite pronoun "anyone."

Using Grammar in Writing

Agreement in number	Watch out for plural subjects that don't end in *s* (*men, women*) and for collective nouns that refer to groups acting as individuals (*the jury argue*). Watch out for subjects ending in *s* that take singular verbs (*news, physics*).
Words between subjects and verbs	A phrase or clause between a subject and a verb can add important details. Just be sure the verb agrees with its subject.
Sentences beginning with *here* or *there*	Beginning a sentence with *here* or *there* can emphasize the subject, which often follows the verb. (*Here is the pen. There are the fingerprints.*)
Compound subjects	When combining subjects with *or* or *nor,* make sure the verb agrees with the part closest to it. When combining subjects with *and,* make sure the verb is plural.
Indefinite pronouns	When you make a generalization in which the subject is an indefinite pronoun, be sure the verb agrees in number with the pronoun.

PRACTICE AND APPLY

Another student interested in forensics has written the letter below. Use the guidelines above to correct the sentences that contain errors in subject-verb agreement.

STUDENT MODEL

Dear Ms. Beck:

Your appearances on *TV Trial* is always a pleasure to watch. In my opinion, your comments and explanations about DNA evidence has been particularly informative. While doing research for a school report on this subject, I recently came across a puzzling question. Here, briefly, is the facts that I do not understand.

On the one hand, according to my reading, identical twins has the same DNA. On the other hand, also according to my reading, identical twins' fingerprints are different. Is this true? If so, how is it possible? Don't our DNA determine our physical characteristics, including our fingerprints?

Any information or research tips you can offer is sure to be helpful. Thank you so much for your time and your advice.

Mixed Review

A. Agreement in Number, Compound Subjects, and Other Problem Subjects
Read this passage. Then write answers to the questions below it.

> **LITERARY MODEL**
>
> **(1)** The final footnote on The Great Taos Bank Robbery was not written until February 4, 1958. **(2)** After the surrender, officers found the two refreshingly frank about their activities. **(3)** In due course, Joe Gomez and Frederick Smith were accused by the U.S. District Attorney of conspiring to violate the provisions of the Federal Banking Act and their case was placed on the winter docket for consideration by the Federal Grand Jury. **(4)** Unfortunately, grand jury proceedings are secret so we will never know exactly what happened when the case was presented. **(5)** We do know that the jury returned a "no bill," which indicates—at the very least—that the jurors could not be convinced that Gomez and Smith took their pistols into the Taos bank with felonious intentions.
>
> —Tony Hillerman, "The Great Taos Bank Robbery"

1. In sentence 1, what verb agrees with the subject *footnote?*
2. In sentence 2, if *found* were in the present tense, would you use *find* or *finds* to agree with the subject?
3. In sentence 3, what is the subject of *were accused?*
4. In sentence 4, what subject does *are* agree with?
5. In summarizing sentence 5, would you say "The jury was not convinced about the intentions of the accused" or "The jury were not convinced about the intentions of the accused"? Explain your choice.

B. Subject-Verb Agreement
Write the verb form that agrees with the subject of each sentence.

1. "The Great Taos Bank Robbery" (reveal, reveals) Hillerman's humor.
2. Most of his fiction (seem, seems) more brooding and serious.
3. (Do, Does) the names Joe Leaphorn and Jim Chee sound familiar?
4. Each (is, are) well-known to mystery fans.
5. Both (work, works) for the Navajo police in Hillerman's novels.
6. The Navajo reservation, located in New Mexico, Arizona, and Utah, (cover, covers) a wide territory.
7. All of Hillerman's books (offer, offers) insights into Navajo life.
8. There (is, are) interesting differences between Leaphorn and Chee.
9. (Have, Has) Leaphorn or Chee solved more cases?
10. Almost every year, one of Hillerman's books (make, makes) the bestseller list.

Choose the best way to write each underlined section and mark the letter of your answer. If the underlined section needs no change, mark the choice "Correct as is."

Mystery writing is livelier and more varied than ever. A choice of styles ranging from gentle whodunits to nail-biting thrillers <u>keeps</u> fans asking
(1)
for more. <u>Anyone, no matter how choosy, have</u> only to visit the nearest
(2)
bookstore to find adventure and intrigue. <u>Writers like Agatha Christie</u>
(3)
<u>and Arthur Conan Doyle has created</u> great detectives and brain-teasing

plots. <u>From America's past comes mysteries</u> written by Edgar Allan Poe
(4)
and Nathaniel Hawthorne. <u>There is Asian, Hispanic, Native American,</u>
(5)
<u>and African-American detectives</u>—all with their devoted fans! One

hundred and fifty years of mystery writing has produced some of the

greatest stories in fiction.

---

1. A. has kept
   B. is keeping
   C. keep
   D. Correct as is

2. A. Anyone, no matter how choosy, has
   B. Anyone, no matter how choosy, will have
   C. Anyone, no matter how choosy, have had
   D. Correct as is

3. A. Writers like Agatha Christie and Arthur Conan Doyle has been creating
   B. Writers like Agatha Christie and Arthur Conan Doyle have created
   C. Writers like Agatha Christie and Arthur Conan Doyle creates
   D. Correct as is

4. A. From America's past are coming mysteries
   B. From America's past has come mysteries
   C. From America's past come mysteries
   D. Correct as is

5. A. There was Asian, Hispanic, Native American, and African-American detectives
   B. There has been Asian, Hispanic, Native American, and African-American detectives
   C. There are Asian, Hispanic, Native American, and African-American detectives
   D. Correct as is

Student Help Desk

Subject-Verb Agreement at a Glance

Verbs should agree with their subjects in number.

A **singular** subject **requires** a **singular** verb.

Plural subjects **require** **plural** verbs.

Tricky Cases

Verb phrase The first helping verb should agree with the subject.	He **has been judging** this case. **They have been judging** this case.
Words between subject and verb Block out these words when deciding what verb form to use.	The **facts** in this case **are** clear.
Indefinite-pronoun subject Singular pronouns take singular verbs; plural pronouns take plural verbs. Some pronouns can be singular or plural.	**Everyone wants** to attend the trial. **Many expect** a guilty verdict. **None** of the pie **was stolen.** **None** of the pies **were stolen.**
Compound subject containing *and* Always use a plural verb.	The **lawyer and** the **judge argue** about a point of law.
Compound subject containing *or* **or** *nor* The verb should agree with the subject closest to it.	Neither the **lawyers nor** the **judge** **agrees.** Neither the **judge nor** the **lawyers** **agree.**
Collective noun Can be singular (a unit) or plural (individuals).	The **staff is meeting.** The **staff disagree** about what to say.
Singular noun ending in s Often use a singular verb.	The **news is** not good.
Title, amount, time Often use a singular verb.	**Three days is** a long time to deliberate.

Other Agreement Problems

Predicate nominative Make sure the verb agrees with the subject, not with the predicate nominative.	The best **evidence** **is** DNA fingerprints. DNA **fingerprints** **are** the best evidence.
Question Convert the question into a statement to find the subject.	(Do, does) the fingerprint match the suspect's prints? The **fingerprint** **does match** the suspect's prints.
Sentence beginning with • *here or there* • **phrase** Turn the sentence around to find the subject.	There (is, are) no verdict yet. No **verdict** **is** there yet. Out of the courtroom (come, comes) the suspect and his lawyers. The **suspect** and his **lawyers** **come** out of the courtroom.

SUBJECT-VERB

The Bottom Line

Checklist for Subject-Verb Agreement

Have I . . .

_____ correctly identified the simple subject and predicate in each clause?

_____ checked for agreement after changing a subject?

_____ checked that *don't* and *doesn't* are used correctly?

_____ checked whether indefinite-pronoun subjects are singular or plural?

_____ checked that verbs agree with the nearest parts of compound subjects containing *or* or *nor*?

_____ checked whether all subjects that end in s are really plural?

_____ put questions and other inverted sentences in normal order to check agreement?

_____ found the true subjects in sentences beginning with *here* or *there*?

Using Pronouns

If you disappoint me again, I'll put a price on your head so large you won't be able to go near a civilized system for the rest of your short life.

Buzzards will tear your eyes out!

Theme: Heroes and Villains

Good Guys Versus Bad Guys

From the *Odyssey,* to the tales of the knights of the Round Table, and to *Star Wars,* stories about heroes and villains capture our imaginations. Heroes and villains threaten and insult each other and boast about their own greatness, and they all use pronouns to do it. Read the quotations above. Could these characters have threatened their enemies without using pronouns?

Write Away: Threats and Boasts

Use your imagination or memory to write some boasts that a modern hero might make. Add to it some nonviolent threats that might scare a modern enemy. Underline the pronouns you use, and save your work in your 🗁 **Working Portfolio.**

Choose the best way to write each underlined word and mark the letter of your answer. If the underlined section needs no change, mark the choice "Correct as is."

Heroes in stories usually have great strength or speed and carry a powerful weapon with <u>them</u>, such as a strong bow or an intergalactic ray
(1)
gun. Some, like Odysseus or Luke Skywalker, occasionally have a god or another special force working with <u>them</u>. However, villains also have
(2)
physical power and <u>his</u> own weapons. In order to win, heroes have to be
(3)
smarter than <u>them</u>. Heroes must outwit <u>they're</u> enemies. Most of <u>us</u>
(4)   (5)   (6)
readers enjoy stories that involve trickery, humor, and contests of wits. We root for the good guys in battles of brains between the villains and <u>they</u>.
(7)
<u>Its</u> the underdog hero, <u>whom</u> has no weapons except <u>their</u> brain, that we
(8)   (9)   (10)
like best.

---

1. A. themselves
   B. him
   C. himself
   D. Correct as is

2. A. him
   B. himself
   C. themselves
   D. Correct as is

3. A. his or her
   B. their
   C. there
   D. Correct as is

4. A. themselves
   B. him
   C. they
   D. Correct as is

5. A. them
   B. their
   C. there
   D. Correct as is

6. A. we
   B. our
   C. his
   D. Correct as is

7. A. theirselves
   B. us
   C. them
   D. Correct as is

8. A. It has
   B. Their
   C. It's
   D. Correct as is

9. A. whoever
   B. who
   C. whose
   D. Correct as is

10. A. theirs
    B. his or her
    C. them
    D. Correct as is

PRONOUNS

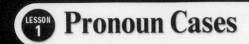

Pronoun Cases

❶ Here's the Idea

▶ **Personal pronouns take different forms depending on how they are used in sentences. The form of a pronoun is called its case.**

There are three pronoun cases: nominative, objective, and possessive. The chart below lists all of the personal pronouns and organizes them by case, number (singular or plural), and person.

Personal Pronouns			
	Nominative	**Objective**	**Possessive**
Singular			
First person	I	me	my, mine
Second person	you	you	your, yours
Third person	he, she, it	him, her, it	his, her, hers, its
Plural			
First person	we	us	our, ours
Second person	you	you	your, yours
Third person	they	them	their, theirs

❷ Why It Matters in Writing

When writers create first-person dialogue in a narrative, they use all forms of pronouns, just as people do when they speak. Notice how many pronouns Odysseus uses when describing his reaction to his archenemy, the Cyclops.

LITERARY MODEL

I would not heed **them** [shipmates] in **my** glorying spirit, but let **my** anger flare and yelled:

'Cyclops, if ever mortal man inquire

how **you** were put to shame and blinded, tell **him**

Odysseus, raider of cities, took **your** eye:

Laertes' son, **whose** home's on Ithaca!'

—Homer, *Odyssey*

Nominative and Objective Cases

① Here's the Idea

Personal pronouns change their case depending on whether they function as subjects or objects.

Nominative Case

▶ **Personal pronouns that function as subjects or as predicate nominatives are in the nominative case.**

I like the legends of King Arthur. He united the knights.
↖SUBJECT   ↖SUBJECT

Be particularly careful to use the nominative case when the pronoun is part of a compound subject.

Queen Guinevere and he were wife and husband.
↑   ↖COMPOUND SUBJECT

A **predicate pronoun** also takes the nominative case. A predicate pronoun follows a linking verb and renames the subject of the sentence.

It was he who gathered the knights of the Round Table.
↖PREDICATE PRONOUN

The following chart shows the nominative form of personal pronouns.

Nominative Pronoun Forms			
	First Person	**Second Person**	**Third Person**
Singular	I	you	he, she, it
Plural	we	you	they

In conversation, people often use the wrong case for a pronoun in the predicate pronoun position. Make sure you use the nominative case for predicate pronouns in formal writing.

It's her. (INCORRECT)

It's she. (CORRECT)

PRONOUNS

Objective Case

▶ **Personal pronouns that function as direct objects, indirect objects, or the objects of prepositions are in the objective case.**

Merlin the Wizard, Arthur's friend, helped him.
DIRECT OBJECT

Merlin gave him loyalty.
INDIRECT OBJECT

Most of Arthur's knights were also loyal to him.
OBJECT OF PREPOSITION

Also use the objective case of the pronoun when it is part of a compound object construction.

The knights pledged allegiance to both Guinevere and him.
COMPOUND OBJECT OF PREPOSITION

Objective Pronoun Forms			
	First Person	**Second Person**	**Third Person**
Singular	me	you	him, her, it
Plural	us	you	them

Compound Constructions To make sure you are using the correct case in a compound construction, look at each part separately.

Here's How Choosing the Correct Case

Lancelot loved both Arthur and (she, her).
(She, Her) and Arthur both loved Lancelot.

1. Try each pronoun from the compound construction alone in the sentence.

Lancelot loved she. → **Lancelot loved her.** (objective case correct)

She loved Lancelot. → **Her loved Lancelot.** (nominative case correct)

2. Choose the correct case for the sentence.

Lancelot loved both Arthur and her.

She and Arthur both loved Lancelot.

Always use the objective case after the preposition *between.*

Guinevere's heart was torn between Arthur and him.

❷ Why It Matters in Writing

Most stories have many characters and many opportunities for the misuse of pronouns. Whenever you revise a story, check your pronoun cases.

STUDENT MODEL

For a long time, one chair at King Arthur's Round Table remained empty. Anyone who tried to sit in it died instantly. When Galahad and his servant arrived, Arthur invited t̶h̶e̶y̶ *them* to sit at the table. Galahad took the empty chair and lived! The chair had been waiting for someone pure in heart, and that person was h̶i̶m̶ *he*.

❸ Practice and Apply

A. CONCEPT CHECK: Nominative and Objective Cases

Choose the correct form from the pronouns in parentheses.

King Arthur: Legend or History?

1. Although King Arthur is a legendary hero, (he, him) probably existed as a real person as well.
2. While historians think that a real King Arthur existed, (they, them) know little about him.
3. It is (them, they) who say that his legend may be based on a real leader of the fifth or sixth century.
4. The real Arthur may have been a Celtic military leader; (he, him) defended Britain from Anglo-Saxon invaders.
5. So many stories were told about (him, he) that he must have been heroic in real life.
6. The legends that grew from the stories were romances and show (we, us) how people thought knights should behave.
7. In reality, (they, them) were often greedy and violent and used their weapons to get what they wanted.
8. Arthur supposedly brought (they, them) together to improve their morality and the quality of life for citizens.
9. Tales about Arthur were originally oral, but eventually people wrote (they, them) down.
10. Over the course of time, legends grow until (they, them) have little resemblance to the truth.

➜ For a SELF-CHECK and more practice, see the EXERCISE BANK, p. 324.

PRONOUNS

B. REVISING: Providing Pronouns

On your paper, write an appropriate pronoun in the correct case for each numbered blank.

Sir Lancelot was one of the most colorful characters in Arthur's Round Table. Not only was **(1)** _____ popular with the ladies, he held quite a war record as well. In one battle **(2)** _____ knocked five knights off their horses and broke the backs of four of **(3)** _____. As **(4)** _____ became angrier, **(5)** _____ knocked off another 28 knights. When a lady led **(6)** _____ to his enemy, **(7)** _____ succeeded in beheading that enemy and freeing 60 of his fellow knights. Lancelot also loved Queen Guinevere. Even though Guinevere was the queen, **(8)** _____ was almost burned at the stake because of her affair with **(9)** _____. Lancelot raced in on his horse; **(10)** _____ rescued **(11)** _____ and returned **(12)** _____ to King Arthur before being banished to France. When **(13)** _____ read the legend of King Arthur, as told in Sir Thomas Malory's *Morte d'Arthur,* **(14)** _____ will think **(15)** _____ are reading a modern adventure story combined with a soap opera.

C. WRITING

The picture at the right shows a tournament in King Arthur's court. Choose one onlooker and write a paragraph describing the scene from that person's point of view. Underline the pronouns you use, and save the paragraph in your ☐ **Working Portfolio.**

Possessive Case

❶ Here's the Idea

▶ **Personal pronouns that show ownership or relationships are in the possessive case.**

Possessive Pronouns			
	First Person	**Second Person**	**Third Person**
Singular	my, mine	your, yours	his, her, hers, its
Plural	our, ours	your, yours	their, theirs

Possessive pronouns can be used in two ways:

1. A possessive pronoun can be used in place of a noun. The pronoun can function as a subject or an object.

I need a book on Australian myths.

Can I borrow yours? Mine is at home.
　　　　DIRECT OBJECT　　　　SUBJECT

2. A possessive pronoun can be used to modify a noun or a gerund. The pronoun comes before the noun or the gerund it modifies.

We learned their history through our reading.
　　　　　　　　NOUN　　　　　　　　　　GERUND

Remember that a gerund acts as a noun. That's why it can be modified by a possessive pronoun.

　　POSSESSIVE

Our sailing to Australia was a terrific experience.
　　　GERUND

Do not use a possessive pronoun with a participle.
　　　　　　　　　　OBJECTIVE

Our friend watched us sailing away.
　　　　　　　　　PARTICIPLE

For more information on participles and gerunds, see p. 71–75.

Avoid confusing possessive pronouns with their sound-alike contractions. Read the sentences below to help you understand the difference between these two kinds of words.

You're visiting Australia? [You are]　**Your** book is here.

They're painting a scene. [They are] **Their** culture is so old.

There's so much to see. [There is]　We have no songs like **theirs**.

It's too bad we can't stay. [It is]　Each landform has **its** story.

PRONOUNS

❷ Why It Matters in Writing

Using pronouns with *-ing* words can be tricky. When you want to stress the **action,** use a gerund with a possessive pronoun: *His waiting is over.* When you want to stress the **actor,** use the objective form of the pronoun with a participle: *I saw **him waiting** at the corner.*

> **STUDENT MODEL**
>
> Some rock art of the Australian aborigines is thousands of years old. **My** photographing these symbols was the high point of our trip. At one stop, the guide called me over to look at an unusual image. I saw **him** pointing to a six-fingered handprint!

❸ Practice and Apply

A. CONCEPT CHECK: Possessive Case

Write the possessive pronouns in the following sentences.

1. Our Australian friend told us a story from her homeland, the land of the aborigines.
2. She told us about their "dreamtime," a time long ago when our animal ancestors inhabited the earth.
3. People back then talked with the animals, friends of theirs.
4. No people knew how to make fire in those days until their friend Joongabilbil the Chicken Hawk taught them.
5. "Without fire," he said, "your children will starve."

➜ **For a SELF-CHECK and more practice, see the EXERCISE BANK, p. 324.**

B. PROOFREADING: Pronoun Errors

Correct the pronoun errors in each sentence on your paper.

1. Creating a small fire in a tree, he said, "Now take some of my burning branches to you're homes."
2. When they're fires went out, the people came back; and they complaining was noisy.
3. As the people watched his rubbing branches together, Joongabilbil said, "Making fire: this is how its done."
4. "Me replacing your fires daily won't work; you must learn and pass on this knowledge to you're children."
5. This legend of Australia shows that knowledge of fire came from it's unlikely hero, a chicken hawk.

Using *Who* and *Whom*

❶ Here's the Idea

▶ **The case of the pronoun *who* is determined by the function of the pronoun in the sentence.**

Forms of *Who* and *Whoever*	
Nominative	who, whoever
Objective	whom, whomever
Possessive	whose, whosever

Who and *whom* can be used to ask questions and to introduce subordinate clauses.

Who and *Whom* in Questions

Who is the nominative form of the pronoun. In questions, *who* is used as a subject or as a predicate pronoun.

Who knows the story of Mulan, a heroine of Old China?
　SUBJECT

The heroine was who?
PREDICATE PRONOUN

Whom is the objective form. In a question, *whom* is used as a direct or an indirect object of a verb or as the object of a preposition.

Whom did Mulan fool?
　DIRECT OBJECT

She told whom the secret of her identity?
　　　INDIRECT OBJECT

> **Here's How** Choosing *Who* or *Whom* in a Question
>
> **To (who, whom) was the order given?**
>
> **1.** Rewrite the question as a statement.
> **The order was given to (who, whom).**
>
> **2.** Figure out whether the pronoun is used as a subject, an object, a predicate pronoun, or the object of a preposition. Then choose the correct form.
> **The order was given to whom.** (*whom* is the object of the preposition *to*)
>
> **3.** Use the correct form in the original question.
> **To whom was the order given?**

PRONOUNS

Who and Whom in Subordinate Clauses

One of the trickiest pronoun situations involves using *who* and *whom* in clauses. In such cases, look only at how the pronoun functions within the clause.

▶ **Use *who* when the pronoun is the subject of a subordinate clause.**

SUBORDINATE CLAUSE

It's the rebel chief who is threatening the borders.

SUBJECT

▶ **Use *whom* when the pronoun is an object in a subordinate clause.**

SUBORDINATE CLAUSE

The chief whom we all fear most is a rebel.

DIRECT OBJECT

Here's How **Choosing *Who* or *Whom* in a Clause**

No one knows (who, whom) wrote the *Ballad of Mulan*.

1. Identify the subordinate clause in the sentence.
   (who, whom) wrote the *Ballad of Mulan*

2. Is the pronoun used as the subject of the clause? Is the pronoun used as the object in the clause? (You may have to rewrite the clause to decide.)
   The pronoun is the subject of the clause. *Who* is the correct choice.
   Who wrote the *Ballad of Mulan*?

3. Choose the correct pronoun for the sentence.
   No one knows who wrote the *t*

Don't assume that *whomever* is correct after the preposition *to*. Choose *whoever* or *whomever* based on the pronoun's function in the subordinate clause.

Give credit to (whoever, whomever) wrote the poem.

Give credit to whoever wrote the poem.

❷ Why It Matters in Writing

Writers frequently misuse *who, whom, whoever,* or *whomever* after prepositions, especially in subordinate clauses. What sounds right may not be correct. To avoid mistakes, keep checking the function of the word in the sentence or clause.

Chinese history is filled with stories of invading nomads who caused trouble for whoever was in their way.

A. CONCEPT CHECK: Using *Who* and *Whom*

Choose the correct pronoun from those in parentheses.

Mulan: The Steel Magnolia

1. The Chinese heroine (who, whom) went to war disguised as a man was portrayed in the popular movie *Mulan*.
2. In the movie, Mulan's father, (who, whom) has fought bravely in the past, is ordered to serve in the army once again.
3. Mulan is afraid that her father, (who, whom) she loves very much, is now too old to go to war.
4. To save his life, she disguises herself and goes in his place so that (whoever, whomever) sees her will think she is a man.
5. During the war, the soldiers discover (who, whom) Mulan really is.
6. (Who, Whom) was the real Mulan?
7. Historians think she was a real person about (who, whom) a famous poem was written more than a thousand years ago.
8. The emperor offered her a reward; but Mulan, (who, whom) wished to go home, accepted only a fine horse.
9. The real Mulan's identity was not discovered until comrades with (who, whom) she had fought visited her at home.
10. For (whoever, whomever) is curious, "Mulan" means "magnolia."

➡ **For a SELF-CHECK and more practice, see the EXERCISE BANK, p. 325.**

B. PROOFREADING: Correcting Errors Using *Who* and *Whom*

Find the sentences in which *who* and *whom* are used incorrectly. Correct each sentence that contains an error.

Women Warriors

(1) Many women in history are known for their bravery in battle. **(2)** One was Raziyya Iltutmish, who ruled Northern India from 1236 to 1240. **(3)** Raziyya's father chose his daughter, who he considered superior to his sons, as his successor. **(4)** Riots protesting a woman ruler broke out, and it was Raziyya herself whom led the troops to restore peace. **(5)** Joan of Arc was the French heroine whom, in 1429, helped to drive the English out of France. **(6)** Joan lived to see the coronation of Charles VII, the man for who she had fought so valiantly. **(7)** Deborah Sampson was the first American woman who we know of that joined an army in combat. **(8)** Like Mulan, Sampson, who fought in the Revolution, dressed as a man to hide her gender.

PRONOUNS

Pronoun-Antecedent Agreement

❶ Here's the Idea

▶ **A pronoun must agree with its antecedent in number, gender, and person.** An **antecedent** is the noun or pronoun that a pronoun refers to or replaces.

Agreement in Number

If the antecedent is singular, use a singular pronoun. If the antecedent is plural, use a plural pronoun.

SINGULAR

The *Ramayana* is one of India's greatest epics. It tells stories about heroic characters. Two of them are Rama and Sita, his wife.

PLURAL

Agreement with Compound Subjects Use a plural pronoun to refer to nouns or pronouns joined by *and.*

PLURAL

Rama and Ravana clash when they fight over Sita.

A pronoun that refers to nouns or pronouns joined by *or* or *nor* should agree with the noun or pronoun nearer to it.

REFERS TO

Neither Ravana nor Rama's troops can defeat their foes.

Agreement with Collective Nouns A collective noun, such as *family,* may be referred to by either a singular or a plural pronoun. The number of the collective noun is determined by its meaning in the sentence.

Use a singular pronoun if the collective noun names a group acting as a unit. In the following sentence, *family* refers to the group as a unit and takes a singular pronoun.

REFERS TO

The family finally gives its support to Rama.

Use a plural pronoun if the collective noun shows the members or parts of a group acting individually. In the sentence below, *family* refers to the group as individuals and takes a plural pronoun.

REFERS TO

Rama's family argue over their plans to rescue Sita.

Agreement in Gender and Person

The gender of a pronoun must be the same as the gender of its antecedent. Remember that *gender* refers to the masculine (*he, him, his*), feminine (*she, her, hers*), or neuter forms (*it, its*) of personal pronouns.

Hanuman, the monkey chief, brings his troops to the battle.

Gender-Free Language Don't use only masculine or only feminine pronouns when you mean to refer to both genders. The purpose of gender-free language is to make sure you include everyone.

> **Here's How** **Using Gender-Free Language**
>
> There are two simple ways to rewrite a sentence such as the following.
> **Every reader of the *Ramayana* has his favorite tales.**
> 1. Rewrite the sentence to make the pronoun and its antecedent plural.
>   **Readers of the *Ramayana* have their favorite tales.**
> 2. Use the phrase *his or her* when necessary.
>   **Every reader of the *Ramayana* has his or her favorite tales.**

The person of the pronoun must be the same as the person of its antecedent. REFERS TO

All you fans should buy your tickets for the latest Rama movie.

❷ Why It Matters in Writing

Today's readers are offended by the old-fashioned use of *his* when referring to both males and females. However, *his or her* becomes awkward when used too often. Try making the antecedents and their pronouns plural to avoid awkwardness.

> **STUDENT MODEL**
>
> The **people** of India treasure the *Ramayana* in part because **they** believe that the epic will bring great blessings to **them. They** also adore the characters in the great Indian epic. **Every** Indian child and adult has **his or her** favorite part.

❸ Practice and Apply

A. CONCEPT CHECK: Pronoun-Antecedent Agreement

Choose the correct pronoun from those in parentheses.

Rama and Ravana: Good Against Evil

1. Rama and Ravana are well known in India because of (his, their) roles as the hero and the villain, respectively, of the *Ramayana*.

2. In the epic, either Rama or his half-brother Bharata must give up (his, their) claim to the throne, and Bharata is made king.

3. Rama, his faithful wife Sita, and his loyal supporter Laksmana leave (his or her, their) home to live in the forest.

4. There, the demon king Ravana and his army kidnap Sita and take her away to (his, their) land.

5. Rama and Laksmana are unable to rescue Sita until a band of talking monkeys and bears offers to help (him, them).

6. At the head of the band is (its, their) leader, the mighty monkey-general Hanuman.

7. In a great battle, neither Ravana nor his demons are easy to defeat because of (his, their) ability to change shapes at will.

8. However, Ravana is defeated by Rama's army through (its, their) incredible feats of strength and bravery.

9. Ravana's army must accept (its, their) defeat.

10. Rama and Sita return to (his or her, their) country's capital, where Rama is finally crowned king.

➔ **For a SELF-CHECK and more practice, see the EXERCISE BANK, p. 326.**

B. REVISING: Using Gender-Free Language

Use gender-free language to revise the following sentences. Make sure the verbs and other words agree with their subjects.

The *Ramayana* Around the World

1. An Indonesian can cheer for her favorite character in puppet performances of the *Ramayana*.

2. The epic is often performed as a dance-drama; thus, an actor who wants a role must prove that he can dance as well as act.

3. These interpretations are often performed by a character holding a mask in front of her face.

4. A person from South and Southeast Asia will probably see his beliefs reflected in performances of the *Ramayana*.

5. During a festival in our country, an individual could enjoy himself by watching six different performances of the epic.

Indefinite Pronouns as Antecedents

LESSON 6

❶ Here's the Idea

▶ **A personal pronoun must agree in number with the indefinite pronoun that is its antecedent.**

The number of an indefinite pronoun is not always obvious. Use the chart below when you are trying to determine the number of an indefinite pronoun.

Indefinite Pronouns		Plural	Singular or Plural
Singular		**Plural**	**Singular or Plural**
another	much	both	all
anybody	neither	few	any
anyone	nobody	many	more
anything	no one	several	most
each	nothing		none
either	one		some
everybody	somebody		
everyone	someone		
everything	something		

Indefinite pronouns that end in *one, body,* or *thing* are always singular.

Agreement with Indefinite Pronouns

Use a singular pronoun to refer to a singular indefinite pronoun.

REFERS TO

Each myth has its own heroes and villains.

REFERS TO

Everyone has his or her favorite myth.

Notice that the phrase *his or her* is considered a singular personal pronoun.

Use a plural pronoun to refer to a plural indefinite pronoun.

Both of the Viking chiefs have their loyal followers.

Only a few of us brought our mythology books along.

Indefinite Pronouns That Can Be Singular or Plural

Some indefinite pronouns can be singular or plural. Use the meaning of the sentence to determine whether the indefinite pronoun is singular or plural.

Use the intervening prepositional phrase to help you decide whether the indefinite pronoun is singular or plural.

None of the mythology has lost its appeal.

Since the noun in the prepositional phrase is singular, the pronoun is singular.

Most of the stories have their origins in tribal myths.

Since the noun in the prepositional phrase is plural, the pronoun is plural.

❷ Why It Matters in Writing

If your personal pronouns and their indefinite antecedents don't agree, readers will find your writing confusing.

STUDENT MODEL

During the 700s and 800s, the dreaded

Norse Vikings raided the lands around the

North Sea in Europe. Some raided villages at

night, destroying **most** of it *them* before dawn.

Most refers to *villages* and requires a plural pronoun.

Anyone spotting a fleet of Viking ships

would tell ~~their~~ *his or her* friends to hide in the woods.

Anyone is singular and requires a singular pronoun.

❸ Practice and Apply

A. CONCEPT CHECK: Indefinite Pronouns as Antecedents

Choose the correct pronoun from those in parentheses.

Balder and Loki: Norse Hero and Villain

1. In one Norse myth, all of the gods loved Balder, (his, their) gentle partner.

2. Most were upset when (he, they) heard a prophecy that the gentle Balder would soon die.

3. Balder's mother traveled around the world to ask all the beings to give (its, their) promise not to harm Balder.

4. Each gave (its, their) promise, except for the tiny mistletoe plant, which she forgot to ask.

5. Everybody believed that (his or her, their) friend would be protected by his mother's actions.

6. The gods didn't know that (his or her, their) friend was still doomed.

7. Loki, who was jealous because few gave (his or her, their) love to him, made an arrow from the mistletoe plant.

8. The gods were playing a game; each tossed (his or her, their) arrow or stone at Balder, but none hurt him.

9. When Loki gave his mistletoe arrow to one of the gods, (he, they) threw it at Balder and killed him.

10. Balder's death plunged the gods into grief so deep that no one ever gave Loki (his or her, their) forgiveness.

➔ **For a SELF-CHECK and more practice, see the EXERCISE BANK, p. 326.**

B. EDITING: Making Pronouns Agree

Edit the following paragraph by correcting the errors in pronoun-antecedent agreement.

Hero Rabbit

In an Incan fable, the animals in the jungle had a meeting to choose the jaguar or the lion as king. Everyone came to the meeting to cast their vote except the rabbit. Many gave his or her votes to the jaguar, but the same number voted for the lion. To break the tie, someone had to volunteer their services to carry the rabbit to the meeting. The jaguar, thinking that the rabbit would repay the favor by voting for him, volunteered. The rabbit, however, voted for the lion because the lion was more peaceful. The jaguar learned that one who has their ideals well guarded cannot be easily swayed, even if you do him a favor.

LESSON 7 Pronoun Reference Problems

❶ Here's the Idea

▶ **The referent of a pronoun should always be clear.**

Indefinite Reference

Indefinite reference is a problem that occurs when the pronoun *it, you,* or *they* does not clearly refer to a specific antecedent. You can fix this problem by rewording the sentence and eliminating the pronoun or by replacing the pronoun with a noun.

Indefinite Reference	
Awkward	**Revised**
In the "Superheroes" article, **it** discussed only three women.	The "Superheroes" article discussed only three women.
In the article, **they** state that girls aren't interested in superheroes.	The author of the article states that girls aren't interested in superheroes.
In other publications, however, **you** learn that girls are interested.	Other publications, however, claim that girls are interested.

General Reference

A **general reference** problem occurs when the pronoun *it, this, that, which,* or *such* is used to refer to a general idea rather than to a specific antecedent. You can fix the problem by rewriting the sentence.

General Reference	
Awkward	**Revised**
The sidekick is weak and vulnerable, **which** makes the character appealing.	The sidekick's weakness and vulnerability make the character appealing.
Sidekicks don't like dangerous situations. **That** is how most people feel.	Like most people, sidekicks don't like dangerous situations.

Ambiguous Reference

Ambiguous means "having two or more possible meanings." An **ambiguous reference** problem occurs when a pronoun could refer to two or more antecedents. You can eliminate an ambiguous reference problem by rewriting the sentence to clarify what the pronoun refers to.

Ambiguous Reference

Awkward	Revised
Princess Xena and Gabrielle were featured in a 1990s TV show. **She** inspired a series of books as well.	Princess Xena and Gabrielle were featured in a 1990s TV show. Xena inspired a series of books as well.
Xena's allies help her overcome her enemies. **They** usually come from another kingdom.	Xena's allies, who usually come from another kingdom, help her overcome her enemies.

❷ Why It Matters in Writing

Using indefinite, general, or ambiguous references can make your writing very confusing. Make sure your pronoun references are always clear so they show logical relationships among the ideas in your sentences.

STUDENT MODEL

DRAFT

In an article on the Internet, **it** says that Xena's village was attacked by an evil warlord when she was a young girl. Xena and her mother fought the invaders until **they** were driven out of the village. As a result of the experience, Xena discovered a sense of power in war. **It** inspired her to leave home and begin a life dedicated to waging war

REVISION

An article on the Internet explains that Xena's village was attacked by an evil warlord when **Xena** was a young girl. Xena and her mother fought the invaders until **the invading forces** were driven out of the village. As a result of the experience, Xena discovered a sense of power in war. **This new feeling** inspired her to leave home and begin a life dedicated to waging war.

❸ Practice and Apply

A. CONCEPT CHECK: Pronoun Reference Problems

Rewrite the following sentences to correct indefinite, general, and ambiguous pronoun references. (There may be more than one way to rewrite a sentence.)

Xena's Friends and Enemies

1. Before Xena became a heroine, she honed her warrior skills, but it was her human skills that were lacking.
2. It was for leaving her army; she paid the price by going through the gauntlet.
3. No warriors had survived it before her.
4. It was two lines of warriors clubbing the person—Xena—who ran through.
5. After surviving it, Hercules helped her start becoming a heroine.
6. Xena's archenemy is Callisto the Warrior Queen; her friends include Gabrielle the Amazon Princess and the handsome thief Autolycus.
7. When Gabrielle met Xena, her chief weapons were her quick wit and intelligence.
8. Autolycus enjoys danger, which probably attracts Xena.
9. In one episode, you learned that Xena was responsible for the death of Callisto's parents.
10. This made Callisto vow that she would destroy Xena.

➡ **For a SELF-CHECK and more practice, see the EXERCISE BANK, p. 327.**

B. REVISING: Eliminating Pronoun Reference Problems

Revise the following paragraph; eliminate any pronoun reference problems.

Wonder Woman

She became the first female superhero when she appeared in comic books in the 1940s. More than 60 years later, you could see Wonder Woman come to life in a TV movie starring Cathy Lee Crosby. Then in 1976, Lynda Carter appeared as the main character in the *Wonder Woman* television series. From episode to episode, they covered everything from hostile alien life forms to a mad scientist to a computerized dating service. The last episode aired in 1979. Nonetheless, it paved the way for shows featuring other superheroines—like Xena.

Other Pronoun Problems

❶ Here's the Idea

▶ **Pronouns can be used with an appositive, in an appositive, or in a comparison.** The guidelines in this lesson can help you choose the correct pronoun in each of these situations.

Pronouns and Appositives

An appositive is a noun or a pronoun that follows another noun or pronoun for the purpose of identifying or explaining it.

The cartoonist, my friend, created the popular superhero.
　　　　　　　⬆ APPOSITIVE

***We* and *Us* with Appositives** The pronouns *we* and *us* are often used with appositives. The nominative case, *we*, is used when the pronoun is a subject. The objective case, *us*, is used when the pronoun is an object.

We artists dream about creating our own superhero strip.
　⬆APPOSITIVE

Don't tell us beginners that it's impossible.
　　　　⬆APPOSITIVE

Follow these guidelines to decide whether to use the nominative case or the objective case.

> **Here's How** Using *We* and *Us*
>
> **No problem is too hard for (we, us) superheroes.**
>
> **1.** Drop the appositive from the sentence and read the sentence twice, using one of the pronoun choices each time.
>
> **No problem is too hard for we.**
>
> **No problem is too hard for us.**
>
> **2.** Often the "sound" will instantly tell you the right choice. Otherwise, determine whether the pronoun is a subject or an object. In this sentence, the pronoun is the object of the preposition *for.*
>
> **3.** Write the sentence and use the correct case.
>
> **No problem is too hard for us superheroes.**

Pronouns in Appositives A pronoun used as an appositive is in the case it would take if the noun were missing.

The publisher paid the students, Mario and him, for the strip.　　　　　　　　APPOSITIVE ⬆

The pronoun case is determined by the function of the noun it identifies. In this sentence, *students* is the direct object; so the pronoun in the appositive is in the objective case.

Follow these steps to figure out which pronoun case to use in an appositive.

Here's How **Using Pronouns in Appositives**

> **The reporters, Clark Kent and (she, her), are working together.**

1. Rewrite the sentence with the appositive by itself.

> **Clark Kent and (she, her) are working together.**

2. Then try each pronoun in the appositive alone. Notice that in this sentence, you have to use a singular verb for each singular pronoun.

> **she is working; her is working**

3. Determine whether the pronoun is a subject or an object. In this sentence, the pronoun is a subject.

4. Write the sentence and use the correct case.

> **The reporters, Clark Kent and she, are working together.**

Pronouns in Comparisons

A comparison can be made using *than* or *as* to begin a clause.

> **Clark Kent is more clumsy than I am.**
>
> **No one looks as nervous as he does.**

When you omit some words from the final clause in a comparison, the clause is called **elliptical.**

> **I knew she would be braver than I.**

If you have trouble determining the correct pronoun to use in an elliptical clause, try filling in the unstated words.

> **Roger can draw Superman as well as (he, him).**
>
> **Roger can draw Superman as well as he [can].** (CORRECT)
>
> **Roger can draw Superman as well as him [can].** (INCORRECT)

Notice that the meaning you want to express can affect the choice of a pronoun.

> **I like the hero better than they.**
>
> (This sentence means "I like the hero better than they do.")
>
> **I like the hero better than them.**
>
> (This sentence means "I like the hero better than I like them.")

❷ Why It Matters in Writing

Using pronouns correctly in comparisons or with appositives helps your readers understand your meaning better. Proper usage helps identify pronouns as actors or as receivers of action.

STUDENT MODEL

Dear Ms. Alvarez,

    We

~~Us~~ aspiring stuntwomen, **Chin Yau and ~~me~~,** *I* showed some

of our falls to Peter Bell, who stages action scenes in movies.

Our friends, Nat and Bill, showed off for him too. He said that

we were more agile than ~~them~~ *they*!

❸ Practice and Apply

A. CONCEPT CHECK: Other Pronoun Problems

Choose the correct pronoun from those in parentheses.

Christopher Reeve: A Real Hero

1. (We, Us) movie fans knew that the role of Superman in the *Superman* movies was played by Christopher Reeve.
2. When we heard that Reeve had been seriously injured in an accident, it shocked and saddened (we, us) listeners.
3. We sympathized with the whole Reeve family—his wife, his three children, and (he, him).
4. Christopher Reeve said that before his accident, he thought heroes were women and men who performed more courageous acts than (we, us) ordinary people.
5. After his accident, he said that (we, us) ordinary people become heroes when we show the "strength to persevere and endure in spite of overwhelming obstacles."

→ **For a SELF-CHECK and more practice, see the EXERCISE BANK, p. 328.**

B. WRITING

Find your **Write Away** boasts and threats from page 178 in your 📁 **Working Portfolio.** Add two boasts or threats that use pronouns in comparisons.

Real World Grammar

Incident Report

Whether we're talking with friends or testifying in court, we're often asked to report what we saw and heard. Eyewitnesses sometimes write up a report like the one below. Pronouns help clarify who did what. Notice how the writer added and corrected pronouns to clarify the quick draft he had made.

Saturday, June 9, 7 P.M., Clark St. Beach

We
~~Us~~ guards—Vince and ~~me~~ [*I*]—were patrolling the beach. About 300 yards offshore were a sailboat and a Jet Ski with a teenaged driver. Suddenly we heard a loud crack! The Jet Ski had hit the sailboat! *We* ~~Saw~~ the sailboat with its mast down, the Jet Ski circling on ~~it's~~ [*its*] side, and three heads bobbing up and down in the waves.

Vince shouted, *We've* "~~Got~~ to help them!" He plunged into the water and began swimming toward the crash site. I followed. Vince is a faster swimmer than ~~me~~ [*I*], but ~~it~~ [*he*] still took about three minutes of hard swimming to get there. We heard a man, [*who*] was bobbing in the water, shout for help. [*To us.*] He screamed, "Find my little girl! [*She's*] Over there!" Looking at where he pointed, we couldn't see [*anyone*]. Vince [*Vince*] swam in the general direction and dived underwater. When ~~he~~ [*Vince*] surfaced, the man shouted, "Farther to the right!" Vince swam farther and dived again. [*He*] Stayed down a long time and emerged about 100 yards from where [*he*] had gone under. Gasping for breath, [*he*] came up holding a drowned girl [*who*] looked like a rag doll.

"Jack," Vince said to me, "Get that Jet Ski. [*We've*] Got to get her to shore." By this time, I had reached the teenager, ~~who's~~ [*whose*] head was bleeding. The father was clinging to [*his*] broken sailboat.

> *It's* is a contraction, not a possessive pronoun.

> *It* has no referent.

> *He* is unclear.

> *Who's* is a contraction, not a possessive pronoun.

Using Grammar in Writing

Unclear reference	Help your readers track the action by making sure that every pronoun clearly refers to one antecedent.
Possessive pronouns	Avoid spelling mistakes! Don't confuse contractions with possessive pronouns.
Pronoun-antecedent agreement	Clarify how many people you're referring to by making sure every pronoun matches its antecedent in number and gender.
Pronoun case	Watch out for appositives and intervening phrases that might cause you to use the wrong case.

PRACTICE AND APPLY: Clarifying with Pronouns

Jack, the eyewitness, didn't have time to finish correcting his draft. Write the pronouns, including *which* and *who,* as well as personal pronouns, that will help him clarify the events in the rest of his report.

I shouted to the teenager, "Stay with the sailboat while Vince takes **(1)** _____ Jet Ski."

I told the dad to stay with the sailboat too. "Vince has got to get **(2)** _____ daughter to shore."

Quickly we got the Jet Ski to Vince, **(3)** _____ climbed on while I held the girl. I handed **(4)** _____ the girl, **(5)** _____ he took to shore immediately.

I swam back to the sailboat, to **(6)** _____ we all clung for support. Within minutes Vince came back. **(7)** _____ told the dad, "Paramedics are there. **(8)** _____ are trying to resuscitate **(9)** _____ daughter. You take this Jet Ski to shore to check on **(10)** _____ ."

As the dad left, we righted the sailboat and waited for the beach speedboat to pick **(11)** _____ up. By the time **(12)** _____ got to shore, the little girl had been revived. Holding **(13)** _____ dad's hand, she was awake and breathing normally. Her dad hugged Vince and told **(14)** _____ , "You saved **(15)** _____ little girl's life! How can I ever thank you?"

Jack and Vince, who saved the lives of three victims, both will receive Citizen Hero Awards.

Dave Cameron
Chief of Police

Mixed Review

A. Using Pronouns Read the passage. Then write the answers to the questions below it.

Many have heard of Scheherazade, the legendary storyteller, but **(1)** <u>they</u> may not know her own story. **(2)** <u>She</u>, a heroine in her own right, agreed to marry the cruel King Shahriyar, **(3)** <u>whom</u> other women feared because he used to murder his brides. Anyone who married the king lost **(4)** <u>her</u> life. Neither Scheherazade nor her sister Dunyazad feared for **(5)** <u>her</u> life because they had a plan to save themselves and the other women. The plan was that the night after the wedding, Dunyazad would ask Scheherazade to tell a story. **(6)** <u>She</u> would then start a tale so enchanting that the king, **(7)** <u>who</u> loved stories, would spare her life in order to hear the end the next night . . . and the next, and so on. Scheherazade's stories make up *The Thousand and One Nights*. **(8)** <u>It</u> includes the tales of Sindbad the Sailor and of Aladdin and his magic lamp. Scheherazade's plan worked, because there was no better storyteller than **(9)** <u>she</u>. The tales continued for 1001 nights, during which time Scheherazade had three children. She and all the women knew that **(10)** <u>their</u> lives were safe because Scheherazade's qualities as a wife, mother, and storyteller had made the king fall in love with her and repent his cruelty.

1. What is the antecedent of *they?*
2. Why is the nominative case correct for the pronoun *She?*
3. Why is the objective case correct for the pronoun *whom?*
4. What is the antecedent of *her?*
5. What are the antecedents of *her?*
6. What is the antecedent of *She?*
7. What is the case of *who?* Why would *whom* be incorrect?
8. What is the antecedent of *it?* Why would *they* be incorrect?
9. What case is the pronoun *she?* Why would *her* be incorrect?
10. What are the antecedents of *their?* Why would *her* be incorrect?

B. Pronoun Reference Problems The six italicized words in the passage below have indefinite, general, or ambiguous references. Rewrite the paragraph to eliminate the reference problems. (There may be more than one way to eliminate the problem.)

Penelope, Odysseus' wife, was pretty smart herself. Many suitors wanted to marry her to get Odysseus' wealth, *whom* they assumed was dead. She delayed each suitor for years by saying that she would accept *them* when she finished her weaving. Every night she pulled out what she'd done by day, so she never got anywhere with *it.* She fooled the suitors for three years, and they never caught on to *it.* In the nick of time, before she had to go through with *it,* Odysseus came home and killed *them.*

Choose the best way to write each underlined word or word group and mark the letter of your answer. If the underlined section needs no change, mark the choice "Correct as is."

We superhero fans also enjoy the not-so-super hero whom is a little
(1)   (2)
smaller than Superman. We've grown to know and love Underdog,

Superchicken, and The Tick, even though he can't leap tall buildings in a
(3)
single bound. Perhaps fans enjoy these characters because they don't take

they're lives very seriously. George of the Jungle, for example, is a funny
(4)
Tarzan type. George's story begins when gorillas raised he from a baby.
(5)
Now he's become the klutzy king of the jungle whom is crashing from tree
(6)
to tree. George's best friends are a talking gorilla and an elephant who

wishes to be a dog. However, a beautiful woman named Ursula comes

between them and he. Him is leaving the jungle because of her. George
(7)   (8)   (9)
moves to San Francisco, where him and Ursula live hilariously ever after.
(10)

---

1. A. us
   B. our
   C. whoever
   D. Correct as is

2. A. he
   B. they
   C. who
   D. Correct as is

3. A. their
   B. there
   C. they
   D. Correct as is

4. A. themselves
   B. their
   C. them
   D. Correct as is

5. A. it
   B. him
   C. himself
   D. Correct as is

6. A. whomever
   B. who
   C. whoever
   D. Correct as is

7. A. they and him
   B. they and he
   C. them and him
   D. Correct as is

8. A. He
   B. His
   C. Them
   D. Correct as is

9. A. she
   B. hers
   C. anyone
   D. Correct as is

10. A. they
    B. them
    C. he
    D. Correct as is

Student Help Desk

Using Pronouns at a Glance

Nominative Case		Objective Case		Possessive Case	
I	we	me	us	my, mine	our, ours
you	you	you	you	your, yours	your, yours
he	they	him	them	his	their, theirs
she		her		her, hers	
it		it		its	

Use this case when
- the pronoun is a **subject**
- the pronoun is a **predicate pronoun**

Use this case when
- the pronoun is the **direct object**
- the pronoun is the **indirect object**
- the pronoun is the **object of a preposition**

Use this case for
- pronouns that show **ownership or relationship**

Pronoun Pitfalls

Who's	contraction: Who is	**Who's** your hero?
Whose	possessive form	**Whose** muscles are bigger?
They're	contraction: They are	**They're** the bravest women.
Their	possessive form	**Their** speed is amazing.
You're	contraction: You are	**You're** extremely talented.
Your	possessive form	**Your** brilliance is known everywhere.

Strictly Singles

Pronouns that end in *-one, -body,* or *-thing* are always singular.	someone somebody something	anyone anybody anything

Tricks to Fix Pronouns

Pronouns in Comparisons

Example: Superman is stronger than (**he**, him).

Trick: Add the missing word or words: than **he** is.

Pronouns and Appositives

Examples: Give (**we**, us) fans an example of your strength.

The heroes, Vince and (**I**, me), received awards.

Trick: Drop the appositive and figure out how the pronoun works in the sentence: Give **us** an example.
I received an award.

Pronouns in Compounds

Example: Please save Alana and (I, **me**) from the monster!

Trick: Drop the other part of the compound and figure out how the pronoun works in the sentence: Please save **me**!

PRONOUNS

The Bottom Line

Checklist for Using Pronouns

Have I . . .

____ used the nominative case for pronouns that are subjects and predicate pronouns?

____ used the objective case for pronouns that are objects?

____ used the possessive case for pronouns that show ownership?

____ used *who* and *whom* correctly?

____ made sure that all pronouns agree with their antecedents in number, gender, and person?

____ used the correct cases of pronouns in compounds, comparisons, and appositives?

____ made sure the pronoun referent is always clear and correct?

Using Modifiers

Tarantulas:

Fact and Fiction

The tarantula is one of the most feared spiders of all and has been the star of several horror films. Yet many people would be surprised to learn that this spider makes a loyal, affectionate pet! It can be more tame than a hamster. The spider will bite only if provoked, and its "deadly" venom is not harmful to humans.

Theme: Animal Legends and Myths

Believe It or Not!

The modifiers in the movie poster *(giant, crawling)* evoke frightening images, but what about the modifiers in the article? Notice how they paint an entirely different picture of this "crawling terror." Used correctly, modifiers can help your readers imagine and feel what you are writing about.

Write Away: Attack of the Killer Goldfish!

Describe a common pet, such as a kitten, rabbit, hamster, or goldfish, in the language of a horror-movie poster. Then write a brief, straightforward description of the animal. Save the work in your 📁 **Working Portfolio.**

Choose the best way to write each underlined section and mark the letter of your answer. If the underlined section needs no change, mark the choice "Correct as is."

<u>Snakes evoke real strong reactions in many people.</u> Some are terrified
(1)

of both poisonous and nonpoisonous snakes. Such fears are probably

behind some of the far-fetched beliefs about these reptiles.

<u>For example, despite the tales, flying snakes haven't never existed.</u>
(2)

<u>In fact, snakes don't even soar good.</u> They just fall gracefully out of trees.
(3)

They can even fall from great heights without being hurt, and this ability

can help them escape predators.

<u>An even more sillier tale states that if you cut a snake into pieces, it</u>
(4)

<u>can put itself back together.</u> This is totally untrue. <u>A sliced-up snake is as</u>

<u>dead as any corpse.</u>
(5)

---

1. A. Snakes evoke real stronger
      reactions in many people.
   B. Snakes evoke real strongly
      reactions in many people.
   C. Snakes evoke really strong
      reactions in many people.
   D. Correct as is

2. A. For example, despite the tales,
      flying snakes haven't never,
      ever existed.
   B. For example, despite the tales,
      flying snakes have never
      existed.
   C. For example, despite the tales,
      no flying snakes have never
      existed.
   D. Correct as is

3. A. In fact, snakes don't even soar
      real good.
   B. In fact, snakes don't even soar
      well.
   C. In fact, snakes don't even soar
      real well.
   D. Correct as is

4. A. An even sillier tale states that
      if you cut a snake into pieces, it
      can put itself back together.
   B. An even most silly tale states
      that if you cut a snake into
      pieces, it can put itself back
      together.
   C. An even more silliest tale
      states that if you cut a snake
      into pieces, it can put itself
      back together.
   D. Correct as is

5. A. A sliced-up snake is as dead as
      a corpse.
   B. A sliced-up snake is as dead as
      any other corpse.
   C. A sliced-up snake is as dead as
      corpses.
   D. Correct as is

Using Adjectives and Adverbs

❶ Here's the Idea

Modifiers are words that give information about, or modify, the meanings of other words. Adjectives and adverbs are common modifiers.

For a review of adjectives and adverbs, see pp. 17–22.

Using Adjectives

▶ **Adjectives modify nouns and pronouns.** They answer the questions *which one, what kind, how many,* and *how much.* In the revision below, the writer adds adjectives to give the reader more specific information.

STUDENT MODEL

DRAFT
In England, people believed that carrying a spider in a pouch around the neck would prevent sickness.

REVISION
In **medieval** times, **many English** people believed that carrying a **small, harmless** spider in a **cloth** pouch around **their** necks would prevent **dreadful** sicknesses.

> Proper adjectives are capitalized.

> More than one adjective can be used with the same noun or pronoun.

> Most adjectives come before the words they modify.

Words classified as other parts of speech can be used as adjectives.

Words Used as Adjectives	
Nouns	**cloth** pouch, **silk** shirt
Possessive pronouns	**their** necks, **her** head, **your** idea
Demonstrative pronouns	**this** house, **that** road, **these** hills, **those** people
Participles	**living** spider, **dreaded** plague

A **predicate adjective** follows a linking verb and modifies the subject of a clause.

The spider looked harmless and small.

Using Adverbs

▶ **Adverbs modify verbs, adjectives, and other adverbs.** They answer the questions *where, when, how,* and *to what degree.* Adverbs such as *so, very, most, more,* and *ever* intensify the meanings of the words they modify.

STUDENT MODEL

A Cherokee story explains how Spider **very cleverly** steals the sun. Half the world is **always** dark, and the other half **always** light. Spider travels **far** to save her people.

> Tells how Spider does something—*very* stresses the cleverness

> Indicate when and where

Notice that an adverb can be placed before or after a verb it modifies.

Place modifiers like *only* and *even* next to the words they modify. Changing their positions will change the meanings of sentences.

Only she stole the sun. (No one else did it.)

She only stole the sun. (She merely stole it; she didn't destroy it.)

She stole only the sun. (She didn't steal anything else.)

❷ Why It Matters in Writing

How important are modifiers? Read the following passage without the highlighted words. What critical information would be missing?

STUDENT MODEL

    Certain poisonous spiders have a **well-deserved** reputation for being **dangerous.** If you **ever** see a **black** spider with a **red hourglass** mark on **its** belly, move **away quickly! Its** bite is **poisonous.**

A. CONCEPT CHECK: Using Adjectives and Adverbs

On a separate sheet of paper, write each italicized word in these sentences, then indicate whether it is used as an adjective or as an adverb.

Spider Lore

1. Around the world, *superstitious* beliefs about spiders *still* persist.

2. *Some* people say that if you *accidentally* step on a spider, rain will come.

3. If *this* idea were true, it would be raining *everywhere,* all the time.

4. In Tahiti, people see the *web-spinning, lowly* spider as a shadow of the gods.

5. They teach children, *big* or *small, never* to harm any spider.

6. *South Sea* islanders say that if you see a spider drop *down* in front of you, you will receive a present.

7. Find a *tiny* spider on your clothes and you'll *soon* receive money.

8. In *Ozark folk* belief, discovering a web with your initials in it near a door brings you good luck *forever.*

9. Spiders have *often* been used in *traditional* medicine.

10. One *interesting* remedy involves rolling a *live* spider in butter and swallowing it!

➜ **For a SELF-CHECK and more practice, see the EXERCISE BANK, p. 329.**

B. WRITING: Creating Captions

Read the cartoon below and identify the modifiers the author uses. Then substitute and add your own modifiers to make the images more frightening or less frightening. For example, you might write "The *small gray* octopus, *alone* and *scared,* oozes *slowly* across the beach."

Calvin and Hobbes by Bill Watterson

LESSON 2 Problems with Modifiers

❶ Here's the Idea

Writers may confuse an adjective with an adverb, use a double negative, or add an extra *here* or *there.* Can you find the five mistakes this writer made with modifiers?

STUDENT MODEL

(1) My grandmother tells urban myths real well. **(2)** Most people can't hardly tell if they're true or not. **(3)** She said that once a koala in a zoo felt badly after eating too many oily eucalyptus leaves. **(4)** This here koala was so full of oil that his fur caught fire when he sat on a heater! **(5)** You won't find no proof of this story, though.

Answers: (1) really well, not real well; (2) can hardly, not can't hardly; (3) felt bad, not felt badly; (4) This koala, not This here koala; (5) won't find any, not won't find no

Read on to find out how you can avoid these mistakes.

Adverb or Adjective?

It's easy to confuse adjectives and adverbs. For example, you might think all words that end in *ly* are adverbs, but some *ly* words—such as *lonely* and *lowly*—function as adjectives.

The lonely scientist turned a lowly insect into a radioactive terror.

Many words have both adjective and adverb forms. If you're not sure which form of a word to use, look at the word that it modifies. If the modified word is a noun or pronoun, use the adjective form. If it's a verb, adjective, or adverb, use the adverb form.

Some stories about real people are really strange.

Some words can function as either adjectives or adverbs depending on how they are used.

A weird tale may appear in the daily newspaper. (ADJECTIVE)
I read the newspaper daily. (ADVERB)

Two pairs of modifiers in particular cause writers problems: *good/well* and *bad/badly.*

Good = Adjective

A good urban myth has some truth to it. (*what kind* of myth? *good* myth)

MODIFIES

The koala feels good today. (It feels happy.)

Well = Adjective or Adverb

MODIFIES

Animals eat well in the zoo. (eat *how?* eat *well*)
↑ ADVERB

MODIFIES

The animal looks well today. (It looks healthy.)
↑ ADJECTIVE

Bad = Adjective

MODIFIES

A bad myth is too phoney to be true. (*what kind* of myth? *bad* myth)

MODIFIES

The koala felt bad after eating. (It felt sick or unhappy.)

Badly = Adverb

MODIFIES

He tells stories badly. (tells stories *how? badly*)

 Never write "He feels badly" or "She looks badly" when referring to someone's state of mind or health. You are saying the person literally *feels* (touches things) poorly or *looks* (sees things) poorly.

Double Negatives

In school and business writing, avoid the use of **double negatives**—two negative words in a single clause. Use only one negative word to express a negative idea.

NONSTANDARD: **I can't hardly believe that people flushed pet alligators into the sewers.**

STANDARD: **I can hardly believe . . .**
I can't believe . . .

NONSTANDARD: **You won't find no proof for this story.**

STANDARD: **You won't find any proof for this story.**
You will find no proof for this story.

 The words *hardly, barely,* and *scarcely* often appear as parts of double negatives. When you use one of these words, make sure that there are no other negative words in the same clause.

This, That, These, Those

This, that, these, and *those* are demonstrative pronouns that can be used as adjectives. There are only three rules you need to remember when using these words as adjectives.

1. They must agree in number with the words they modify.

These kinds of myths stem from half-truths. (PLURAL)

This kind of myth stems from half-truths. (SINGULAR)

2. Never use *here* or *there* with demonstrative adjectives. The adjective already points out which one; it doesn't need any help.

NONSTANDARD: **This here sewer worker saw an alligator.**

STANDARD: **This sewer worker saw an alligator.**

3. Never use the pronoun *them* as an adjective in place of *these* or *those.*

NONSTANDARD: **Them people have written a book about urban myths.**

STANDARD: **These people (Those people) have written a book about urban myths.**

❷ Why It Matters in Writing

In many real-world situations, such as applying for a job, the use of double negatives, *here* or *there* with demonstrative adjectives, or *them* as an adjective could make you appear less qualified.

STUDENT MODEL

Job Application—draft

I ~~can't~~ can't hardly believe how this job matches my experience with kids ages 7 to 10. For the past year, I've been a volunteer at a skating rink, working with these ~~here~~ grade-school kids.

MODIFIERS

❸ Practice and Apply

A. CONCEPT CHECK: Problems with Modifiers

For each sentence, write the correct choice of the words in parentheses.

Dog Catches Intruder!

1. Urban myths appear (frequent, frequently) in newspapers.
2. One example of (this type, these type) of story concerns a choking guard dog.
3. A woman comes home, and her dog is choking (bad, badly).
4. She (quick, quickly) takes the dog to a veterinarian and leaves it there.
5. She (hasn't, has) scarcely returned home when the phone rings.
6. The vet has found three fingers lodged (firm, firmly) in the dog's throat.
7. The vet shouts, "Don't waste (no, any) time! Get out of the house!"
8. The woman calls the police, who drive (rapid, rapidly) to her home.
9. They search the house (good, well) for intruders.
10. They find a (real, really) scared burglar hiding in the closet— with three fingers missing!

➜ For a **SELF-CHECK** and more practice, see the **EXERCISE BANK**, p. 329.

B. EDITING AND PROOFREADING: Correcting Errors

Rewrite these sentences, correcting errors in the use of modifiers.

Track of the Cougar

(1) Haven't you never heard of the cougar attacks in several Western towns? (2) These type of stories sound like urban myths, but they're true! (3) In recent years, people have been moving steady into cougars' mountain territories. (4) A few joggers have been injured real bad by the big cats, who think people are prey. (5) For this reason, people and cougars can't live together very good.

C. WRITING: Revising Paragraphs

Look over the **Write Away** pieces in your ⬜ **Working Portfolio** and correct any modifier errors you find.

LESSON 3 · Using Comparisons

❶ Here's the Idea

Have you ever said something like "I think horror films are better than mysteries"? If so, you have used a modifier to compare two or more things. Adjectives and adverbs have two forms that can be used to make comparisons: the comparative form and the superlative form.

Making Comparisons	
An adjective or adverb modifies a word and makes no comparison.	In most legends, Coyote is a **smart** trickster.
The **comparative** compares two persons, places, or things.	Coyote is **smarter** than Wolf at outwitting people.
The **superlative** compares three or more persons, places, or things.	Coyote is the **smartest** of all the animals.

Regular Comparisons

Most modifiers are changed in regular ways to show comparisons.

Regular Comparisons		
Rule	**Comparative**	**Superlative**
Add -er or -est		
• to a one-syllable word	tough**er**	tough**est**
• to many two-syllable words	happi**er**	happi**est**
Use more or most		
• with some two-syllable words to avoid awkward sounds	**more** helpless (*not* helplesser)	**most** helpless (*not* helplessest)
• with words of more than two syllables	**more** important	**most** important
• with adverbs ending in *ly*	**more** quickly	**most** quickly

Never use the superlative form when comparing only two things.

NONSTANDARD: **Of the two stories, which was the most exciting?**

STANDARD: **Of the two stories, which was the more exciting?**

Irregular Comparisons

Some modifiers have irregular comparative and superlative forms.

He thinks storytelling is good and practical jokes are better, but tricks to get rich are the best of all.

Common Irregular Forms

Adverb or Adjective	Comparative	Superlative
good	better	best
well	better	best
far	farther, further	farthest, furthest
bad	worse	worst
much	more	most
many	more	most
little	less, lesser	least

❷ Why It Matters in Writing

Understanding the differences between comparative and superlative forms can help you choose the correct forms in your work. You'll avoid mistakes like those in the model below.

STUDENT MODEL

Ranchers and wildlife experts are learning that coyotes are better at surviving than wolves ever were. For instance, of the two animals, coyotes are ~~the smartest~~ *smarter* at finding new sources of food. However, the *most* importantest factor may be that whenever people kill coyotes, the survivors have more pups than usual. There are more coyotes today than there were 100 years ago!

❸ Practice and Apply

A. CONCEPT CHECK: Using Comparisons

For each sentence, write the correct comparative or superlative form.

Coyote, Iktome, and the Rock (from a Sioux Story)
1. Coyote and his friend Iktome discovered the (most remarkable, remarkablest) rock.
2. "I think this rock has power," Coyote said. He gave it his (better, best) blanket to keep it warm in the chill weather.
3. As they traveled on, the weather became (worse, worser).
4. Iktome was cold, but Coyote was (colder, coldest).
5. "That rock has (less, least) feeling than I do. I'm going to get my blanket back. Stupid rock—why does it need a cover?"
6. However, the more Coyote pulled, the (harder, hardest) the rock held on to the blanket.
7. Coyote finally yanked it off and ran, every step taking him (fartherest, farther) away from the rock.
8. Behind him, he heard a rumbling sound getting (louder, loudest) every moment.
9. The rock squashed Coyote (flatter, flattest) than a rug and wrapped itself in the blanket again.
10. The (best, better) advice is "If you have something to give, give it forever."

➡ **For a SELF-CHECK and more exercises, see the EXERCISE BANK, p. 330.**

B. WRITING: Interpreting Graphs

Home on the Range
This graph compares animal ranges in 1850 and 1990. For each blank in the sentence below, write a comparative or superlative form of *many* or *few*.

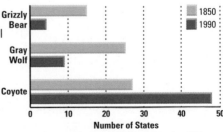

Source: *The Nature of North America*, 1998.

1. In 1850 gray wolves lived in _____ states than grizzly bears.
2. In 1990 gray wolves could be found in far _____ states than in 1850.
3. Of the three animals, coyotes live in the _____ states.
4. Grizzly bears can be found in the _____ states.

MODIFIERS

Problems with Comparisons

LESSON 4

❶ Here's the Idea

When using modifiers to compare two or more things, writers may commit two errors: double comparisons and illogical comparisons.

Double Comparisons

▶ **Do not use both *-er* and *more* to form a comparative. Do not use both *-est* and *most* to form a superlative.** Double comparisons are always incorrect.

NONSTANDARD: **The actor's eyes were more yellower than a wolf's.**

STANDARD: **The actor's eyes were yellower than a wolf's.**

NONSTANDARD: **He wears the most hairiest makeup I've ever seen.**

STANDARD: **He wears the hairiest makeup I've ever seen.**

Illogical Comparisons

▶ **When you are comparing something that is part of a larger group to the group itself, use *other* or *else* to avoid an illogical comparison.** In the following sentence, the writer meant to compare the werewolf to other monsters. But is that what the sentence says?

NONSTANDARD: **I think a werewolf is more mysterious than any monster.**

WEREWOLF   MONSTERS

Because the werewolf is a kind of monster, too, the writer should have written the sentence this way:

STANDARD: **I think a werewolf is more mysterious than any other monster.**

CHAPTER 9

❷ Why It Matters in Writing

Correct comparisons help the reader understand what you are comparing and to what degree.

STUDENT MODEL

Modern filmmakers have created ~~more~~ scarier and *more* realistic werewolves than filmmakers in the past. The *best* ~~better~~ of the werewolf films is *An American Werewolf in London*. It won an Oscar in 1982 for makeup. I think it was more frightening than any *other* film of the year.

❸ Practice and Apply

CONCEPT CHECK: Problems with Comparisons

Correct the illogical and double comparisons in the following sentences. If a sentence contains no error, write *Correct*.

How to Make a Werewolf

1. *The Wolf Man* (1941) was the most scariest film of its time.
2. The movie made Lon Chaney, Jr., more popular than any actor in his family.
3. In those days, film had fewer special effects than modern movies have.
4. Filmmakers created special effects with a far more slower technique, called stop-motion photography.
5. The technique involved shooting footage one frame at a time, in a process more time-consuming than any special effect.
6. The most easiest way to create a werewolf was to apply fake hair a little at a time, shooting a few frames at each stage.
7. The actor looked hairier than anyone on the movie set.
8. In modern werewolf movies, computers and robotics are used to create more better monsters.
9. *An American Werewolf in London* had the most wildest makeup, including extra long fangs on the werewolf.
10. The transformation looked stranger than in earlier movies.

→ **For a SELF-CHECK and more exercises, see the EXERCISE BANK, p. 330.**

Grammar in Literature

Setting the Scene with Modifiers

Modifiers help writers

- create a vivid image of a person, place, or thing
- provide key details and information in only a few words
- compare two or more people, places, or things

In the following excerpt, the author uses modifiers to describe a dog's reaction to extreme cold.

CHAPTER 9

To Build a Fire

Jack London

At the man's heels trotted a dog, a big native husky, the proper wolf dog, gray-coated and without any visible or temperamental difference from its brother, the wild wolf. The animal was depressed by the tremendous cold. It knew that it was no time for travelling. Its instinct told it a truer tale than was told to the man by the man's judgment. In reality, it was not merely colder than fifty below zero; it was colder than sixty below, than seventy below. It was seventy-five below zero. Since the freezing point is thirty-two above zero, it meant that one hundred and seven degrees of frost obtained. The dog did not know anything about thermometers. Possibly in its brain there was no sharp consciousness of a condition of very cold such as was in the man's brain. But the brute had its instinct. It experienced a vague but menacing apprehension that subdued it and made it slink along at the man's heels, and that made it question eagerly every unwonted movement of the man as if expecting him to go into camp or to seek shelter somewhere and build a fire.

Adjectives paint a vivid picture of the dog.

Comparisons are used to tell how cold it was and to contrast the dog's feeling about the conditions with the man's.

Adjectives and adverbs describe the dog's reaction to the conditions.

Using Modifiers to Provide Key Information

Adjectives	In descriptions, it's better to use a few selected adjectives than to pile them up and slow your readers down *(big native husky* versus *big, handsome, steel-eyed native husky).*
Adverbs	Words that intensify, such as *very, so,* and *extremely,* can be overused. For example, instead of using *very often,* choose a more precise modifier, such as *frequently.*
Comparisons	With just a word or two ("... it was *colder* than sixty below, ...") you can quickly convey differences between people or things.

PRACTICE AND APPLY: Choosing Effective Modifiers

Read the following passage. Then choose modifiers from the list to fill in the blanks.

golden	precious	ancient Greek
this	several	brilliantly
one-eyed	jealously	always

(1) In _(what kind?)_ legends, the griffin _(how?)_ guards a treasure of jewels and gold. **(2)** _(which one?)_ fabulous beast has the head and wings of an eagle and the body of a lion. **(3)** His only enemies are the _(what kind?)_ fighters known as the Arimaspians. **(4)** These warriors are _(when?)_ after the griffin's _(what kind?)_ treasure. **(5)** In some stories, _(how many?)_ griffins pull the chariot of the sun across the sky. **(6)** Their _(what kind?)_ wings shine _(how?)_ as they fly high above the earth.

Mixed Review

A. Adjectives and Adverbs Read the following passage. Then answer the questions below it.

> LITERARY MODEL
>
> **(1)** The country Fox and the city Cat were chatting one day. **(2)** The Fox bragged forever about all his tricks. **(3)** "I am so good! No matter what the danger, I have one hundred tricks to save myself." **(4)** The humble Cat said, "I have only one trick—climbing a tree. If it fails, I'm lost." **(5)** "One trick?" that proud Fox sneered. **(6)** "What if an eagle swoops down on you? **(7)** I must say, you are really stupid." **(8)** Suddenly a pack of baying hounds burst upon the two startled animals. **(9)** The Cat dashed so quickly up a tree he almost reached the top. **(10)** The unlucky Fox tried all his clever tricks but was caught by the hounds anyway.
>
> —*Aesop's Fables*

1. What nouns are used as adjectives in sentence 1?
2. Which word in sentence 2 is an adverb?
3. Is the word *good* in sentence 3 an adjective or an adverb?
4. What are the two adjectives in sentence 4?
5. What kind of adjective is the word *that* in sentence 5?
6. What question does the adverb *down* answer in sentence 6?
7. Which word in sentence 7 is a predicate adjective?
8. What participles are used as adjectives in sentence 8?
9. What are the adverbs in sentence 9?
10. In sentence 10, what questions do the adjectives *unlucky, all,* and *clever* answer?

B. Using Comparisons If an underlined word or phrase contains an error, write the correct word or phrase. If there is no error, write *Correct.*

There **(1)** <u>isn't no other</u> animal as mysterious as the cat. In the countries formerly known as Burma and Siam, cats were held in the **(2)** <u>most highest</u> regard. **(3)** <u>Those kind of feelings</u> were probably based on ancient beliefs about the animal's magical powers. Temple cats, in particular, were cared for really **(4)** <u>good.</u> People treated them better than **(5)** <u>any cat</u>. **(6)** <u>Them cats</u> were the guardians of the people who had died. Some were even **(7)** <u>more holier</u> because they were buried alive in the tombs of royalty. Of course, their **(8)** <u>biggest</u> challenge was to escape through holes in the tombs. Once they did, **(9)** <u>those here</u> cats were taken back to the temple. They were given **(10)** <u>real expensive</u> food and treated like gods and goddesses!

Choose the best way to write each underlined section and mark the letter of your answer. If the underlined section needs no change, mark the choice "Correct as is."

Some people are afraid of the most tiniest housefly. Imagine, then, how
(1)
frightening a fly the size of a car would be. Makers of horror films take

them scary prospects seriously. Their insect fright movies are more
(2)   (3)
terrifying than many horror films.

In *Them!* atomic testing is blamed for enormous ants roaming the New

Mexico desert. The ants are defeated in a real big battle in the Los
(4)
Angeles sewer system. In *Beginning of the End,* radioactivity creates a

plague of giant locusts. At first, authorities can't hardly believe that
(5)
everyone in Ludlow, Illinois, has vanished. Then a huge swarm of locusts

heads for Chicago. The situation seems hopeless until the hero lures the

locusts into Lake Michigan, where they drown.

---

1. A. Some people are afraid of the tinier housefly.
   B. Some people are afraid of the most tinier housefly.
   C. Some people are afraid of the tiniest housefly.
   D. Correct as is

2. A. Makers of horror films take this scary prospects seriously.
   B. Makers of horror films take these scary prospects seriously.
   C. Makers of horror films take these here scary prospects seriously.
   D. Correct as is

3. A. Their insect fright movies are more terrifying than many other horror films.
   B. Their insect fright movies are more terrifying than horror films.
   C. Their insect fright movies are more terrifying than any films.
   D. Correct as is

4. A. The real ants are defeated in a big battle in the Los Angeles sewer system.
   B. The ants are defeated in a really big battle in the Los Angeles sewer system.
   C. The ants are real defeated in a big battle in the Los Angeles sewer system.
   D. Correct as is

5. A. At first, authorities can't scarcely believe that everyone in Ludlow, Illinois, has vanished.
   B. At first, authorities can hardly believe that everyone in Ludlow, Illinois, has vanished.
   C. At first, authorities can't never believe that everyone in Ludlow, Illinois, has vanished.
   D. Correct as is

MODIFIERS

Student Help Desk

Using Modifiers at a Glance

Adjectives	Modifier	Comparative	Superlative
tell which one, what kind, how many, how much	green	greener	greenest
	gigantic	more gigantic less gigantic	most gigantic least gigantic
Adverbs			
tell when, where, how, to what extent	greedily	more greedily less greedily	most greedily least greedily

Crafty Comparisons

	Comparative Form	Superlative Form
One-syllable words	Add -er.	Add -est.
Two-syllable words	Add -er or more.	Add -est or most.
Words with more syllables	Add more.	Add most.

Remember . . .

- Never use -er and more (more higher) or -est and most (most highest) together.
- Never use -est or most to compare only two things.
- Always use else or other when comparing one member of a group to the whole group.

Frank and Ernest by Thaves

© 1992 Thaves. Reprinted with permission. Newspaper dist. by NEA, Inc.

CHAPTER 9

Adjective or Adverb?

Adverb really, badly, well	They drive **badly.** He **really** wants to go. She plays **well.**
Adjective real, good, well, bad	It's a **real** story. I made a **bad** mistake. That's a **good** idea. They feel **good** (happy). She looks **well** (healthy). I feel **bad.**

Use the adverb form if . . .

the word modifies a verb, an adjective, or another adverb and tells how, when, where, or to what degree: **Crow behaved badly.**

Use the adjective form if . . .

the word modifies a noun or pronoun and tells which one, what kind, how much, or how many: **He stole food from his good friends.**

OR

the word follows a linking verb and refers to the subject: **He felt bad about what he did.**

The Bottom Line

Checklist for Using Modifiers

When I use modifiers, do I . . .

____ place them close to the words they modify?

____ choose the correct adverb or adjective forms?

____ avoid double negatives?

____ avoid using *them* for *these* or *those?*

____ avoid using *here* or *there* with demonstrative pronouns used as adjectives?

When I make comparisons, do I . . .

____ always use *-er* or *more* when comparing only two things?

____ avoid double comparisons and illogical comparisons?

Capitalization

If you're a STAR TREK fan, come and meet other "TREKKERS"; enter the costume contest for best ferengi, romulan, or vulcan; and learn to speak klingon at the world's biggest star trek convention.

Theme: Unusual Events

Calling All Trekkers!

Red alert! The person who wrote this ad needs to brush up on the rules of capitalization. Why do you think it's important to capitalize some letters and not others? For example, what is the difference in meaning between the words *Enterprise* and *enterprise?* between the words *Federation* and *federation?*

Write Away: An Event to Remember
Write a paragraph describing a memorable event from the last school year. It might be an unusual event or simply one that you found enjoyable. Save your paragraph in your **Working Portfolio.**

Diagnostic Test: What Do You Know?

For each underlined group of words, choose the letter of the correct revision.

Are you a follower of *The Next Generation, deep space nine, Voyager,* or
(1)
the original *Star Trek* series with captain James T. Kirk as commanding
(2)
officer of the starship *Enterprise?* If so, you may be interested in
conventions sponsored by Starfleet: The International Star Trek Fan
(3)
Association. if you're thinking, "That would be interesting," I would like to
(4)
tell you about some contests held at such conventions. You might enter a
paper-airplane contest in which each plane must be made by its Captain
(5)
and must carry one United States penny during flight. You might enter a
costume contest for the best-dressed Starfleet officer, alien, or Greek god.
(6)
Instead of attending a convention, you might prefer to take courses in
literature, history, or other subjects at Starfleet academy, which has
(7)
"campuses" all over the world, including Officer's Command college in
(8)
Harbord, new south Wales, Australia. You could even attend the Vulcan
(9)
Academy of Science (vas) and take courses such as thermodynamics,
(10)
Volcanology I, and logic.

1. A. Follower
   B. *The next generation*
   C. *Deep Space Nine*
   D. Correct as is

2. A. Captain
   B. james t. kirk
   C. Commanding Officer
   D. Correct as is

3. A. international
   B. fan
   C. association
   D. Correct as is

4. A. If you're thinking
   B. that
   C. Interesting
   D. Correct as is

5. A. captain
   B. Penny
   C. Flight
   D. Correct as is

6. A. Officer
   B. Alien
   C. God
   D. Correct as is

7. A. Literature
   B. History
   C. Academy
   D. Correct as is

8. A. officer's command college
   B. officer's
   C. College
   D. Correct as is

9. A. harbord
   B. New South Wales
   C. new South Wales
   D. Correct as is

10. A. VAS
    B. Thermodynamics
    C. Logic
    D. Correct as is

People and Cultures

① Here's the Idea

People's names and titles, the names of the languages they speak, and the religions they practice are all proper nouns and should be capitalized.

Names and Initials

▶ **Capitalize people's names and initials.**

Toni Morrison	Franklin Delano Roosevelt	R. L. Stine
Lyndon B. Johnson	Sandra Cisneros	B. B. King

Personal Titles and Abbreviations

▶ **Capitalize titles and abbreviations of titles that are used before names or in direct address.**

Professor Stevens	Dr. Martin Luther King, Jr.
Chief Justice William H. Rehnquist	Lt. Col. Eileen Collins

Sgt. Kaspar escorted Ambassador Nakamora to the dinner.

▶ **Capitalize abbreviations of titles even when they follow names.**

Emilio Estefan, **Jr.**	Stephen Baker, **C.E.O.**
Michelle Phillips, **Ph.D.**	

▶ **Capitalize a title of royalty or nobility only when it precedes a person's name.**

Queen Elizabeth I

Sir Winston Churchill

King Henry VIII

Count Victor

The poetry reading was attended by Sir Robert.

The audience included the prince and princess.

CHAPTER 10

Family Relationships

▶ **Capitalize words indicating family relationships only when they are used as parts of names or in direct address.**

Aunt Ruth   Uncle Ed   Grandma Johnson

When my mother and Aunt Betty were children, did you read poetry to them, Grandfather?

 In general, do not capitalize a word referring to a family relationship when it follows a person's name or is used without a name.

Ben, my brother, likes writing poetry.

The Pronoun *I*

▶ **Always capitalize the pronoun *I*.**

My friends and I had never been to a poetry slam before.

Ethnic Groups, Languages, and Nationalities

▶ **Capitalize the names of ethnic groups, races, languages, and nationalities, along with adjectives formed from these names.**

English   Spanish   Cherokee
Chinese   Swahili   German

Religious Terms

▶ **Capitalize the names of religions, religious denominations, sacred days, sacred writings, and deities.**

Religious Terms	
Religions	Christianity, Judaism, Islam
Denominations and sects	Sunni, Baptist, Methodist
Sacred days	Ramadan, Easter, Passover
Sacred writings	Bible, Koran, Torah
Deities	Allah, God

 Do not capitalize the words *god* and *goddess* when they refer to gods of ancient mythology.

Athena was the Greek goddess of wisdom.

❷ Practice and Apply

A. CONCEPT CHECK: People and Cultures

Identify and rewrite the words that contain capitalization errors in the following sentences.

Poetry Slam!

1. A poetry slam is a competition in which readers perform original poems that are rated by a panel of Judges.
2. "The difference between a slam and a traditional poetry reading," reports ms. malaika fisher, "is the level of energy."
3. Love, hate, death, Religion, and other topics about which people feel strongly are typical subjects of the poems.
4. Anyone is welcome to read at a slam, from your Dentist to your Grandmother.
5. All poets are welcome, from beginners to distinguished poets such as linda gregg, a teacher at a prestigious university.
6. If there is ever a poetry slam in my area, i plan to attend it.
7. Poetry slams take place in more than 100 american cities.
8. Now they are being held in other countries as well, with poets reading in languages such as german and swedish.
9. As Marc k. Smith, the Father of the poetry slam, says, "The performance of poetry is an art—just as much an art as the art of writing it."
10. Because of his role in originating and popularizing the poetry slam, smith has been nicknamed slampapi.

➜ **For a SELF-CHECK and more practice, see the EXERCISE BANK, p. 331.**

B. REVISION: Capitalization Errors

Identify and correct all capitalization errors in this family tree.

ROWINSKI FAMILY

dr. miroslav rowinski (dr. anna ross pell)

Monika (Chris r. Oslecki, c.e.o.)   uncle Bob (professor Maria Lopez)

Paulina   Marianna (gen. kevin r. Cavanaugh)

kevin, jr.   tracy   anna

First Words and Titles

LESSON 2

❶ Here's the Idea

First words in sentences, most lines of poetry, quotations, and outline entries are capitalized. Greetings and closings in letters and important words in titles are capitalized.

Sentences and Poetry

▶ **Capitalize the first word of every sentence.**

Many people enjoy reenacting historical events.

▶ **Capitalize the first word in every line of traditional poetry.**

> **LITERARY MODEL**
>
> Listen, my children, and you shall hear
> Of the midnight ride of Paul Revere,
> On the eighteenth of April, in Seventy-five;
> Hardly a man is now alive
> Who remembers that famous day and year.
>
> —Henry Wadsworth Longfellow, "Paul Revere's Ride"

Modern poets often choose not to begin each line with a capital letter. You also have this choice in writing your own poems.

Quotations

▶ **Capitalize the first word of a direct quotation if it is a complete sentence.** Do not capitalize a direct quotation if it is a fragment of a sentence.

The e-mail said, "Is anyone interested in reenacting a battle?"

One player says reenactments are "the closest we can get to time travel."

▶ **In a divided quotation, do not capitalize the first word of the second part unless it starts a new sentence.**

"We have the costumes," the e-mail continued, "but we need history experts."

"Join our group," the writer said. "You'll have fun."

CAPITALIZATION

Parts of a Letter

▶ **In a letter, capitalize the first word of the greeting, words such as *Sir* or *Madam*, and the first word of the closing.**

May 20, 200-

Civil War Reenactors
1800 W. Wheeling St.
Boston, MA 02124
Dear Sir:
   I would be very interested in joining your group. I've read a lot about American history, and I've always wanted to take part in a reenactment. Please send me more information.

Yours truly,
Ellen Hobson

Outlines

▶ **Capitalize the first word of each entry in an outline, as well as the letters that introduce major subsections.**

I. Historical reenactments

   A. Reenactments of events in American history

      1. Famous battles

      2. Nonmilitary events

Titles

▶ **Capitalize the first word, the last word, and all other important words in a title. Do not capitalize conjunctions, articles, or prepositions of fewer than five letters.**

Titles	
Books	*The Catcher in the Rye, The Old Man and the Sea*
Plays and musicals	*The Devil and Daniel Webster, West Side Story*
Short stories	"The Gift of the Magi," "To Build a Fire"
Magazines and newspapers	*People, National Geographic, New York Times*
Movies	*The Phantom Menace, Gone with the Wind*
Television shows	*The Simpsons, The Today Show*
Works of art	*The Thinker, Ophelia*
Poems	"My Papa's Waltz," "The Road Not Taken"

❷ Practice and Apply

A. CONCEPT CHECK: First Words and Titles

Identify and rewrite the words that contain capitalization errors in the following sentences.

Reenact It

1. each year, Civil War reenactors gather at Gettysburg, Pennsylvania, to reenact the battle that took place there.
2. One reenactment takes place at the Yingling Farm, where the movie *gettysburg* was filmed.
3. If you ask a participant, "are you an actor?" he or she may reply, "no, I'm a reenactor."
4. Newspapers like the *Civil War news* and magazines like *Camp Chase gazette* provide information for reenactors.
5. reenactors are not professional actors, but people who get together to reenact historical events.
6. "some groups specialize in reenacting battles," explained the tour guide.
7. The poem "Concord hymn," by Ralph Waldo Emerson, commemorates the first battle of the American Revolution, a good subject for a reenactment.
8. another kind of reenactment occurs at Renaissance fairs.
9. If you go to a Renaissance fair, people will be dressed like characters from Shakespeare's *Twelfth night* and *the Tempest*.
10. You might see a Shakespeare reenactor as he composes the line "shall I compare thee to a summer's day?"

➜ **For a SELF-CHECK and more practice, see the EXERCISE BANK, p. 332**

B. EDITING AND PROOFREADING: Capitalization Errors

Find and correct 15 capitalization errors in this letter.

dear mr. oliver,

    I thought you would like to know that I did something educational this summer! last week we went to a Renaissance fair. The whole fair is a dramatization of a day when Queen Elizabeth I leads a procession through an English village. everyone talks and dresses like characters out of *romeo And juliet*. A girl dressed as a lady in waiting said to us, "give ye good day, my lords and ladies," and we answered, "'Tis a passing fair day." there were jugglers, tumblers, and dancers; there were musicians playing and singing songs like "greensleeves" and "o mistresse mine."

sincerely,

Julia

CAPITALIZATION

Places and Transportation

❶ Here's the Idea

The names of specific places, celestial bodies, landmarks, and vehicles are capitalized.

Geographical Names

▶ **In geographical names, capitalize each word except articles and prepositions.**

Geographical Names	
Divisions of the world	Arctic Circle, Northern Hemisphere
Continents	South America, Australia, Africa
Bodies of water	Pacific Ocean, Snake River, Lake Michigan
Islands	West Indies, Long Island, Canary Islands
Mountains	Mount Rainier, Alps, Allegheny Mountains
Other landforms	Grand Canyon, Mohave Desert, Rock of Gibraltar
Regions	Eastern Europe, Scandinavia, Latin America
Nations	Spain, Saudi Arabia, Czech Republic
States	Maine, Texas, South Carolina
Counties and Townships	Alameda County, Middlebury Township
Cities and towns	Houston, San Francisco, Evanston
Roads and streets	Fifth Avenue, Lake Shore Drive, Main Street

Directions

▶ **Capitalize the words *north*, *south*, *east*, and *west* when they name particular regions of the country or world or are parts of proper names.**

Interesting festivals are held all over the country, from the West Coast to the East Coast, in the North and in the South.

Each year, the Apple Butter Festival is held in West Virginia.

Do not capitalize words that indicate general directions or locations.

To get to the fair, drive north on Route 17.

Bodies of the Universe

▶ **Capitalize the names of planets and other specific objects in the universe.**

Halley's Comet   Venus   Pleiades

▶ **Do not capitalize *sun* and *moon*. Capitalize *earth* only when it is used with other capitalized astronomical terms. Don't capitalize *earth* when it is preceded by the article *the* or when it refers to land or soil.**

Of all the inner planets, only Earth and Mars have satellites.

The earth is rich in nutrients.

Buildings, Bridges, and Other Landmarks

▶ **Capitalize the names of specific buildings, bridges, monuments, and other landmarks.**

Washington Monument	Empire State Building
London Bridge	Gateway Arch

Pat sent me a postcard of the Golden Gate Bridge.

Planes, Trains, and Other Vehicles

▶ **Capitalize the names of specific airplanes, trains, ships, cars, and spacecraft.**

Vehicles	
Airplanes	*Flyer* (the Wright brothers' first successful airplane)
Trains	*Super Chief*, *City of New Orleans*
Ships	U.S.S. *Constitution*, *Half Moon*
Cars	*Civic*, *Mustang*
Spacecraft	*Sputnik 1*, space shuttle *Columbia*

CAPITALIZATION

Capitalization **237**

❷ Practice and Apply

A. CONCEPT CHECK: Places and Transportation

For each sentence, write correctly the words that should be capitalized. If a sentence is correct, write *Correct.*

Flip That Flapjack!

1. Every year in liberal, kansas, in the united states of america, one day a year is designated International Pancake Day.

2. Liberal is in seward county, in southwestern Kansas.

3. On the other side of the atlantic ocean, in the british isles, the people of olney hold a similar celebration.

4. Olney is located in a county called buckinghamshire.

5. Women in Liberal compete against women in Olney in a race that is the only official one of its kind on the earth.

6. The race begins on pancake boulevard in liberal and at the market square in Olney.

7. You will not find a similar race in continental europe or in any other town in the united states.

8. The tradition began in 1445, even before Columbus's *Niña*, *pinta*, and *santa maría* set sail.

9. In a town in england, a woman who was making pancakes heard the church bells ringing and, not wanting to be late, ran to the church with skillet in hand.

10. Whether you come from the east or the west, visit liberal and celebrate Pancake Day with friends and family.

➜ **For a SELF-CHECK and more practice, see the EXERCISE BANK, p. 333.**

B. EDITING AND PROOFREADING: Capitalization Errors

Identify and correct ten capitalization errors in this paragraph.

The Festivals of Texas

The state of texas may have the most unusual festivals in the United States. For example, the city of san antonio starts off each year by draining the river and inviting residents to roll in the mud or throw mud at photos of their city council members. The world's biggest rattlesnake roundup takes place in sweetwater, where Texans collect about 6,000 pounds of rattlers and fry thousands of pounds of rattlesnake steaks. In shamrock, Texas, on St. Patrick's Day, everyone adds *O'* to his or her name. People in this town gather to kiss a slab of the Blarney Stone imported from cork, ireland. In dublin, Texas, festivals feature Irish dancers and an Irish stew cook-off. San Antonio dyes the river green and renames it the river shannon.

LESSON 4 Organizations and Other Subjects

❶ Here's the Idea

Capitalize the names of organizations, historical events and documents, and months, days, and holidays.

Organizations and Institutions

▶ **Capitalize all important words in the names of organizations, institutions, stores, and companies.**

University of New Mexico

National Association of Manufacturers

Madison Township Middle School

Bernard's Fine Foods

Chicago Public Library

Kansas Department of Agriculture

 Do not capitalize words such as *school*, *company*, *church*, *college*, and *hospital* when they are not used as parts of names.

Abbreviations of Organization Names

▶ **Capitalize abbreviations of the names of organizations and institutions.**

ABA (American Bar Association)

UCLA (University of California, Los Angeles)

OAS (Organization of American States)

USAF (United States Air Force)

Historical Events, Periods, and Documents

▶ **Capitalize the names of historical events, periods, and documents.**

The League of Nations was formed after World War I.

Historical Events, Periods, and Documents	
Events	American Revolution, Civil War
Documents	Declaration of Independence, Bill of Rights
Periods	Middle Ages, Roaring Twenties

Time Abbreviations and Calendar Items

▶ **Capitalize the abbreviations B.C., A.D., B.C.E., C.E., A.M., and P.M.**

According to Roman legend, Rome was founded in 753 **B.C.**

The restaurant is open from 7:00 **A.M.** to 10:00 **P.M.**

▶ **Capitalize the names of months, days, and holidays but not the names of seasons.**

March	summer	Memorial Day
Thanksgiving	Friday	spring

The activities will begin on Saturday, April 17, at 9 **A.M.**

When the name of a season is used in the title of a festival or celebration (**Winter Carnival**), capitalize it.

Special Events, Awards, and Brand Names

▶ **Capitalize the names of special events and awards.**

Super Bowl	Olympic Games
Newbery Medal	Academy Awards

The Chilean poet Pablo Neruda won the Nobel Prize for literature in 1971.

▶ **Capitalize the brand names of products but not common nouns that follow brand names.**

Strongstik adhesive tape   Power Pack batteries

School Subjects and Class Names

▶ **Capitalize the names of school subjects only when they refer to specific courses.** (Do, however, capitalize proper nouns and adjectives in all such names.)

geometry	American history
French	American History I

▶ **Capitalize the word *freshman, sophomore, junior,* or *senior* only when it is used as part of a proper noun or in a direct address.**

The Senior Council will meet next Thursday.

Please take your seats, Freshmen.

❷ Practice and Apply

A. CONCEPT CHECK: Organizations and Other Subjects

For each sentence, write correctly the words that should be capitalized. If a sentence is correct, write *Correct*.

Bug Watch

1. Every april, purdue university plays host to an unusual event called the bug bowl.

2. This curious spring carnival was originated by Tom Turpin, an entomology professor.

3. Turpin, who teaches entomology 105, sees the event as a way to help people understand insects better.

4. One part of the weekend-long happening is a parade of cars decorated to look like different kinds of bugs.

5. A highlight is the cockroach race, the winner of which receives an award called the old open can—a bronzed garbage can with a cockroach on top.

6. In bug bowl 98, penn state challenged purdue to a Big Ten Spit-Off to see who would hold the cricket-spitting record.

7. People have eaten insects since before the stone age, and those attending can taste foods made with insects.

8. In 1995 the carnegie foundation for the advancement of teaching declared Turpin the "indiana professor of the year."

9. The award was presented by the council for advancement and support of education, or case for short.

10. The bug bowl is part of springfest, which offers nearly 100 activities and events.

➡ **For a SELF-CHECK and more practice, see the EXERCISE BANK, p. 333.**

B. MIXED REVIEW: Capitalization Errors

Rewrite the following newspaper ad, correcting all capitalization errors.

Section

LAKE CENTRAL HIGH SCHOOL CLASS OF '91 REUNION

Date	friday, september 7, 2001	saturday, september 8, 2001
Time	7:00 p.m. - 1:00 a.m.	1:00 p m, - whenever
Event	alumni dinner and dance	old gold picnic
Location	springfield country club	lincoln park
	2080 w. jefferson rd.	

Capitalization **241**

Real World Grammar

Itinerary

At some point, you may have the responsibility of creating an itinerary. An **itinerary** is a written record, schedule, or account of a journey. An itinerary should include the date, time, and location of each stop, highlights of the attractions, and other important information related to your trip. When you capitalize words appropriately, you help your reader distinguish general terms from specific names.

ITINERARY

DATE: Friday, june 29
EVENT: Uptown Poetry Slam
LOCATION: Old Mill Books, Chicago, Illinois
HIGHLIGHTS: Reading by class member callie ortiz at 8:00 P.M.

DATE: Saturday, June 30
EVENT: Pioneer Days
LOCATION: Utica, Illinois, outside of Starved Rock state park
HIGHLIGHTS: Craft displays, reenactment of the battle of starved rock

DATE: Sunday, July 1
EVENT: Bristol Renaissance faire
LOCATION: 12550 120th avenue, Kenosha, Wisconsin
HIGHLIGHTS: medieval games at 11:00 A.M., parade at 1:00 P.M.

Capitalize:

names of months

people's names

national and state parks

names of historical events

events

names of streets

names of historical periods

PRACTICE AND APPLY: Creating an Itinerary

Your science club is planning a field trip to the East Coast for March 19–25. Use the following information about tourist attractions to create an itinerary like the one on the preceding page. Be sure to capitalize words appropriately.

DATE: WEDNESDAY, MARCH 22
ATTRACTION: CAPE COD MUSEUM OF NATURAL HISTORY
LOCATION: ROUTE 6A
BREWSTER, MASSACHUSETTS
HIGHLIGHTS: SEAL CRUISE ABOARD *BEACHCOMBER*, WORKING BEEHIVE AT 9:30 A.M., WHALE EXHIBIT, WILDFLOWER GARDEN

DATE: FRIDAY, MARCH 24
ATTRACTION: PHILADELPHIA INSECTARIUM
LOCATION: 8046 FRANKFORD AVENUE
PHILADELPHIA, PENNSYLVANIA
HIGHLIGHTS: WORLDWIDE BUTTERFLY COLLECTION, EXOTIC BEETLE COLLECTION, LIVE TERMITE TUNNEL, CAMOUFLAGE INSECTS

DATE: MONDAY, MARCH 20
ATTRACTION: NATIONAL MUSEUM OF DENTISTRY
LOCATION: UNIVERSITY OF MARYLAND
BALTIMORE, MARYLAND
HIGHLIGHTS: LIFE-SIZE MODEL OF "IRON JAW" ACT, GEORGE WASHINGTON'S TEETH, TOOTH JUKEBOX

Mixed Review

A. Capitalization Read the following passage. On a separate sheet of paper, explain why each underlined word or phrase is capitalized.

Who is Punxsutawney Phil? Does **(1)** <u>Groundhog Day</u> ring a bell? Punxsutawney Phil is the official groundhog weather prognosticator who makes an appearance once a year on **(2)** <u>Gobbler's Knob</u> in **(3)** <u>Punxsutawney, Pennsylvania</u>. The official celebration is traced back to **(4)** <u>February 2, 1886</u>, when Clymer Freas wrote in the **(5)** <u>*Punxsutawney Spirit*</u>, **(6)** "<u>Today</u> is Groundhog Day and up to the time of going to press the beast has not seen its shadow." Groundhog Day is rooted in a tradition associated with the holiday of **(7)** <u>Candlemas</u>. On February 2, halfway through winter, people would wait for the sun to come out. If the day turned out to be sunny, they would expect six more weeks of wintry weather. In 1993 **(8)** <u>Columbia Pictures</u> released the comedy **(9)** <u>*Groundhog Day*</u>, starring Bill Murray. Although it was filmed in Woodstock, Illinois, some names of Punxsutawney businesses, including **(10)** <u>The Smart Shop and Stewart's Drug Store</u>, were used in the movie. Whether you believe in Phil's forecast or not, he's been right about 39 percent of the time.

B. Editing and Proofreading Rewrite the ad below, using the capitalization rules presented in this chapter.

If you're a STAR TREK FAN, come and meet other "TREKKERS"; enter the costume contest for best ferengi, romulan, or vulcan; and learn to speak KLINGON at the opening of this attraction.

C. Revision For each capitalization error, write the word correctly.

Chocolate, Sweet Chocolate!
Oakdale Chamber of commerce
590 north Yosemite avenue
Oakdale, california 95361

dear Sir or madam:

I understand you are looking for interesting, mouthwatering chocolate concoctions to feature at the Oakdale Chocolate Festival to be held may 15 and 16. I am the author of <u>The Chocolate lover's Guide</u> and teach chocolate 101 at Calorie college, and I have a few recipes that might interest you. I recently exhibited my creations at the International Festival Of Chocolate in london.

Please send me information about the festival in Oakdale.

Sincerely Yours,

c. Barr

For each underlined group of words, choose the letter of the correct revision.

On a quiet <u>Sunday in a cabin on the slopes of the volcano kilauea</u>, the
(1)
first things <u>Sonny Ching saw when he woke up were the trophies</u>. His
(2)
students had won both the women's and the men's competition in the
annual <u>Merrie monarch Festival</u> hula competition. The festival, a
(3)
celebration of traditional Hawaiian culture, is named for the last Hawaiian
king, <u>king david kalakaua</u>, who worked to preserve his people's rich
(4)
heritage of music and dance. It is held in the city of <u>Hilo, on the island of</u>
(5)
<u>hawaii</u> in <u>the state of Hawaii. Each Spring</u>, at the festival, groups of
(6)
dancers compete and are rated by judges, but as the 1995 <u>miss aloha hula</u>,
(7)
Tracy Vaughan, said, "<u>I didn't come here to win. I came to show how much</u>
(8)
<u>i love the hula</u>." Before the competition, dancers honor the ancient fire
<u>Goddess Pele and her sisters</u>. "Hula is the language of the heart," <u>the king</u>
(9)
<u>once said, "And therefore the heartbeat of the Hawaiian people</u>."
(10)

1. A. sunday
   B. volcano
   C. Kilauea
   D. Correct as is

2. A. sonny
   B. ching
   C. Trophies
   D. Correct as is

3. A. merrie
   B. Monarch
   C. merrie monarch festival
   D. Correct as is

4. A. King David Kalakaua
   B. king David Kalakaua
   C. King david kalakaua
   D. Correct as is

5. A. hilo
   B. Island of Hawaii
   C. Hawaii
   D. Correct as is

6. A. State of Hawaii
   B. each spring
   C. Each spring
   D. Correct as is

7. A. Miss Aloha Hula
   B. miss Aloha Hula
   C. Miss
   D. Correct as is

8. A. i didn't come here to win
   B. i came to show
   C. how much I love the hula
   D. Correct as is

9. A. goddess pele
   B. goddess Pele
   C. Sisters
   D. Correct as is

10. A. King
    B. "and therefore the heartbeat . . ."
    C. hawaiian
    D. Correct as is

CAPITALIZATION

Student Help Desk

Capitalization at a Glance

People and **C**ultures

First **W**ords and **T**itles

Places and **T**ransportation

Organizations and **O**ther **S**ubjects

To Capitalize or Not to Capitalize: Nouns

Common	Proper
college	Smith College
island	Easter Island
hall	Orchestra Hall
mountains	Rocky Mountains
war	Civil War
club	Chess Club
museum	Metropolitan Museum of Art

Capitalization Tips — Do Capitalize

The first word of a sentence	Who wrote the poem "Annabel Lee"?
The first word in every line of a traditional poem	It was many and many a year ago, In a kingdom by the sea, —Edgar Allan Poe, "Annabel Lee"
A family word used as a name or in direct address	Susan saw the parade with Uncle Ed.
The first and last words and other important words in a title	*To Kill a Mockingbird*
The name of a particular person, place, planet, event, brand, or the like	Professor Jones plans to take his geography class on a trip to the Grand Canyon.

Capitalization Pitfalls — Don't Capitalize

The first word in every line of some modern poems	I am fourteen and my skin has betrayed me —Audre Lorde, "Hanging Fire"
A family word used as a common noun	My uncle competed for the city record in the pie-eating contest.
The name of a season used as a common noun	Every spring, people demonstrate their wacky talents in the festival.
A class name used as a common noun	She is a senior.
A compass direction not used as a proper noun	The festival is held on Route 41, just south of North Shore Avenue.

The Bottom Line

Checklist for Capitalization

Have I capitalized . . .

____ people's names and initials?

____ personal titles before names?

____ names of ethnic groups, races, languages, and nationalities?

____ names of religions and other religious terms?

____ names of bodies of the universe?

____ names of monuments, bridges, and other landmarks?

____ names of planes, trains, and spacecraft?

____ names of historical events, periods, and documents?

____ names of special events, awards, and brands?

Punctuation

PRINCIPAL

Theme: Games and Hobbies

A Treasure Hunt

You're trying to figure out where a rival school's team has left your school mascot. Is it "Go to the Quick Mart, (then) past the Chicken Shack" or "Go to the Quick Mart (that is) past the Chicken Shack"? Without proper punctuation marks, this message makes no sense.

Write Away: Return It or Else!

If you were one of the students whose school mascot was stolen by the rival school, how would you respond to the ransom note? Write a short letter to the editor of your school newspaper, giving your opinion about the playing of pranks on rival schools. Save your writing in your ▭ **Working Portfolio.**

For each numbered item, choose the letter of the best revision.

> Can you imagine the popularity the game of chess has had over the
> (1)
> years. For some, people chess is more than a competitive game. In
> (2)
> Marostica Italy, a ceremony takes place every other year to celebrate
> (3)
> a game of chess. The townspeople dress up as chess pieces in
>
> festive colorful costumes and act out the game. The origin of this event
> (4)
> goes back to the 15th century, when two rival suitors; challenged each
> (5)
> other to a game of chess; each wanted to marry the local lord's daughter.
> (6)
> To emphasize the importance of the challenge the game was played in
> (7)
> front of an audience. Today the town "reenacts" this 15th-century duel on a
> (8)
> giant chessboard while an announcer calls out the moves from a tower. . .
> (9)   (10)

1. A. Can you imagine?
   B. Can you imagine the
      popularity the game of chess
      has had over the years?
   C. Can you imagine the
      popularity; the game of chess
      has had over the years?
   D. Correct as is

2. A. For some people,
   B. For some people:
   C. For some people—
   D. Correct as is

3. A. Marostica, Italy,
   B. Marostica—Italy,
   C. "Marostica Italy,"
   D. Correct as is

4. A. festive colorful, costumes
   B. festive, colorful costumes
   C. festive colorful—costumes
   D. Correct as is

5. A. two rival suitors:
   B. two rival suitors'
   C. two rival suitors
   D. Correct as is

6. A. the local, lord's daughter
   B. the local lords daughter
   C. the local lords' daughter
   D. Correct as is

7. A. To emphasize the importance
      of the challenge,
   B. To emphasize the importance,
      of the challenge
   C. To emphasize the "importance"
      of the challenge
   D. Correct as is

8. A. re—enacts
   B. re enacts
   C. reenacts
   D. Correct as is

9. A. "chess board"
   B. chess—board
   C. chess-board
   D. Correct as is

10. A. tower?
    B. tower!
    C. tower.
    D. Correct as is

Periods and Other End Marks

❶ Here's the Idea

Periods, question marks, and exclamation points—together known as **end marks**—are used to indicate the end of sentences. Periods are also used in several other ways.

Periods

▶ **Use periods at the end of all declarative sentences and most imperative sentences.**

Declarative Sentence
Chess is a strategic game**.**

Imperative Sentence
Follow the rules**.**

▶ **Use periods at the end of most sentences containing indirect questions.** An indirect question tells what someone has asked without giving the exact wording.

The student asked how chess is played**.**

Other Uses of Periods

▶ **Use periods after initials and after most abbreviations.**

Gen**.** George Washington   3 lb**.** 10 oz**.**
Dr**.** Michael C**.** Scott

▶ **Use a period after each number or letter in an outline or list.**

Outline	List
I**.** Traditional games	1**.** Board games
A**.** Board games	2**.** Tile games
1**.** Chess	3**.** Target games
2**.** Backgammon	4**.** Card games
B**.** Tile games	

Question Marks

▶ **Use a question mark at the end of an interrogative sentence.**

Do you know who has won the most championships**?**

Exclamation Points

▶ **Use an exclamation point to end an exclamatory sentence or after a strong interjection (a word that shows feeling or imitates a sound).**

Hurrah **!**   We won the game **!**   What a game **!**

Don't overuse exclamation points. They lose their effectiveness if used too frequently, as in the sentences below.

Chess is the most competitive game! It requires skill and concentration! Tension mounts as each player attacks the enemy king!

❷ Practice and Apply

CONCEPT CHECK: Periods and Other End Marks

Write these sentences, inserting periods, question marks, and exclamation points where needed.

Chess Geniuses

1. Can a child learn to play chess at three years of age
2. Bobby Fischer, the first American to win the world championship, learned the moves of chess at the age of six
3. Many people wonder why Fischer lost his title in 1975
4. He simply refused to play the Russian challenger Anatoly Karpov under federation rules
5. Anatoly Karpov won the title by default. Amazing
6. Karpov, a child prodigy, learned to play chess at the age of four
7. How did Karpov dominate world competition from the mid-1970s to the mid-1980s
8. In 1985, he lost the championship title to Gary Kasparov
9. Kasparov became the youngest champion in the history of the game, and in 1996 he defeated a powerful chess computer
10. If you want to write a report on chess, follow this outline:
I History of chess
A Ancient precursors
1 Persia
2 Europe
B Modern chess

➜ **For a SELF-CHECK and more practice, see the EXERCISE BANK, p. 334.**

Commas in Sentence Parts

❶ Here's the Idea

Commas can make the meaning of sentences clearer by separating certain sentence elements. However, using too many commas can cause more confusion than leaving them out.

Commas in Series

▶ **In a series of three or more items, use a comma after every item except the last one.**

Bungee jumping has joined the ranks of **surfboarding ,** **skateboarding ,** and **sky surfing** as an extreme sport.

A person who wants to bungee jump can go to professional sites and jump from **bridges ,** **hot-air balloons ,** and **tall buildings.**

▶ **Use commas after *first, second,* and so on when they introduce items in a series.**

Participants are asked to follow three simple rules: **first ,** secure the bungee cord for safety; **second ,** do not attempt to hold on to anything; and **third ,** have fun.

▶ **Use commas between adjectives of equal rank that modify the same noun.**

A **young ,** **adventurous** man jumped off a 300-foot bridge.

To tell whether a series of adjectives requires a comma, place the word *and* between the adjectives. If the sentence still makes sense, replace *and* with a comma. Likewise, if you can change the order of the adjectives without changing the meaning of the sentence, place a comma between them.

Commas with Introductory Elements

▶ **Use a comma after an introductory word or a mild interjection such as *oh* or *well*.**

Oh, bungee jumping is not for the faint-hearted.

However, if you are a thrill-seeker, then this is the perfect hobby.

▶ **Use a comma after an introductory prepositional phrase that contains one or more other prepositional phrases.**

At the beginning of the jump, a person feels a rush of emotions.

▶ **Use a comma after an infinitive phrase, a participial phrase, or an adverb clause that begins a sentence.**

PARTICIPIAL PHRASE
Taking a deep breath, the jumper prepares for the dive.

ADVERB CLAUSE
When the jump is over, the exhilaration remains.

Commas with Interrupters

▶ **Use commas to set off words that interrupt the flow of thought in a sentence.**

Bungee jumping, **by the way**, can be done in groups.

A seven-person team, **for example**, has jumped in a specially designed basket.

Common Interrupters			
however	I suppose	by the way	of course
therefore	moreover	in fact	furthermore
for example	I believe	after all	nevertheless

▶ **Use commas to set off nouns of direct address.** A noun of direct address names the person or people being spoken to. Nouns of direct address can be either proper nouns or common nouns, as these examples show.

David, do you know anyone who has gone bungee jumping?

If you want to learn more about bungee jumping, **ladies and gentlemen**, try a search on the Internet.

▶ **Use commas to set off nonessential appositives.** An appositive is a word or phrase that identifies or renames a noun or pronoun. A nonessential appositive adds information about a noun or pronoun in a sentence in which the meaning is already clear.

NONESSENTIAL

Paul**, my brother,** has gone bungee jumping in Australia.

An essential appositive provides information that is needed to explain the preceding noun or pronoun. It requires no commas.

ESSENTIAL

His friend **Sheila** will jump from a hot-air balloon in August.

> Without the appositive the word *friend* could refer to any friend.

❷ Practice and Apply

CONCEPT CHECK: Commas in Sentence Parts

Write the words that should be followed by commas. If no commas are necessary in a sentence, write *None.*

An Ancient Ritual or a Modern Craze?

1. Bungee jumping has been called the human yo-yo the brain-squasher and the leap of faith.
2. Although bungee jumping is a recent invention the craze has already spread around the world.
3. Bungee jumping is a must-do activity for people visiting or living in places like France Australia and Mexico.
4. However this sudden craze is nothing new to the people of Pentecost Island in the South Pacific.
5. Our modern hobby is their version of an ancient tribal ritual that tests manhood.
6. The men it is said leap from towers 50 to 80 feet high, attached by just enough vine for their heads to barely touch the ground.
7. No this ritual is not a make-believe story.
8. In 1979 members of Oxford University's Dangerous Sports Club heard stories about the ritual and decided to test their own courage with a jump.
9. Wearing tuxedos and top hats they jumped off the 245-foot Clifton Bridge in Bristol, England.
10. A. J. Hackett a New Zealander brought bungee jumping to public attention when he jumped from the Eiffel Tower.

➡ **For a SELF-CHECK and more practice, see the EXERCISE BANK, p. 335.**

More Commas

LESSON 3

① Here's the Idea

Commas to Avoid Confusion

▶ **Use a comma whenever readers might misinterpret a sentence without it.**

UNCLEAR: Before the rodeo cowboys competed against one another for fun.

CLEAR: Before the rodeo, cowboys competed against one another for fun.

Commas with Quotations

▶ **Use commas to separate direct quotations from explanatory words like *he said, Greg replied,* and *Sheila asked.*** If the explanatory words precede the quotation, insert a comma before the quoted words.

Mr. Cruz said, "The rodeo was born during the era of the cattle industry, in the 1860s and 1870s."

If the explanatory words interrupt a quotation, insert a comma inside the quotation marks before the explanatory words and another comma after the explanatory words.

"Cowboys would gather together," **Mr. Cruz said,** "and compete against one another in steer roping and bronco riding."

If the explanatory words follow a quotation, insert a comma inside the quotation marks before the explanatory words.

"Today cowboys compete against each other for monetary awards," **added Mr. Cruz.**

Commas in Compound Sentences

▶ **Use a comma to separate independent clauses joined by a conjunction in a compound sentence.**

Rodeos are held in many parts of the United States, **but** they are also popular in Mexico, Canada, and Australia.

 Do not use a comma to separate the parts of a two-part compound predicate.

Many Western regions claim to be the birthplace of the rodeo and hold annual exhibitions to celebrate the Old West.

Commas with Nonessential Clauses

▶ **Use commas to set off nonessential clauses.** A nonessential clause adds extra information to a sentence but is not necessary to the meaning of the sentence.

Trick riding and fancy roping, **which are virtually unknown to rodeo fans today,** were popular events during the 1920s and 1930s.

Essential clauses are necessary to the meaning of sentences and are not set off with commas.

Fancy roping originated among those Mexican horsemen who are known as *charros*.

Commas in Letters, Place Names, and Dates

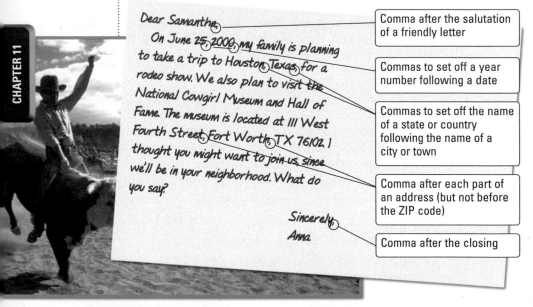

Dear Samantha,

On June 25, 2000, my family is planning to take a trip to Houston, Texas, for a rodeo show. We also plan to visit the National Cowgirl Museum and Hall of Fame. The museum is located at 111 West Fourth Street, Fort Worth, TX 76102. I thought you might want to join us, since we'll be in your neighborhood. What do you say?

Sincerely,
Anna

Comma after the salutation of a friendly letter

Commas to set off a year number following a date

Commas to set off the name of a state or country following the name of a city or town

Comma after each part of an address (but not before the ZIP code)

Comma after the closing

Peanuts by Charles Schulz

A. CONCEPT CHECK: More Commas

Write the words that should be followed by commas in these sentences. If a sentence is correct, write *Correct.*

College for Cowboys

1. Scottsdale Arizona is home to the Arizona Cowboy College.
2. In 1989, Lloyd Bridwell started his own college after watching some commercials for trade schools.
3. Bridwell offers his course up to eight times a year and accepts up to eight students per course.
4. The course which lasts a week teaches students basic cowboy skills.
5. Not only do students wake before sunrise and cook over campfires but they also learn about cattle grazing, branding, and roping.
6. Before leaving students gain an understanding of the demands of life on a ranch.
7. In a recent interview one of Bridwell's students said "This has completely changed my life."
8. Bridwell's appreciation of the cowboy way of life comes from his father who once competed in rodeos.
9. After high school Lloyd worked as a ranch hand and cowboy for four years before going off to college and in 1986 he opened an equestrian training center.
10. Anyone who is interested in taking Bridwell's course should be prepared to work hard.

➡ **For a SELF-CHECK and more practice, see the EXERCISE BANK, p. 335.**

B. PROOFREADING: Adding Commas

Proofread the following letter for punctuation errors. Write the words that should be followed by commas in the letter.

Dear Chris

On August 25, 2000 a few of us got together to visit the Cowboy Hall of Fame in Oklahoma City Oklahoma. Its museum has a great art exhibit devoted to the American West. You would have loved it!

The museum has works by Frederic Remington who was born in Canton New York and Charles Russell from St. Louis. If you find yourself in Oklahoma City, visit the museum. Its address is 1700 NE. 63rd St. Oklahoma City OK. I hope you enjoy the postcard.

Sincerely
Julie

PUNCTUATION

Semicolons and Colons

❶ Here's the Idea

A semicolon marks a break in a sentence; it is stronger than a comma but not as strong as a period. A colon indicates that a list, a quotation, or some form of explanation follows.

Semicolons

▶ **Use a semicolon to join the parts of a compound sentence if no coordinating conjunction is used.**

The first recorded Olympics took place in 776 B.C. in Olympia, Greece **;** only one athletic event was held that year—a footrace of about 193 meters (210 yards).

▶ **Use a semicolon before a conjunctive adverb that joins the clauses of a compound sentence.** Conjunctive adverbs include *therefore, however, otherwise, consequently,* and *moreover.* These usually function as introductory words and need to be followed by commas.

The first 17 ancient Olympics featured only footraces and ended in one day **; however,** the program changed in the 18th Olympics, when wrestling and the pentathlon were added.

▶ **When commas occur within parts of a series, use semicolons to separate the parts.**

The first modern Olympics were held in Athens, Greece **;** the second in Paris, France **;** and the third in St. Louis, Missouri.

Colons

▶ **Use a colon to introduce a list of items.** Colons often follow words like *these* or *the following.*

The pentathlon included the following events **: discus throw, long jump, javelin throw, running, and wrestling.**

Never use a colon after a verb or a preposition.

The spectators watched 〰 wrestling, boxing, and chariot races.

▶ **Use a colon between two independent clauses when the second explains or summarizes the first.**

Before the games the athletes had to affirm their eligibility to compete **: they swore a solemn oath to Zeus.**

▶ **Use a colon to introduce a long or formal quotation.**

Before the athletes were allowed to begin their two-day march to Olympia, the judges gave a few words of caution**:** **"If you have practiced hard for Olympia and if you have not been lazy or done anything dishonorable, then go forward with confidence. But if you have not trained yourselves this way, then leave us and go where you choose."**

The following chart shows other uses of colons.

Uses of Colons	
Greetings of business letters	Dear Sir or Madam**:** Dear Ms. McDonough**:**
Times of day	12**:**00 A.M. 9**:**30 P.M.
References to some holy books	Psalms 23**:**7 Qur'an 75**:**22

❷ Practice and Apply

CONCEPT CHECK: Semicolons and Colons

Write each word that should be followed by punctuation, indicating whether the punctuation should be a semicolon or a colon. If a sentence is correct, write *Correct.*

The Olympics: A Heroic Tradition

1. The pentathlete was the most admired athlete in ancient Greece athletes in Athens and Sparta began their training at a young age.

2. Although the style and grace of an athlete were important, winning was more important athletes who took first place were regarded as heroes.

3. Historical records show that statues were built as a tribute to the winners however, these statues were destroyed.

4. Lists of Olympic winners were compiled by several writers Hippias of Elis, the Greek philosopher Aristotle, and the Roman historian Sextus Julius Africanus.

5. Today a first-place athlete gets a gold medal a second-place one, a silver medal and a third-place one, a bronze medal.

➡ **For a SELF-CHECK and more practice, see the EXERCISE BANK, p. 336.**

Quotation Marks

LESSON 5

❶ Here's the Idea

Quotation marks are used to indicate that a statement made by another person is being quoted word for word.

▶ **Use quotation marks at the beginning and at the end of a direct quotation.**

Bill **said,** "My favorite sport is baseball."

Quotation marks are not used with an indirect quotation—that is, a retelling of what a person said, thought, or wrote.

Bill **said that** his favorite sport is baseball.

▶ **Use single quotation marks around a quotation within a quotation.**

"President Franklin D. Roosevelt once said, 'Major league baseball has done as much as any one thing in this country to keep up the spirit of the people,'" stated Mr. Pennebaker.

> When both quotations end at the same place, include both single and double closing quotation marks.

Divided Quotations

Sometimes a direct quotation is divided into two or more parts by explanatory words (*he said, she exclaimed, they reported*). In such cases use quotation marks before and after each part of the quotation.

"The first baseball game between two organized teams," **Mr. Pennebaker explained,** "was in Hoboken, New Jersey, on June 19, 1846."

> Commas separate explanatory words from the quotation.

When the second part of a divided quotation is a new sentence, use a capital letter. If the sentence is not new, do not capitalize the second divided quotation.

"In 1845 Alexander Cartwright started the Knickerbocker Base Ball Club of New York," **Mr. Pennebaker told us.** "He is known as the father of organized baseball for his contribution."

Long Quotations

▶ **If one speaker's words continue for more than a paragraph, each paragraph should begin with a quotation mark. However, a closing quotation mark should not be used until the end of the entire quotation.**

Sonia said, " Who do you think has the record for the most home runs in a season? Is it Babe Ruth, Joe DiMaggio, Sammy Sosa, or Mark McGwire? ⎯ " Babe Ruth is my favorite. "

> No quotation mark at the end of first paragraph

Quotation Marks with Other Punctuation

Punctuation Guide	
Mark	**Inside or Outside Closing Quotation Mark?**
Period or comma	inside
	He told us, "The Cincinnati Red Stockings were the first professional baseball team."
Question mark or exclamation point	**inside if the quotation itself is a question or exclamation**
	"You know that baseball is considered the national pastime, don't you?" he asked.
	outside if the sentence containing the quoted material is a question or explanation
	Do you think anyone here knows the song "Take Me Out to the Ball Game"?
Colon or semicolon	outside
	Baseballs used from the mid-1800s until about 1920 were "dead"; when hit, they didn't travel as far as those used today.

PUNCTUATION

Dialogue

▶ Dialogue is conversation between two or more people. Begin a new paragraph each time the speaker changes, and use a separate set of quotation marks for each speaker's words.

LITERARY MODEL

"I'm playing outfield," she said. "I don't like the responsibility of having a base."

"Yeah, I can understand that," I said, though I couldn't. "There's a band in Dixford tomorrow night at nine. Want to go?"

—W. D. Wetherell, "The Bass, the River, and Sheila Mant"

Titles

▶ Use quotation marks around the titles of magazine articles, chapters, short stories, TV episodes, essays, short poems, and songs.

"One Throw" (SHORT STORY)

"Baseball and Softball: A Comparative Study" (ESSAY)

"Picking Dandelions in the Outfield" (POEM)

❷ Practice and Apply

A. CONCEPT CHECK: Quotation Marks

Write the following sentences, inserting quotation marks (and commas) where necessary. If a sentence is correct, write *Correct*.

Baseball Legends

1. Whoever wants to know the heart and mind of America one famous educator wrote had better learn baseball.
2. Most young Americans learn about this game, and they delight in stories about legendary players like Babe Ruth and Joe DiMaggio said my teacher, Mr. Richards.
3. Babe Ruth once daringly pointed to center field while at bat and then smashed the next ball over the center-field fence.
4. If I'd missed that homer after calling it Babe Ruth later told a sportswriter I'd have looked like an awful fool.

5. Another time Ruth was reported as saying All I can tell 'em is I pick a good one and sock it. I get back to the dugout and they ask me what it was I hit and I tell 'em I don't know except it looked good.
6. In 1941 Joltin' Joe DiMaggio hit safely in 56 consecutive games.
7. His nerves are steady as his bat the sportswriters declared.
8. During the 56 games of the streak, DiMaggio's batting average was .408.
9. Ernest Hemingway even mentioned him in the book *The Old Man and the Sea;* its main character says I would like to take the great DiMaggio fishing.
10. As long as baseball is the national pastime Mr. Richards exclaimed we will continue to hear about great baseball players who make history!

➡ For a SELF-CHECK and more practice, see the EXERCISE BANK, p. 337.

B. PROOFREADING: Adding Quotation Marks

On your paper, write the sentences that require quotation marks, inserting the needed punctuation.

PROFESSIONAL MODEL

I am one of the few people I know who hate sports. I can confess to having never watched the Super Bowl. Furthermore, it baffles me how anyone can remember which baseball teams are in the National League and which are in the American League. I do, however, enjoy humorous stories and quotations about baseball, particularly the remarks of Yogi Berra, the former New York Yankees catcher. Once a reporter asked Yogi, How did you like school when you were growing up, Yogi? Yogi replied, Closed. Another time Yogi commented, You can't think and hit at the same time. I also like humorous books about baseball, especially Joe Garagiola's *Baseball Is a Funny Game.* One Detroit Tigers pitcher is quoted as saying, All the fat guys watch me and say to their wives, See, there's a fat guy doing okay. Nothing, however, has made me want to go see a baseball game in person. If the people don't want to come out to the park, Yogi once observed, nobody's going to stop 'em.

Other Punctuation

❶ Here's the Idea

Other punctuation marks include hyphens, apostrophes, dashes, and parentheses. Like commas, semicolons, and colons, these punctuation marks help clarify your writing.

Hyphens

▶ **Use a hyphen if part of a word must be carried over from one line to the next.**

> Ancient stargazers were intrigued and fascinated by the move-
> ments of the planets and other heavenly bodies.

Only divide words of two or more syllables. Never divide one-syllable words like *growl* or *weight,* and do not leave a single letter at the end or beginning of a line. For instance, these divisions would be wrong: *e-lection, cloud-y.*

▶ **Use hyphens in compound numbers from twenty-one to ninety-nine.**

> eighty - eight constellations   twenty - five astronomers

▶ **Use hyphens in fractions.**

> one - third of the students   three - fourths of the course

▶ **Use hyphens in certain compound nouns.**

> cross - references   great - grandfather

▶ **Use a hyphen between words that function as a compound adjective before a noun.**

> The Milky Way is a much - studied galaxy.

Such a compound is not usually hyphenated when it follows the noun it modifies.

> The Milky Way galaxy has been much studied.

Do not use a hyphen between an adverb ending in *-ly* and the adjective it modifies.

> Over the years many people have conducted carefully timed observations of comets.

Use a hyphen after the prefixes *all-, ex-,* or *self-* (as in *all-around, ex-president,* and *self-employed*). If in doubt, use the dictionary to check hyphenation.

Apostrophes

▶ **Use apostrophes to form the possessive forms of nouns.**

   Singular noun + **'s**: student**'s**, instructor**'s**, writer**'s**

Use an apostrophe and *s* even if the singular noun ends in *s: Carlos's.*

   Plural noun + **'**: boys**'**, books**'**, Smiths**'**

Plural nouns that do not end in *s* take an apostrophe and *s: women's, children's.*

Add only an apostrophe to a classical name ending in *s: Jesus', Moses', Zeus'.*

▶ **To form the possessive of an indefinite pronoun, use an apostrophe and s.**

   everybody + **'s** = everybody**'s**
   someone + **'s** = someone**'s**

Do not use apostrophes in possessive personal pronouns: *hers, ours, yours, its, theirs.* Do not confuse the possessive form *its* with the contraction *it's* (*it is*).

   It**'s** fun to watch the space show in the planetarium.
   Compared with **its** tail, a comet's nucleus is extremely small.

▶ **Use an apostrophe and s to form the plural of a letter, a numeral, or a word referred to as a word.**

   ABC**'s**   two *n***'s**
   three 4**'s**   *yes***'s** and *no***'s**

▶ **Use an apostrophe to show the omission of numerals in a date.**

   the summer of **'**99 (the summer of 1999)

If it is not clear what century is intended, write out the entire year number.

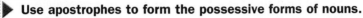

▶ **Use an apostrophe in a contraction.** In a contraction words are joined with one or more letters left out. An apostrophe shows where the letter or letters have been omitted.

they**'**re = they are   shouldn**'**t = should not

Dashes

▶ **Use dashes to signal an abrupt change of thought or set off an idea that breaks into the flow of a sentence.**

Stargazing and comet tracking **—two of the oldest pastimes—** are not just for astronomers.

▶ **Use a dash after a series to indicate that a summary statement follows.**

Halley, Encke, and Klemola **—** each of these people had a comet named after him.

 Do not overuse dashes, especially in formal writing. They can make your writing appear too casual. Also, do not use dashes to replace semicolons or periods.

Parentheses

▶ **Use parentheses to set off material that is loosely related to the sentence or paragraph in which it occurs.**

Ancient stargazers created the constellations **(such as Orion, the great hunter, and Leo, the lion)** by connecting the bright stars with imaginary lines.

If a complete sentence enclosed in parentheses stands alone, it is punctuated and capitalized like any other sentence.

Constellations were named for gods, people, animals, and objects. **(Actually, this is how we got the zodiac.)**

When a parenthetical sentence occurs within another sentence, it does not begin with a capital letter. An end mark is included only if the parenthetical sentence is a question or exclamation.

On clear, dark nights you can see up to 3,000 stars with the naked eye **(can you believe it?)**, but only a few comets are are bright enough to be seen with the naked eye.

CONCEPT CHECK: Other Punctuation

Proofread the following draft for punctuation errors. Write the underlined passages, inserting or deleting hyphens, apostrophes, dashes, and parentheses where necessary. If an underlined passage is correct, write *Correct*.

STUDENT MODEL

The Curse of Halley's Comet

For centuries, people believed that comets **(1)** <u>heavenly bodies that move in large elliptical orbits about the sun</u> were omens of catastrophe. Though the moon, the sun, and the stars were familiar, **(2)** <u>a comets characteristics</u> were unknown. To some people, a comet's tail resembled a woman's unbound hair **(3)** <u>a traditional sign of mourning</u>. Others thought the tail resembled a sword **(4)** <u>an omen of death and war</u>. Several historical documents point to massive chaos when a comet made **(5)** <u>it's appearance</u>. In 1066 **(6)** <u>Halleys comet</u> was first sighted in April and remained visible for two months **(7)** <u>long enough to cause both the English and the Normans great distress</u>. According to historians, the **(8)** <u>intensely-feared comet</u> was blamed for **(9)** <u>Englands' defeat in the Battle of Hastings</u>. Halley's return in 1456 created such a stir that people believed that the comet caused illness, a **(10)** <u>mysterious red-rain</u>, and the births of **(11)** <u>two headed animals</u>.

Although the physical structure of comets was clearly known by the 1900s, **(12)** <u>scientific observations—at the time—aroused new fears</u>. Astronomers at the **(13)** <u>University of Chicago's Yerkes Observatory</u> discovered a poisonous gas within the tail of Halley's comet. Within days, newspaper headlines warned people of the "danger." Before Halley's return in 1910, some people constructed **(14)** <u>gas-proof rooms</u>, while others purchased an assortment of gimmicks **(15)** <u>comet pills, inhalers, comet insurance, and conjure bags</u> to protect themselves against disaster. Finally, in 1986 (Halley's final appearance in the 20th century) some people had comet parties, while others thought that the comet would crash into the North Pole and end life.

➡ **For a SELF-CHECK and more practice, see the EXERCISE BANK, p. 338.**

PUNCTUATION

Ellipses and Italics

LESSON 7

❶ Here's the Idea

Ellipses indicate that material has been left out. **Italics** (represented by underlining in handwritten or typewritten material) are used to set off certain words, phrases, and titles.

Ellipses

▶ **Use an ellipsis (. . .) to indicate an omission of words or an idea that trails off.** If you use an ellipsis at the end of a sentence, make sure you include a period before it.

> **PROFESSIONAL MODEL**
>
> Although marathon runners are admired for their perseverance, they are also considered a bit insane. . . . The thought of the striking midday sun beaming its rays into our bodies at 97° is enough to make some of us sit in front of an icebox all day long. But what about those individuals who run . . . out of necessity?

 Do not omit words from a quoted passage if doing so changes the passage's meaning.

UNCLEAR: The article says, "The athlete would be in great shape . . . to run the marathon."

CLEAR: The article says, "The athlete would be in great shape—in about a year or so after rebuilding physical stamina—to run the marathon."

Italics

▶ **Use italics to set off letters referred to as letters and words referred to as words.**

Do you know where the word *marathon* originated?

Can you write a paragraph that contains no *e*'s?

▶ **Use italics to set off foreign words and phrases.**

au revoir   *ad infinitum*

Words and abbreviations that have become part of the English language, however, are not italicized: faux pas, gringo, etc., et al.

CHAPTER 11

▶ **Use italics to set off the titles of books, newspapers, magazines, plays, movies, television series, book-length poems, long musical compositions, and works of art.**

    Romeo and Juliet (PLAY)   *Road Rules* (TV SERIES)

❷ Practice and Apply

A. CONCEPT CHECK: Italics

Write these sentences, underlining words that should be italicized. Also, indicate which words, if any, are incorrectly italicized.

Marathon Tidbits

1. According to *The World Book Encyclopedia,* the word marathon refers to a footrace of about 26 miles (42 kilometers).
2. In Runner's World, Owen Anderson wrote that a person training for a marathon should have fun and enjoy the workout—the health benefits will inevitably follow.
3. You've probably heard of the *Boston Marathon,* but did you know that marathons are run in Chicago, New York, Los Angeles, and many other cities around the world?
4. In World-Class Marathoners, Nathan Aaseng wrote about Abebe Bikila, a first-time marathoner who shocked the world by running barefoot in the 1960 *Olympics.*
5. If you are looking for a list of marathon champions, you may want to read the ESPN Information Please Sports Almanac, which is published annually.

→ **For a SELF-CHECK and more practice, see the EXERCISE BANK, p. 339.**

B. REVISING: Using Ellipses

Write this passage, using ellipses to cut it to four lines.

PROFESSIONAL MODEL

    Hundreds of hours, hundreds of miles, and now I'm here, with hundreds, thousands of regular people like me. We are packed together on a downtown Los Angeles avenue, a throbbing swarm of gel soles, mesh shirts, and digital watches. An unspoken but persistent question hovers over most of the 19,000 racers: Will I make it?

        —Michael Konik, "Marathon Man," *Men's Fitness*

Real World Grammar

Business Letter

Business letters require complete clarity, since they often contain important dates, order numbers, addresses, and lists of items. When you write a business letter, always proofread your draft for punctuation errors that can lead to miscommunication and can delay a reply.

Hang Gliding
ADVENTURES

Your source for
hang gliding
information

1400 Green Street
San Francisco CA 94133
May 27 2001

> Insert commas in addresses and in the date.

Hang Gliding Adventures
2552 North Canal St.
San Francisco CA 94166

Dear Sir or Madam

> Use a colon after the salutation of a business letter.

About two weeks ago I called your 800 number and asked for some information about your training centers, particularly Hang Gliding Adventures I. The literature I received covered the basics lessons safety hang-gliding locations and equipment. I am now requesting additional information. Do you have a list of shops where I can find a beginners glider, or can I buy a used glider over the Internet

> Use a colon to introduce a list of items.

> Insert commas between items in a series.

Please call me at (415) 555-5512 between 3:00 P. M. and 5:00 P. M. with the information I requested. Thank you for your assistance.

> Insert an apostrophe in a possessive noun.

Sincerely
Erica Springfield

> Use an appropriate end mark.

> Insert a comma after the closing.

Proofread this letter for incorrect or missing commas, periods, colons, and parentheses. Rewrite the letter correctly.

3155 W Orchard St
Boulder CO, 80304
June 15 2001

Omega Corporation
4636 State Street
Seattle WA, 98107

Dear Sir or Madam

On April 20 I ordered pairs of your Omega 2000 running shoes Omega Silver Series aerobic shoes and Omega Gold Star in-line skates through your advertisement in *Runner's Guide.* The advertisement stated that if I purchased a pair of Omega 2000 serial #2345 and Omega Silver Series serial #2346 before May 29 I would receive a $40 refund. However your company failed to give me a refund when I received the bill.

I am enclosing a copy of the dated check for your records. Please send me my refund as soon as you clear up the misunderstanding

Sincerely

Sarah G Collins

Buy Direct and Save
Omega athletic shoes and in-line skates

Omega Corporation

$40 Rebate
When you purchase
2 pairs of shoes from
the Omega Series
SEE DETAILS BELOW.

PUNCTUATION

Mixed Review

A. Punctuation: Comma, Hyphen, Quotation Marks, End Marks For each numbered item, explain why the highlighted punctuation is used.

> **LITERARY MODEL**
>
> **(1)** "Perhaps , " said General Zaroff , "you were surprised that I recognized your name. You see, I read all books on hunting published in English, French, and Russian. I have but one passion in my life, Mr. Rainsford, and it is the hunt."
>
> **(2)** " You have some wonderful heads here, " said Rainsford as he ate a particularly well cooked filet mignon. " That Cape buffalo is the largest I ever saw . "
>
> "Oh, that fellow. Yes, he was a monster."
>
> **(3)** "Did he charge you?"
>
> "Hurled me against a tree," said the general. "Fractured my skull. But I got the brute."
>
> "I've always thought," said Rainsford, "that the Cape buffalo is the most dangerous of all big game."
>
> For a moment the general did not reply; he was smiling his curious **(4)** red-lipped smile. Then he said slowly: "No. You are wrong, sir. The Cape buffalo is not the most dangerous big game."
>
> —Richard Connell, **(5)** " The Most Dangerous Game "

Look at the letter you wrote for the **Write Away** on page 248 or another piece from your 🗂 **Working Portfolio.** Proofread the piece for punctuation errors.

B. Proofreading Write the underlined groups of words, inserting the correct punctuation.

How would you feel if you were trapped inside **(1)** a ring a bullring, to be precise with a ferocious bull that weighed 1,000 pounds **(2)** 450 kilograms or more? In countries such as **(3)** Spain Portugal Mexico and France, bullfighting is a traditional pastime. **(4)** The bullfighter called a matador is considered a national hero. The matador is accompanied by assistants called **(5)** banderilleros these assistants provoke the bull with a cape that is magenta on one side and yellow on the other. **(6)** Since the bull is colorblind it can only detect the movement of the cape. If the matador performs gracefully **(7)** actually, when he endangers himself enough to give the spectators a thrill the crowd will applaud and shout, **(8)** Ole! If the **(9)** matadors efforts have been moderately successful, the *presidente,* usually a local official, rewards him with one of the **(10)** bull's ears an exceptional performance merits two ears.

For each numbered item, choose the letter of the best revision.

How much do you think an <u>empty glass bottle</u> is <u>worth or, better yet,</u>
(1)   (2)
how much would you be willing to pay for an empty bottle? <u>The average</u>

<u>person might say, "Empty bottles have no value."</u> <u>However</u> to an antique-
(3)   (4)
bottle collector, a bottle can be worth hundreds, even thousands, of dollars.

Richard Rushton-Clem of <u>Lewisburg Pennsylvania</u> purchased an <u>unusual,</u>
(5)   (6)
<u>pickle bottle</u> (more commonly known as a pickle jar) for $3. <u>Clem—a former</u>
(7)
antique-shop owner, had an idea that the bottle was worth more than $3, but

he never imagined it was worth thousands of dollars. He decided to sell it

over the Internet to the highest bidder; the reserve price was set at $275.

<u>An interested buyer:</u> confirmed that the bottle was a rare <u>11-inch amber</u>
(8)
<u>Willington pickle bottle</u>. In the end, there were about 57 bids.
(9)
A Pennsylvania doctor purchased <u>Mr. Clems</u> $3 bottle for $44,100.
(10)

---

1. A. empty, glass bottle
   B. empty glass-bottle
   C. empty glass, bottle
   D. Correct as is

2. A. worth, or better yet
   B. worth or better yet,
   C. worth, or, better yet,
   D. Correct as is

3. A. The average person might say,
      "empty bottles have no value."
   B. The average person might say:
      empty bottles have no value.
   C. The average person might say,
      "Empty bottles have no value?"
   D. Correct as is

4. A. However—
   B. However:
   C. However,
   D. Correct as is

5. A. Lewisburg, Pennsylvania
   B. Lewisburg-Pennsylvania
   C. Lewisburg, Pennsylvania,
   D. Correct as is

6. A. unusual pickle bottle
   B. unusual-pickle bottle
   C. unusual pickle, bottle
   D. Correct as is

7. A. Clem,—a former
   B. Clem: a former
   C. Clem, a former
   D. Correct as is

8. A. An interested buyer,
   B. An interested buyer—
   C. An interested buyer
   D. Correct as is

9. A. "11 inch" amber Willington
      pickle bottle
   B. 11-inch amber, Willington
      pickle, bottle
   C. 11-inch, amber, Willington,
      pickle, bottle
   D. Correct as is

10. A. Mr. Clems'
    B. Mr. Clem's
    C. Mr. Clems's
    D. Correct as is

Student Help Desk

Punctuation at a Glance

Hyphenating Compound Adjectives

Join Us

Tips to Remember	
Always use a hyphen after the prefix *all, ex,* or *self.*	George is very **self-reliant.**
Never use a hyphen if each adjective could be used separately.	His performance showed a **trendy '90s** style.
Never use a hyphen when one of the words ends in *-ly.*	Sonia showed off her **lovely rare** watch.
Never hyphenate a compound containing the words *very* and *most.*	This is the **most anticipated** movie of the year.

Apostrophes
Little Marks That Make a Big Difference

Type of Word	Possessive
singular noun school, girl, Tess	school**'**s, girl's, Tess**'**s
plural noun ending in s teachers, cars, Joneses	teachers**'**, cars**'**, Joneses**'**
plural noun not ending in s children, women, people	children**'**s, women**'**s, people**'**s
indefinite pronoun everyone, anybody	everyone**'**s, anybody**'**s

Punctuating Titles

Names Up in Lights

Quotation Marks

Magazine article	"America's Pastime Returns in the Summer of '98"
Chapter title	Chapter 1, "Fast-Pitch Softball—No Speed Limits"
Short story	"One Throw"
Essay	"Baseball and Softball: A Comparative Study"
Short poem	"Picking Dandelions in the Outfield"
Song	"Take Me Out to the Ball Game"

Italics

Book title	*The Adventures of Huckleberry Finn*
Newspaper	*Chicago Sun-Times*
Magazine	*Newsweek*
Play	*A Midsummer Night's Dream*
Movie	*The Silence of the Lambs*
TV series	*The X-Files*
Work of art	*The Night Café*
Book-length poem	*Paradise Lost*
Long musical composition	*The Nutcracker Suite*

PUNCTUATION

The Bottom Line

Checklist for Punctuation

Have I . . .

____ ended every sentence with the appropriate end mark?

____ used commas to separate items in series?

____ used semicolons to separate independent clauses in compound sentences whose parts are not joined with conjunctions?

____ used a dictionary to verify hyphenated words?

____ used apostrophes in possessive nouns?

____ used parentheses to enclose material that is loosely related to what surrounds it?

____ used italics and quotation marks correctly to set off titles of books, magazine articles, stories, artworks, and songs?

Quick-Fix Editing Machine

You've worked hard on your assignment. Don't let misplaced commas, sentence fragments, and missing details lower your grade. Use this Quick-Fix Editing Guide to help you recognize grammatical errors and make your writing more precise.

① Sentence Fragments

What's the problem? Part of a sentence has been left out.
Why does it matter? A fragment doesn't convey a complete thought.
What should you do about it? Find out what is missing and add it.

What's the Problem?

Quick Fix

What's the Problem?	Quick Fix
A. A subject is missing. Disappeared into cyberspace.	**Add a subject.** **My homework** disappeared into cyberspace.
B. A verb is missing. Something strange on my disk.	**Add a verb.** Something strange **is** on my disk.
C. A helping verb is missing. My friends saying that I couldn't lose it.	**Add a helping verb.** My friends **were** saying that I couldn't lose it.
D. Both a subject and a verb are missing. Somewhere on the hard drive.	**Add a subject and a verb to make an independent clause.** **I'll** probably **find** it somewhere on the hard drive.
E. A subordinate clause is treated as if it were a sentence. Because I spent two hours on my homework.	**Combine the fragment with an independent clause.** **I'm frustrated** because I spent two hours on my homework. <div align="center">**OR**</div>**Delete the conjunction.** ~~Because~~ I spent two hours on my homework.

For more help, see Chapter 5, pp. 116–119.

QUICK FIX

② Run-On Sentences

What's the problem? Two or more sentences have been run together.

Why does it matter? A run-on sentence doesn't show where one idea ends and another begins.

What should you do about it? Find the best way to separate the ideas or to show the proper relationship between the two.

What's the Problem?

Quick Fix

A. The end mark separating two complete thoughts is missing.

I practice the violin every day the dog always howls.

Add an end mark and start a new sentence.

I practice the violin every day. **The** dog always howls.

B. Two sentences are separated only by a comma.

Singing dogs may be funny on TV, in real life they can drive you crazy.

Add a coordinating conjunction.

Singing dogs may be funny on TV, **but** in real life they can drive you crazy.

OR

Change the comma to a semicolon.

Singing dogs may be funny on TV**;** in real life they can drive you crazy.

OR

Replace the comma with an end mark and start a new sentence.

Singing dogs may be funny on TV. **In** real life they can drive you crazy.

OR

Make one of the independent clauses into a subordinate clause.

Although singing dogs may be funny on TV, in real life they can drive you crazy.

For more help, see Chapter 5, pp. 120–121.

3 Subject-Verb Agreement

What's the problem? A verb does not agree with its subject in number.

Why does it matter? Readers may regard your work as careless.

What should you do about it? Identify the subject and use a verb that matches it in number.

QUICK FIX

What's the Problem?

Quick Fix

What's the Problem?	Quick Fix
A. A verb agrees with the object of a preposition rather than with the subject. The animation of **cartoons are** fascinating.	Mentally block out the prepositional phrase and make the verb agree with the true subject. The **animation** ~~of cartoons~~ **is** fascinating.
B. A verb agrees with a word in a phrase that comes between the subject and the verb. I, as well as my **friends, are** the first in line for animated films.	Mentally block out the phrase and make the verb agree with the true subject. **I,** ~~as well as my friends,~~ **am** the first in line for animated films.
C. A verb doesn't agree with an indefinite-pronoun subject. **Each** of us **plan** to make cartoons our life.	Decide whether the pronoun is singular or plural and make the verb agree with it. **Each** of us **plans** to make cartoons our life.
D. A verb in a contraction doesn't agree with its subject. **It don't** seem like a waste of time to us.	Use a verb in a contraction that agrees with the subject. **It doesn't** seem like a waste of time to us.
E. A singular verb is used with a compound subject that contains *and*. **Celeste and Jono wants** to open a studio someday.	Use a plural verb. **Celeste and Jono want** to open a studio someday.

For more help, see Chapter 7, pp. 158–171.

What's the Problem?

Quick Fix

| **F.** A verb doesn't agree with the nearest part of a compound subject containing *or* or *nor*. | Use a verb that agrees with the subject closest to the verb. |

Neither my friends nor **my teacher think** animation is a boring topic.

Neither my friends nor **my teacher thinks** animation is a boring topic.

G. A verb doesn't agree with the true subject of a sentence beginning with *here* or *there*.

Mentally turn the sentence around so that the subject comes first, and make the verb agree with it.

There is many new techniques in animated films.

There **are** many new **techniques** in animated films.

H. A singular subject ending in *s, es, or ics* is mistaken for a plural.

Watch out for these nouns and use singular verbs with them.

Mathematics are useful in learning those techniques.

Mathematics is useful in learning those techniques.

News of the techniques **were featured** in several magazine articles.

News of the techniques **was featured** in several magazine articles.

I. A collective noun referring to a single unit is treated as plural (or one referring to individuals is treated as singular).

If the collective noun refers to a single unit, use a singular verb.

Our **group are** working on a storyboard.

Our **group is** working on a storyboard.

J. A period of time isn't treated as a single unit.

Use a singular verb whenever the subject refers to a period of time as a single unit.

Two weeks aren't enough time to learn how to draw!

Two weeks isn't enough time to learn how to draw!

For more help, see Chapter 7, pp. 158–171.

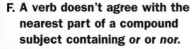

QUICK FIX

4 Pronoun Reference Problems

What's the problem? A pronoun does not agree in number or gender with its antecedent, or an antecedent is unclear.

Why does it matter? Lack of agreement or unclear antecedents can cause confusion.

What should you do about it? Find the antecedent and make the pronoun agree with it, or rewrite a sentence to make the antecedent clear.

What's the Problem?	Quick Fix
A. A pronoun doesn't agree with an indefinite-pronoun antecedent. **Each** of the team members cast **their** vote.	Decide whether the indefinite pronoun is singular or plural, and make the pronoun agree with it. **Each** of the team members cast **his or her** vote.
B. A pronoun doesn't agree with the nearest part in a compound subject joined by *nor* or *or*. Neither the doctor nor the **nurses** hurt **herself** when I dropped the tray of glasses.	Find the nearest simple subject and make the pronoun agree with it. Neither the doctor nor the **nurses** hurt **themselves** when I dropped the tray of glasses.
C. A pronoun doesn't have an antecedent. In the handbook **it** says to put safety first.	Rewrite the sentence to eliminate the pronoun. The handbook says to put safety first.
D. A pronoun's antecedent is vague or indefinite. I guess **they** knew I was coming.	Change the pronoun to a specific noun. I guess **the supervisor** knew I was coming.
E. A pronoun could refer to more than one noun. The **supervisor** and the **nurse** talked, and **she** assigned me to pillow duty.	Substitute a noun for the pronoun to make the reference specific. The supervisor and the nurse talked, and **the supervisor** assigned me to pillow duty.

For more help, see Chapter 8, pp. 190–198.

What's the problem? A pronoun is in the wrong case.

Why does it matter? Readers may regard your writing as sloppy and careless, especially if your writing is supposed to be formal.

What should you do about it? Identify how the pronoun is being used and replace it with the correct form.

What's the Problem?

Quick Fix

A. A pronoun that follows a linking verb is in the wrong case.

The funniest student in school is **him.**

Always use the nominative case after a linking verb.

The funniest student in school is **he.**

OR

Reword the sentence.

He is the funniest student in school.

B. A pronoun used as the object of a preposition is not in the objective case.

Geoff tries his jokes out on Marie and **I.**

Always use the objective case when a pronoun is the object of a preposition.

Geoff tries his jokes out on Marie and **me.**

C. The wrong case is used in a comparison.

Not even Drew Carey is funnier than **him.**

Complete the comparison and use the appropriate case.

Not even Drew Carey is funnier than **he (is).**

D. *Who* or *whom* is used incorrectly.

When we need a laugh, **who** do we call? Geoff!

Use *who* if the pronoun is a subject, *whom* if it is an object.

When we need a laugh, **whom** do we call? Geoff!

E. A pronoun followed by an appositive is in the wrong case.

Us students even laugh when Geoff is being serious.

Mentally eliminate the appositive to test for the correct case.

We ~~students~~ even laugh when Geoff is being serious.

For more help, see Chapter 8, pp. 181–189.

6 *Who* and *Whom*

What's the problem? A form of the pronoun *who* or *whoever* is used incorrectly.

Why does it matter? The correct use of *who, whom, whoever,* and *whomever* in formal situations gives the impression that the speaker or writer is careful and knowledgeable.

What should you do about it? Decide how the pronoun functions in the sentence to determine which form to use.

What's the Problem?

Quick Fix

A. *Whom* is incorrectly used as a subject.

Whom is making noise in the basement?

Use *who* as the subject of a sentence.

Who is making noise in the basement?

B. *Who* is incorrectly used as the object of a preposition.

With who will you go to check out the noise?

Use *whom* as the object of a preposition.

With whom will you go to check out the noise?

C. *Who* is incorrectly used as a direct object.

Who could I ask?

Use *whom* as a direct object.

Whom could I ask?

D. *Whomever* is incorrectly used as the subject of a sentence or a clause.

Whomever is in the basement, come out now!

Whomever is used only as an object. Use *whoever* as the subject of a clause.

Whoever is in the basement, come out now!

E. *Who's* is incorrectly used as the possessive form of *who*.

Who's house could be this scary?

Always use *whose* to show possession when the possessive form of *who* is needed.

Whose house could be this scary?

For more help, see Chapter 8, pp. 187–189.

⑦ Confusing Comparisons

What's the problem? The wrong form of a modifier is used when making a comparision.

Why does it matter? Incorrectly worded comparisons can be confusing and illogical.

What should you do about it? Use wording that makes the comparison clear.

What's the Problem?

Quick Fix

A. Both -er and more or -est and most are used in making a comparison.

Jamilla is **more luckier** than I.

I used to think I was the **most unluckiest** person on the planet.

Eliminate the double comparison.

Jamilla is ~~more~~ **luckier** than I.

I used to think I was the ~~most~~ **unluckiest** person on the planet.

B. The word other is missing in a comparison where it is logically needed.

I had more bad luck than any student at school.

Add the missing word.

I had more bad luck than any **other** student at school.

C. A superlative form is used where a comparative form is needed.

I'm not sure who has the worst luck— Lorenzo or I.

When comparing two things, always use the comparative form.

My luck never improves; it gets **worse** than Lorenzo's every day.

D. A comparative form is used where a superlative form is needed.

Of the five kids in my family, I am the **more** unfortunate.

When comparing more than two things, use the superlative form.

Of the five kids in our family, I am the **most** unfortunate.

For more help, see Chapter 9, pp. 217–221.

QUICK FIX

8 Verb Forms and Tenses

What's the problem? The wrong form or tense of a verb is used.

Why does it matter? Readers may regard your work as careless or confusing.

What should you do about it? Replace the incorrect verb with the correct form or tense.

What's the Problem?

Quick Fix

What's the Problem?	Quick Fix
A. The wrong form of a verb is used with a helping verb. A thief in the park **had stole** a woman's purse.	**Always use a past participle with a helping verb.** A thief in the park **had stolen** a woman's purse.
B. A helping verb is missing. Agent Lance **seen** the incident happen.	**Add a helping verb.** Agent Lance **had** seen the incident happen.
C. An irregular verb form is spelled incorrectly. Unfortunately, Lance had not **wore** his glasses.	**Look up the correct spelling and use it.** Unfortunately, Lance had not **worn** his glasses.
D. A past participle is used incorrectly. The thief got away long before Lance **seen** him.	**To show the past, use the past form of a verb.** The thief got away long before Lance **saw** him. **OR** **Change the verb to the past perfect form by adding a helping verb.** The thief got away long before Lance **had seen** him.
E. Different tenses are used in the same sentence without a valid reason. Lance **lost** his chance because he **forgets** his glasses.	**Use the same tense throughout the sentence.** Lance **lost** his chance because he **forgot** his glasses.

For more help, see Chapter 6, pp. 134–139.

Misplaced and Dangling Modifiers

What's the problem? A modifying word or phrase is in the wrong place, or it doesn't modify any other word in the sentence.

Why does it matter? The sentence can be confusing or unintentionally funny.

What should you do about it? Move the modifying word or phrase closer to the word it modifies or add a word for it to modify.

What's the Problem?

What's the Problem?	Quick Fix
A. The adverb *even* or *only* is not placed close to the word it modifies. Bats **only** frighten me. I'm afraid of **even** things that look like bats.	**Move the adverb to make your meaning clear.** **Only** bats frighten me. I'm **even** afraid of things that look like bats. **OR** Bats frighten **only** me. Bats don't scare my friends.
B. A prepositional phrase is too far from the word it modifies. During our freshman year **in Kentucky** we went to one of the huge **caves.**	**Move the prepositional phrase closer to the word it modifies.** During our freshman year we went to one of the huge **caves in Kentucky.**
C. A participial phrase is too far from the word it modifies. **Flying near the ceiling,** our class watched the bats.	**Move the participial phrase closer to the word it modifies.** Our class watched the bats **flying near the ceiling.**
D. A participial phrase does not relate to anything in the sentence. **Peering through binoculars,** hundreds of bats were visible.	**Reword the sentence by adding a word for the participial phrase to refer to.** **Peering through binoculars, we** observed hundreds of bats.

For more help, see Chapter 3, pp. 78–79, and Chapter 9, p. 211.

10 Missing or Misplaced Commas

What's the problem? Commas are missing or are used incorrectly.

Why does it matter? Incorrect use of commas can make sentences hard to follow.

What should you do about it? Determine where commas are needed and add or omit them wherever necessary.

What's the Problem?

Quick Fix

A. A comma is missing before the conjunction in a series.

Too many TV talk shows are crude, offensive and depressing.

Add a comma.

Too many TV talk shows are crude, offensive, and depressing.

B. A comma is incorrectly placed after a closing quotation mark.

"These shows are simply a means to show the depressing side of life", noted one TV critic.

Always put a comma before a closing quotation mark.

"These shows are simply a means to show the depressing side of life," noted one TV critic.

C. A comma is missing after an introductory phrase or clause.

Although these shows are about people's problems the problems are rarely solved.

Find the end of the phrase or clause, and add a comma.

Although these shows are about people's problems, the problems are rarely solved.

D. Commas are missing around a nonessential phrase or clause.

Other talk shows which feature entertainers are simply a means to promote various entertainment products.

Add commas to set off the nonessential phrase or clause.

Other talk shows, which feature entertainers, are simply a means to promote various entertainment products.

E. A comma is missing from a compound sentence.

Talk shows waste my time and most of them disgust me.

Add a comma before the coordinating conjunction.

Talk shows waste my time, and most of them disgust me.

For more help, see Chapter 11, pp. 252–257.

⑪ Using Active and Passive Voice

What's the problem? The use of a verb in the passive voice makes a sentence weak.

Why does it matter? Sentences written in the active voice are more interesting to readers than are sentences with verbs in the passive voice.

What should you do about it? Rewrite sentences, and use the active rather than the passive voice.

What's the Problem?

What's the Problem?	Quick Fix
A. The passive voice makes a sentence dull. Twisters **are tracked** and **chased** by tornado watchers.	Use the active voice to revise the sentence. Tornado watchers **track** and **chase** twisters.
B. The passive voice takes the emphasis away from the people performing an action. Storm sightings **are** immediately **plotted** on maps by these eager followers.	Change the voice from passive to active. These eager followers immediately **plot** storm sightings on maps.
C. The passive voice makes a sentence wordy. The unpredictable tornado **has been followed** closely by storm chasers.	Change the voice from passive to active. Storm chasers **followed** the unpredictable tornado closely.

For more help, see Chapter 6, pp. 144–145

Note: The passive voice is effective in the following situations:

to emphasize the receiver of an action or the action itself

This site for the next vacation **was chosen** to avoid tornadoes.

to make a statement about an action whose performer does not have to be specified or is unknown

No tornadoes **have been spotted** in this area since 1995.

12 Improving Weak Sentences

What's the problem? A sentence repeats ideas or contains too many ideas.

Why does it matter? Empty or overloaded sentences can bore readers and weaken the message.

What should you do about it? Make sure that every sentence contains a substantial, clearly focused idea.

What's the Problem?

A. An idea is repeated.

Elizabeth enjoys the best of two worlds because she is bilingual **and speaks two languages fluently.**

B. A single sentence contains too many weakly linked ideas.

In Montreal, Canadians speak French and English, and Elizabeth's home was in Montreal, and Elizabeth learned both languages, so that she spoke both fluently when her family moved to the United States five years ago.

C. Too much information about a topic is crammed into one sentence.

The official language spoken in Montreal is still controversial because many French people settled there, although Canada was once controlled by the British, so some people want French to be Quebec's official language, and some want English.

Quick Fix

Eliminate the repeated idea.

Elizabeth enjoys the best of two worlds because she is bilingual. ~~and speaks two languages fluently.~~

Divide the sentence into two or more sentences while using subordinate clauses to show relationships between ideas.

In Montreal, where Elizabeth was born, both French and English are spoken. When her family moved to the United States five years ago, Elizabeth spoke both languages fluently.

Divide the sentence into two or more sentences, and use subordinate clauses to show relationships between ideas.

Although Canada was once controlled by the British, many French people settled in Montreal. A controversy continues about whether French or English should be the official language of Quebec.

13 Avoiding Wordiness

What's the problem? A sentence contains unnecessary words.

Why does it matter? The meaning of wordy sentences can be unclear to readers.

What should you do about it? Use concise terms and eliminate extra words.

What's the Problem?

What's the Problem?	**Quick Fix**
A. A single idea is unnecessarily expressed in two ways. At 7:00 A.M. **in the morning**, we were waiting at the cold, drafty bus stop.	**Delete the unnecessary words.** At 7:00 A.M. ~~in the morning~~, we were waiting at the cold, drafty bus stop.
B. A sentence contains words that do not add to its meaning. **What I mean to say is that** the four of us were desperately trying to keep warm.	**Delete the unnecessary words.** ~~What I mean to say is that~~ The four of us were desperately trying to keep warm.
C. A simple idea is expressed in too many words. The bus was late **on account of the fact that** it had a flat tire.	**Simplify the expression.** The bus was late **because** it had a flat tire.
D. A clause is used when a phrase would do. The bus driver, **who is** a ten-year veteran, arrived a half-hour late with a brand-new tire and cups of hot cocoa.	**Reduce the clause to a phrase.** The bus driver, ~~who is~~ a ten-year veteran, arrived a half-hour late with a brand-new tire and cups of hot cocoa.

QUICK FIX

14 Varying Sentence Beginnings

What's the problem? Too many sentences begin the same way.

Why does it matter? Lack of variety in sentence beginnings makes writing dull and choppy.

What should you do about it? Reword some sentences so that they begin with prepositional phrases, verbal phrases, or subordinate clauses.

What's the Problem?

Too many sentences in a paragraph start with the same word.

My little sister loves attention. She charms the adults. She flashes her toothless smile. She blows bubbles, and they think she's darling.

My older brother also loves attention. He entertains his friends. He does tricks. He does pratfalls, and they think he's hilarious.

My cousin is rather quiet. She stays in her room for hours. She writes poetry there. She lives in our house, but we sometimes forget she exists.

Quick Fix

Start a sentence with a prepositional phrase.

My little sister loves attention. **With her toothless smile,** she charms the adults. She blows bubbles, and they think she's darling.

OR

Start a sentence with a verbal phrase.

My older brother also loves attention. **Entertaining his friends with tricks and pratfalls is a favorite activity because they think he's hilarious.**

OR

Start a sentence with a subordinate clause.

My cousin is rather quiet. **When she writes poetry, she stays in her room for hours.** We sometimes forget that she lives in our house.

For more help, see Chapter 3, pp. 66–77 and Chapter 4, pp. 92–100.

QUICK FIX

Varying Sentence Structure

What's the problem? A piece of writing contains too many simple sentences.

Why does it matter? Similarity in sentence structure makes writing dull and lifeless.

What should you do about it? Combine or reword sentences to create different structures.

What's the Problem?

The use of too many simple sentences leads to dull or choppy writing.

Members of the school band set a record last Saturday. They raised a thousand dollars. The money was for charity.

They held a "playathon." It was a musical marathon. It lasted 12 hours.

The marathon came to an end. The band members collapsed on the gym floor. The volunteers handed out lip balm, bandages, and refreshments.

Quick Fix

Combine the sentences to form a compound sentence.

Members of the school band set a record last Saturday**, and** they raised a thousand dollars ~~The money was~~ for charity.

OR

Combine the sentences to form a complex sentence.

They held a "playathon," a musical marathon, **that lasted 12 hours.**

OR

Combine the sentences to form a compound-complex sentence.

When the marathon came to an end, the band members collapsed on the gym floor**, and** volunteers handed out lip balm, bandages, and refreshments.

16 Adding Supporting Details

What's the problem? Unfamiliar terms aren't defined, and claims aren't supported.

Why does it matter? Undefined terms and unsupported claims weaken an explanation or persuasive writing.

What should you do about it? Add supporting information to clarify statements and reasons.

QUICK FIX

What's the Problem?

Quick Fix

A. A key term is not defined.

As more people use e-mail, the problem of **UCE** grows.

Define the term.

As more people use e-mail, the problem of UCE **(unsolicited commercial e-mail)** grows.

B. No reason is given for an opinion.

The flood of electronic junk mail is bad.

Add a reason.

The flood of electronic junk mail is bad **because it slows down the e-mail system.**

C. No supporting facts are given.

Consumers must be careful.

Add supporting facts.

The Federal Trade Commission reports that a lot of the junk mail is fraudulent; therefore, consumers must be careful.

D. No examples are given.

Consumers should arm themselves with information.

Add examples.

Consumers should arm themselves with information, **such as the tips from the "Internet Fraud Watch" Web site.**

17 Avoiding Clichés and Slang

What's the problem? A piece of formal writing contains clichés or slang expressions.

Why does it matter? Clichés do not convey fresh images to readers. Slang is inappropriate in formal writing.

What should you do about it? Reword sentences to replace the clichés and slang with clear, fresh expressions.

What's the Problem?

Quick Fix

A. A sentence contains a cliché.

After a morning of packing and stacking boxes of goods for the hurricane victims, the volunteers **were so hungry they could have eaten a horse.**

Eliminate the cliché and use a fresh description or explanation.

After a morning of packing and stacking boxes of goods for the hurricane victims, the volunteers **swooped down on the donated lunches like ravenous vultures.**

B. A sentence contains inappropriate slang.

Everyone agreed that working for the hurricane relief effort was **way cool.**

Replace the slang with more appropriate language.

Everyone agreed that working for the hurricane relief effort was **a rewarding and uplifting experience.**

QUICK FIX

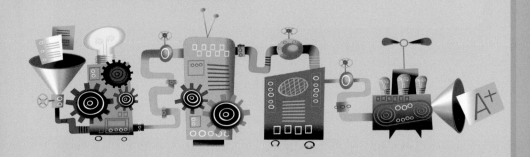

18 Using Precise Words

What's the problem? Nouns, modifiers, or verbs are not precise.

Why does it matter? Writers who use vague or general words do not engage their readers' interest.

What should you do about it? Replace general words with precise and vivid ones.

QUICK FIX

What's the Problem?

Quick Fix

A. Nouns are too general.

The **group** unloaded the **equipment** and marched into the **building.**

Use specific nouns.

The **four members of the Kingpins** unloaded their **bowling bags and uniforms** and marched into the **Shady Lanes Bowling Alley.**

B. Modifiers are too general.

Today they would be facing their **biggest** opponent, the Splits. "We're going to beat the Splits," Ivan said.

Use more precise or vivid adjectives and adverbs.

In a few hours, they would be facing their **fiercest and most feared** opponent, the Splits.

C. A sentence tells about what happens rather than shows it.

The Kingpins **were** tense as they **headed** for lane 21. "We're **going** to beat the Splits," Ivan said.

   "**Let's** warm up," Frank **replied.**

Use precise verbs and modifiers to describe the actions.

Ivan, the team captain, **scanned** the lane numbers. "Well, today's the day we'll **destroy** the Splits' winning streak," he said, his voice **quivering unconvincingly.**

   Frank **lurched** forward. "Let's just find lane 21 and do our warm-ups," he **snapped.**

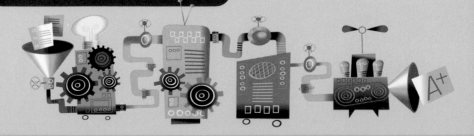

19 Using Figurative Language

What's the problem? A piece of writing is lifeless or unimaginative.

Why does it matter? Lifeless writing bores readers because it doesn't help them form mental pictures of what is being described.

What should you do about it? Add figures of speech to make the writing lively and to create pictures in readers' minds. Do not, however, combine figures of speech that have no logical connection.

What's the Problem?

A. A description is dull and lifeless.

The first Sunday dinner I ever prepared was a failure. Aunt Lydia inspected each forkful.

OR

I couldn't tell if Uncle Lou liked the dinner.

B. Figures of speech that have no logical connection have been used together.

However, my brother, **always as hungry as a great white shark,** was **a human steam shovel,** scooping up great mounds of food and dumping them in his mouth.

Quick Fix

Add a simile.

The first Sunday dinner I ever prepared was a failure. Aunt Lydia inspected each forkful **like a picky shopper examining damaged goods.**

OR

Rewrite the sentence, adding a metaphor.

Uncle Lou was **a statue at our dinner table.** He ate his meal stiffly and silently but never revealed his thoughts.

Delete one of the figures of speech.

However, my brother, ~~always as hungry as a great white shark,~~ was **a human steam shovel,** scooping up great mounds of food and dumping them in his mouth.

20 Paragraphing

What's the problem? A paragraph contains too many ideas.

Why does it matter? A long paragraph doesn't help to signal new ideas and discourages readers from continuing.

What should you do about it? Break the paragraph into smaller paragraphs, each focusing on one main idea. Start a new paragraph whenever the speaker, setting, or focus changes.

What's the Problem?

A. Too many ideas are contained in one paragraph.

Every morning the towering figure of Principal Douglas Mulder stands guard in the hallway. His booming voice has stopped many mischief-makers in their tracks. Few students would guess that Principal Mulder has a hobby that contrasts with his ex-Marine image. Mulder has always loved creating figurines out of glass. Back in his office, Principal Mulder shows off his collection of glass figurines to a new substitute teacher, Mr. Kravitz. Many have admired them, but few knew their origin. "Mr. Mulder, these are impressive!" "I've loved glass-blowing ever since my grandmother first taught me the craft."

Quick Fix

Every morning the towering figure of Principal Douglas Mulder stands guard in the hallway. His booming voice has stopped many mischief-makers in their tracks.

Start a new paragraph to introduce a new idea.

Few students would guess that Principal Mulder has a hobby that contrasts with his ex-Marine image. Mulder has always loved creating figurines out of glass.

Start a new paragraph to change the setting or place.

Back in his office, Principal Mulder shows off his collection of glass figurines to a new substitute teacher, Mr. Kravitz. Many have admired them, but few knew their origin.

Start a new paragraph whenever the speaker changes.

"Mr. Mulder, these are impressive!"

"I've loved glass-blowing ever since my grandmother first taught me the craft."

What's the Problem?

B. An essay is treated as one long paragraph.

Have you ever watched a movie with great special effects and wondered, How did they do that? Many people might be surprised to learn that special efffects involve just a few basic techniques. Some special effects rely on the use of models and miniatures. The shark in *Jaws,* for example, was really depicted by three different mechanical models designed to be used in different scenes. Some of the most complex special effects involve a process called composite photography. For instance, the cartoon characters' actions in the film *Who Framed Roger Rabbit?* were drawn and photographed on one piece of film; the live actors' movements were photographed on another. The two pieces of film were then combined so that the cartoon characters and the humans looked as if they were on screen together. The next time you watch a movie, you won't have to ask how they did that. You'll already know.

Quick Fix

Have you ever watched a movie with great special effects and wondered, How did they do that? Many people might be surprised to learn that special efffects involve just a few basic techniques.

Start a new paragraph to introduce the first main idea.

Some special effects rely on the use of models and miniatures. The shark in *Jaws*, for example, was really depicted by three different mechanical models designed to be used in different scenes.

Start a new paragraph to introduce another main idea.

Some of the most complex special effects involve a process called composite photography. For instance, the cartoon characters' actions in the film *Who Framed Roger Rabbit?* were drawn and photographed on one piece of film; the live actors' movements were photographed on another. The two pieces of film were then combined so that the cartoon characters and the humans looked as if they were on screen together.

Start a new paragraph to give the conclusion.

The next time you watch a movie, you won't have to ask how they did that. You'll already know.

QUICK FIX

Student Resources

Exercise Bank

① The Parts of Speech

1. Nouns (links to exercise A, p. 8)

➡ **1.** *Rock and Roll Hall of Fame:* proper, concrete, singular;
Cleveland: proper, concrete, singular; *visitors:* common,
concrete, plural; *world:* common, concrete, singular

3. *building:* common, concrete, singular; *I. M. Pei:* proper,
concrete, singular; *architect:* common, concrete, singular;
designs: common, concrete, plural

Write each noun. Identify it as common or proper, concrete or
abstract, singular or plural.

1. Like other forms of jazz, swing allows musicians the freedom to
   improvise.
2. Bandleaders like Glenn Miller, Artie Shaw, and Duke Ellington
   popularized the sound.
3. The popular bands that played this music were known as "big
   bands" because they had many musicians.
4. Today, young people have rediscovered the music and dances
   of swing.
5. They are doing the lindy hop, a popular swing dance named
   after Charles Lindbergh, the famous aviator.

2. Personal and Possessive Pronouns (links to exercise A, p. 10)

➡ **1.** *them:* personal   **2.** *he:* personal; *his:* possessive

Write each pronoun and tell whether it is personal or possessive.

1. *La Bohème,* an opera, is loved for its unforgettable characters and
   their romantic lives.
2. The opera focuses on Rodolfo, a poor poet, and Mimì, the woman
   who loves him.
3. When Rodolfo learns Mimì is dying, he can do nothing to help
   her because of his own poverty.
4. They are friends with the other main characters—Marcello, a
   struggling painter, and Musetta, his fickle sweetheart.
5. Mimì dies in the final scene, but only after she and Rodolfo
   have declared their love.

3. Other Kinds of Pronouns (links to exercise A, p. 13)

➜ **2.** *that:* experience **3.** *Someone:* none

Write each pronoun and identify its antecedent, if it has one.

1. Anyone in the market for a violin made by Antonio Stradivari can expect to pay close to a million dollars.
2. Stradivari, who lived from 1644 to 1737, was one of the greatest violinmakers in the history of music.
3. What makes a Stradivarius violin worth a million dollars?
4. Each of the instruments produces a sound unequaled even by those manufactured today.
5. Music lovers or musicians who can afford the price should treat themselves to the finest instrument money can buy.

4. Verbs (links to exercise on p. 16)

➜ **2.** *might scare:* action, *is:* linking

Write each verb or verb phrase and identify it as an action or a linking verb. Underline any auxiliary verbs.

1. All sounds are simply vibrations.
2. Place your hand on your throat as you speak.
3. Can you feel the vibrations?
4. Vibrations travel through the air as invisible sound waves.
5. When the sound waves are a certain frequency, they vibrate the eardrum and the bones in your ear.
6. Nerve endings in your inner ear sense the vibrations, which are sent to your brain as electrical signals.
7. Scientists measure the loudness of sounds in decibels.
8. The units were named in honor of Alexander Graham Bell, who was the inventor of many communication devices.
9. The noise level in a school cafeteria might be rated at about 80 decibels, which sounds almost painful.
10. The loudest rock concerts can produce sound of more than a hundred decibels, which can be harmful to your ears.

5. Adjectives (links to exercise A, p. 18)

→ **1.** *major:* trend
2. *Japanese:* invention

Write each adjective that is not an article in these sentences, along with the word it modifies.

1. For many years, Ravi Shankar has played the sitar.
2. The sitar, a musical instrument with strings, is used to play Indian music.
3. Since 1995 Shankar's talented daughter, Anoushka, has been attracting worldwide attention.
4. She made her professional debut in India at the age of 13 and has since performed in many countries.
5. In 1998, the British Parliament honored Anoushka with a medal for her outstanding contributions to Asian arts.

6. Adverbs (links to exercise A, p. 21)

→ **2.** often, late   **4.** terribly

For each sentence below, write each adverb.

1. For some rock 'n' roll fans, February 3, 1959, will always be "the day the music died."
2. On that particularly stormy day, Buddy Holly and Ritchie Valens died tragically in a plane crash.
3. Valens and Holly had extremely popular rock 'n' roll hits, and they were traveling together on a bus for a concert tour.
4. They were due next in Fargo, North Dakota, and Holly decided to hire a small plane instead.
5. Valens had originally planned not to be on the fatal flight, but, unluckily, he won a seat from another musician in a coin toss.

7. Prepositions (links to exercise A, p. 25)

→ **1.** of(music)   **2.** to its(birth)

For each sentence below, write each prepositional phrase and underline the preposition. Then circle the object of the preposition.

1. Rock 'n' roll got its start in the 1950s and captured fans when it was played on the radio.
2. A few disc jockeys at radio stations across the country began playing rhythm and blues and rock 'n' roll.
3. Rhythm and blues, created and performed by African Americans, was known throughout the South.

4. Without this style of music, rock 'n' roll might never have existed in the form we know today.
5. Chuck Berry, Little Richard, Bo Diddley, and many other early rock 'n' roll stars got their start in rhythm and blues.

8. Conjunctions (links to exercise A, p. 28)

➡ **1.** when, and   **4.** but

For each sentence below, write the conjunctions.

1. In the late 1800s and early 1900s, songwriters had neither radio nor TV to help them sell their songs.
2. In those days, composers and songwriters worked full-time for music publishers.
3. After a song was published as sheet music, stores sold copies to the public.
4. A song's popularity was judged both by how many copies of sheet music it sold and by how much it was sung in theaters and elsewhere.
5. When we talk about hit songs today, we are referring not to the number of copies of sheet music sold but to the number of CDs or cassettes purchased.

9. Interjections (links to exercise on p. 29)

➡ **1.** Great!

Choose the better interjection in each sentence.

1. (Say,/Ouch,) which kind of music do you think cats prefer—classical or disco?
2. (Yuk!/Wow!) How could anyone tell which music they like?
3. (Alas,/Well,) a Japanese researcher measured some cats' heartbeats while the animals listened to different kinds of music.
4. Just tell me the result, (OK?/aha!)
5. (Hey,/Anyway,) the cats preferred soothing music, like classical and New Age, to loud music, like disco or rock.

2 The Sentence and Its Parts

1. Simple Subjects and Predicates (links to exercise A, p. 39)

➡ **1.** Hurricane Andrew, struck   **2.** storm, destroyed

Write the simple subject and simple predicate of each sentence.

1. Lighter-than-air gas lifts airships, or dirigibles, into the air.
2. These aircraft differ from balloons in one important way.
3. Powerful engines move these "ships" through the air.
4. People called large, rigid airships "zeppelins," after their inventor, Count Ferdinand von Zeppelin.
5. This German engineer had designed several zeppelins in the early 1900s.
6. Many passengers traveled overseas on airships before the age of the airplane.
7. Several tragedies ended airship passenger service.
8. On May 6, 1937, the *Hindenburg* exploded in New Jersey.
9. The terrible accident killed 35 of the 97 people aboard.
10. The event remains one of the most famous air disasters of all time.

2. Complete Subjects and Predicates (links to exercise A, p. 42)

➡ **3.** The special effects crew
   5. The real challenge

Write the complete subject and complete predicate of each sentence.

1. Socialite Molly Brown showed remarkable courage at the scene of the *Titanic* tragedy.
2. The sailor in charge of the lifeboat turned out to be unfit for the job.
3. The outspoken and courageous Brown supposedly ordered everyone to start rowing or bailing water.
4. This vigorous work kept the women and children alive in the frigid night air.
5. This courageous act earned Brown the nickname "the unsinkable Mrs. Brown."

3. Compound Subjects and Verbs (links to exercise A, p. 44)

→ 1. <u>Children</u> and <u>adults</u>
   2. <u>signals</u> and <u>triggers</u>

Write the compound parts in each sentence below. Underline the compound subjects once and the compound verbs twice.

1. Matthew Henson and Robert E. Peary reached the North Pole on April 6, 1909.
2. Earlier, Peary had traveled to and explored the polar regions near Greenland.
3. In the 1890s Peary met and hired Henson, an African American, as his personal assistant.
4. Henson organized and went on several of Peary's expeditions.
5. Henson and four Inuit men made it to the North Pole with Peary.
6. The weather and terrain almost defeated the explorers.
7. The resourceful Henson had studied and learned the Inuit language.
8. Both fame and controversy surrounded Peary on his return.
9. Eventually, experts and fellow explorers acknowledged Peary's discovery of the North Pole.
10. Though never as famous as Peary, Henson deserved and received recognition for his role in the expedition.

4. Kinds of Sentences (links to exercise A, p. 46)

→ 1. interrogative   2. declarative

Identify each of the following sentences as declarative, imperative, interrogative, or exclamatory.

1. Wildlife photographer Jim Brandenburg followed a pack of arctic wolves for three summers.
2. Have you ever seen pictures of these beautiful animals?
3. Notice their large ears and sharp eyes.
4. A wolf's sense of smell is thousands of times keener than ours!
5. How did Brandenburg get along with the wolves?
6. He was careful to learn and respect their code of behavior.
7. Did the wolves accept the stranger in their midst?
8. They even seemed sad when he left!
9. Locate Ellesmere Island on a map or globe.
10. This island is where Brandenburg lived as the lone human in the wolves' territory.

5. Subjects in Unusual Positions (links to exercise A, p. 49)

➡ **1.** ships, were   **2.** storm, sprang

On a separate sheet of paper, write the simple subject and the verb of each sentence below. Be sure to include all parts of each verb phrase.

1. There is amazing biodiversity within the Amazon rain forest.
2. Does the forest really cover about a third of South America?
3. In this lush environment live countless species.
4. Consider the different layers of the forest.
5. From the top layer, or upper canopy, come the cries of parrots and of the forest monkeys.
6. Below the canopy are slender trees resembling poles.
7. Is the bottom level called the forest floor?
8. In this zone reside many grazing mammals.
9. Think about the importance of the Amazon rain forest.
10. There still exist many undiscovered species in its midst.

6. Subject Complements (links to exercise A, p. 51)

➡ **1.** mountain, PN
     2. risky, PA

On a sheet of paper, write each subject complement and identify it as a predicate adjective (PA) or a predicate nominative (PN).

1. Kentucky's Mammoth–Flint Ridge cave system is a popular tourist site.
2. This network of caves is the world's longest.
3. One of California's fascinating sites is Death Valley.
4. To some, the valley looks desolate and lifeless.
5. However, it has become a tourist magnet thanks to its warm climate.

7. Objects of Verbs (links to exercise A, p. 53)

➡ **1.** height, DO
     2. Mount Everest, IO; name, DO

Each sentence below contains at least one complement. Write each complement and identify it as a direct object (DO) or an indirect object (IO).

1. Caves fascinate many people.
2. Scientists known as speleologists study these natural formations.
3. Amateur spelunkers explore caves as a hobby.
4. The underground passages offer scientists glimpses of the earth's interior.

5. The bizarre landscapes give spelunkers a special thrill.
6. Every year, thousands of tourists visit these underground worlds.
7. Guides show visitors the spectacular limestone pillars.
8. Electric lights illuminate the underground chambers.
9. The lights give the caves a dramatic air.
10. Sunlight never enters a cave's eerie interior.

③ Using Phrases

1. Prepositional Phrases (links to exercise A, p. 68)

➡ **1.** of outdoor competition, type   **2.** in this sport, participate

Write each prepositional phrase, along with the word or words it modifies.

1. Orienteers are people who compete in woods or across open country on foot.
2. Checkpoints are marked along the course with colored flags.
3. The winner of the contest is the person who reaches all the checkpoints in the fastest time.
4. People without any experience can enjoy orienteering.
5. If anyone is lost for three hours or more, rescue teams start searching.

2. Appositives and Appositive Phrases (links to exercise A, p. 70)

➡ **1.** another championship sprinter, Wilma Rudolph
   2. polio, disease

Write the appositives and appositive phrases in these sentences, along with the words they rename or identify.

1. The sprinter Wilma Rudolph became the first American woman to win three gold medals in a single Olympics.
2. Rudolph grew up in a large family in Tennessee, the Volunteer State.
3. Polio, a viral illness, left the young Rudolph unable to walk.
4. She had also suffered from the illnesses pneumonia and scarlet fever.
5. The Rudolphs, a loving and determined family, helped Wilma overcome her disability.
6. At Tennessee State University, Rudolph joined the women's track team, the Tigerbelles.
7. Her hometown, Clarksville, honored Rudolph with a big parade after the 1960 Olympic Games.

8. During her track career, Rudolph tied and set world records in the short-distance races—the 100-meter and 200-meter runs.
9. Rudolph was "born to inspire," according to her Olympic teammate Isabelle Daniels Holston.
10. The 1977 television movie *Wilma* told the dramatic story of Rudolph's life.

3. Verbals: Participial Phrases (links to exercise A, p. 73)

➡ **1.** steadily declining, interest

Write the participial phrase in each sentence. Then write the noun modified by the phrase.

1. Many teenagers playing on high school football teams have had to quit because they must work after school.
2. Also, parents worried about their children's grades insist that their teenagers concentrate on academics, not sports.
3. In some schools, severely strained budgets have forced administrators to drop their football programs.
4. As a result, National Football League (NFL) officials say they may have to create special academies promoting high school football.
5. Many future professional players may learn their skills at these football academies established by the NFL.

4. Verbals: Gerund Phrases (links to exercise on p. 75)

➡ **1.** Olympic swimming, OP
   2. having her children learn to swim at an early age, PN

Write the gerund phrase in each sentence. Then tell if the phrase functions as a subject (S), an object of a preposition (OP), a direct object (DO), an indirect object (IO), or a predicate nominative (PN).

1. Swimmer Pablo Morales's goal was making the 1992 Olympic team.
2. Watching Pablo swim at the Olympics was difficult for Pablo's father.
3. Mr. Morales coped with the tension by clutching a picture of his late wife.
4. Spectators applauded Pablo's winning of two gold medals.
5. In 1998 Morales returned to the limelight by heading a list of swimmers to be inducted into the International Swimming Hall of Fame.

5. Verbals: Infinitive Phrases (links to exercise A, p. 77)

→ **1.** *to help people in need:* adverb
2. *To give something back to society:* noun

Write each infinitive or infinitive phrase, indicating whether it functions as an adjective, an adverb, or a noun.

1. After the 1997 Masters golf tournament, Tiger Woods was ready to do something for golf.
2. Woods loves to teach at his golf clinics for children.
3. He is involved in First Tee, a project to build affordable golf facilities.
4. First Tee was created to expand children's opportunities in golf.
5. To make golf more popular and ethnically diverse is the project's ultimate goal.
6. At first, Woods didn't plan to inspire people.
7. Even as a small child, he had a goal to be a championship golfer.
8. In August 1996, Woods sought to win a third consecutive U.S. Amateur Championship.
9. To compete for prize money is one reason Woods turned professional.
10. He became the only rookie in golf history to finish among the top five in five consecutive tournaments.

6. Placement of Phrases (links to exercise on p. 79)

→ **1.** Correct
3. Competing for Stanford University, Lambert was awarded the most-valuable-player trophy at the 1997 NCAA championship.

Rewrite these sentences to eliminate misplaced and dangling phrases. If a sentence has no errors in phrase placement, write *Correct.*

1. To be good at volleyball, many skills are required.
2. A player in several different ways must be able to hit the ball.
3. Three of the most common ways of hitting the ball are "digging," "setting," and "spiking."
4. To make a dig, the ball is hit just before it reaches the floor by a player who lunges or squats.
5. For a set, the ball is hit high in the air so that another player can spike it.
6. Making a spike, the ball is hit hard by a player who jumps high, near the net.

7. Having a height of seven to eight feet, it is difficult for young players to spike over a volleyball net.
8. Consisting of six players, good chemistry is required for a volleyball team.
9. Called the forwards, the three players who stand near the net focus on spiking and on blocking the other team's spikes.
10. Called the backs, digging and setting for the forwards is the focus of the other three players.

4 Clauses and Sentence Structure

1. Kinds of Clauses (links to exercise on p. 93)

→ 1. independent
  2. subordinate

Identify the underlined clauses as subordinate or independent.

1. While some scientists map the human genome, others map the genes of simpler animals.
2. They started with viruses and with bacteria, which are single cells.
3. Some biologists study a worm called *Caenorhabditis elegans*, which has a nervous system like that of complex animals.
4. This worm has a transparent body, which makes it easier to study.
5. The biologists, who thought the worm would have about 6,000 genes, found that it had nearly 20,000.
6. The scientists had to sequence 97 million bases, which are the chemical building blocks of DNA.
7. After they had worked for a number of years, scientists had sequenced 99 percent of the worm's genes.
8. That this was a challenging project is clear.
9. Scientists can learn much from this particular worm because it shares many genes with humans.
10. Whatever scientists learn about the *C. elegans* genome may help in finding cures for some diseases.

2. Adjective and Adverb Clauses (links to exercise A, p. 97)

➡ **2.** when the U.S. Army Air Force bought the first Sierra Sam, started

5. that humans could ride anything

Write the adjective and adverb clauses in the following sentences. After each clause, write the word or words that it modifies.

1. Many diseases, even those that are not hereditary, have a genetic component.
2. After scientists learned how genes work, they found that more than 5,000 diseases are caused by a change in one gene.
3. More than half the people who are living in the world today will probably suffer from some form of genetic disease.
4. One such disease is cancer, which starts when the genetic instructions in cells go wrong.
5. Cancer is often caused by cell mutations that occur late in life.
6. The environment can be a factor in certain kinds of cancer, since exposure to toxic chemicals and radiation can affect cells.
7. Some cancer drugs are called "magic bullets" because they are aimed directly at tumor cells.
8. Another genetic disease is sickle cell anemia, which is caused by a recessive gene.
9. Only a person whose parents both carry the sickle cell gene can get the disease.
10. Although scientists still have a lot to learn, they have made much progress in fighting genetic illnesses.

3. Noun Clauses (links to exercise A, p. 99)

➡ **1.** That birth order influences personality, S

2. that first-born children tend to be more conservative and traditional, DO

Write the noun clause in each sentence. Indicate whether the clause is a subject (S), a direct object (DO), an indirect object (IO), a predicate nominative (PN), or an object of a preposition (OP).

1. Many adoptive parents have feared that their children could suffer from being adopted.
2. Therapists looked for certain problems in whoever was adopted.
3. They thought that adopted children would be more likely than other children to have problems at home and in school.

4. What the therapists overlooked was the large number of adopted children who are well-adjusted.
5. They studied whoever was adopted and ignored other factors.
6. The reason some children are adopted is that they were abused or neglected by their birth parents.
7. That abuse and neglect hurt children is clear.
8. Most adopted children recover from whatever affected them early in life.
9. That is why they are as successful as their peers.
10. What researchers have found in several studies of adopted teens is good psychological health.

4. Sentence Structure (links to exercise A, p. 103)

➡ **2.** CD   **4.** CX

Identify each of the following sentences as simple (SS), compound (CD), complex (CX), or compound-complex (CC).

1. Your first name can be a blessing or a curse, depending on what your parents chose.
2. Some people claim that your name affects your relationships, career, and self-esteem.
3. Whoever has an odd name can overcome it or change it.
4. Every first name has conscious or unconscious associations.
5. Many names have literal meanings; for example, the name Margaret comes from a Greek word meaning "pearl."
6. Frederick means "peaceful," and Kevin means "kind" or "gentle," while Herman means "warrior."
7. Many names can be translated into other languages, so the English "John" becomes "Sean" in Gaelic and "Ivan" in Russian.
8. Some parents name their children after relatives, while others choose names that sound good with their last name.
9. Others can't resist a joke, which is how people have been given the names Candy Barr, Mac Aroni, and Merry Christmas.
10. A couple with the last name Beach named their children Rocky, Coral, Sandy, and Pebble.

5 Writing Complete Sentences

1. Sentence Fragments (links to exercise A, p. 119)
Answers may vary.

➜ 1. People have been baking bread since prehistoric times.
   2. About 4,600 years ago, bakers in Egypt learned how to use yeast to make bread rise.

Rewrite the numbered fragments as complete sentences. You may add words to the fragments or combine them with sentences.

Baking soda is used as an ingredient in batter and dough. The soda reacts with acids in various other ingredients, such as milk or lemon juice, and produces carbon dioxide bubbles. **(1) Cause the batter or dough to expand.** Because of its chemical properties, baking soda has many other uses. **(2) Apart from baking.** It neutralizes acids, including stomach acids. **(3) That can cause acid indigestion.** Because many odors can be traced to acids, baking soda can often be used to neutralize the acids and eliminate the odors. **(4) Have probably seen people using baking soda to absorb odors in refrigerators, closets, and litter boxes. (5) To deodorize a locker filled with sneakers and gym clothes!**

2. Run-On Sentences (links to exercise A, p. 121)
Answers may vary.

➜ 1. Julia Child originally had not prepared for a career in the food industry; in fact, she majored in history in college.
   2. During World War II, Child served with a secret intelligence agency. Her assignments took her around the world.

Correct the run-ons below. (There may be more than one way to fix each run-on.) If a sentence is not a run-on, write *Correct*.

1. Fannie Farmer occupies a special place in the history of food writing, in the late 1800s she invented the modern cookbook.
2. Before Farmer created a recipe format that gave exact measurements, cooks used recipes that advised them to add a "pinch" or a "handful" of an ingredient.
3. Farmer's method ensured that a recipe gave the same results each time, it did not matter who did the cooking.

4. Her approach was an immediate success with the American public, the *Boston Cooking School Cook Book,* her first published work, became a bestseller in the United States and was soon translated into French, Spanish, and Japanese.
5. Think of Fannie Farmer the next time you measure out a teaspoon of this or a cup of that while making your favorite recipe!
6. Irma Rombauer was another groundbreaking cookbook author; her book, *The Joy of Cooking,* is generally considered a classic of the genre.
7. Over the years, three generations of Rombauers have been involved in producing various editions of the book, Rombauer's daughter Marion coauthored a major revision that was published in 1951, and her son Ethan was in charge of the revision that came out in 1997.
8. Perhaps cooking is not exactly your cup of tea, perhaps your taste in reading tends toward humor.
9. If this is the case, you might enjoy the essays of Calvin Trillin.
10. Trillin is an author and humorist who has a keen interest in food he clearly enjoys searching out memorable foods, unusual food facts, and remarkable food rituals to share with his readers.

6 Using Verbs

1. The Principal Parts of a Verb (links to exercise A, p. 133)

➜ **1.** made **2.** seeking

Choose the correct form of the verb in parentheses.

1. Night has (fallen, fell) in Florida.
2. The amateur astronomers (prepared, preparing) their gear carefully before coming outside.
3. Everyone has (bringed, brought) binoculars, a telescope, and insect repellent.
4. They (wear, worn) the stinky salve to ward off mosquitoes.
5. In the past, they had been (ate, eaten) alive by the bloodthirsty attackers.
6. They are discussing their sightings when suddenly a shout (rings, rang) out.

7. One observer has (seen, saw) Jupiter and its moons.
8. At 11 P.M., he (swinged, swings) his telescope around to Jupiter again.
9. He (spotting, spots) something strange.
10. Later, he will (found, find) out that two of Jupiter's moons had (make, made) a rare double shadow on the planet.

2. Forming Verb Tenses (links to exercise on p. 136)

➡ **1.** open   **2.** is reading

Write the correct tense or form of each underlined verb in the passage below.

(1) In this day and age, flying around the world <u>was</u> no big deal. **(2)** However, could a person do in the 20th century what Jules Verne's character <u>does</u> in 1872? **(3)** In 1989 Michael Palin and a BBC TV crew accepted the challenge and <u>are attempting</u> to go by land and sea around the globe in 80 days.

(4) Verne's Phileas Fogg and his servant Passepartout <u>have left</u> on their journey from Charing Cross Station. **(5)** Palin and his crew started in London on a train that <u>leaves</u> from Victoria Station. **(6)** In Saudi Arabia, bureaucrats had restricted train travel, so Palin <u>drives</u> through the desert, but his TV crew flew. **(7)** While they <u>will be crossing</u> the Persian Gulf in a small ship called a dhow, Palin became seasick. **(8)** On their trip across the United States by train, they <u>stop</u> in Colorado and went for a ride in a dogsled.

(9) They <u>return</u> to London at the end of 80 days but missed their station because of a bomb scare. **(10)** In the 21st century, probably some traveler <u>will have tried</u> the trip again, keeping the spirit of adventure alive.

3. Using Verb Tenses (links to exercise on p. 140)

➡ **1.** wonder *or* have wondered   **2.** know

Write the correct tense of each underlined verb.

1. As I <u>am reading</u>, I kept wondering what else could happen to Yossi Ghinsberg.
2. He <u>survives</u> the terrors of the river, but he faced other problems on land.
3. It was growing dark, and Ghinsberg <u>has needed</u> food and shelter.
4. He didn't know whether Kevin <u>is looking</u> for him.

5. At one point, when a deadly snake was within striking distance, Ghinsberg <u>becomes</u> angry.
6. He had been keeping his frustration in check, but he suddenly <u>vents</u> his anger against the snake.
7. Driven by hatred, he <u>has picked</u> up a rock and killed the snake with it.
8. As I eagerly turned the page, I <u>wonder</u>—by morning, will he have eaten the snake?
9. I have never been so hungry that I <u>will think</u> of eating a snake.
10. However, I <u>am never</u> in a fight for survival, so I don't know what I would be capable of doing.

4. Shifts in Tense (links to exercise on p. 143)

➡ 1. saw   2. was traveling

For each sentence below, choose the correct verb from the pair shown in parentheses.

1. Did the creators of the Iditarod know that their race (inspires, would inspire) other races?
2. Crossing Alaska in a dogsled sounds crazy, but a bike race in the snow (seems, seemed) even crazier.
3. Nevertheless, the classic Alaskan race (has given, gives) birth to other races that are run on the Iditarod trail.
4. People call these races the Iditasport; besides biking, they (include, included) running, skiing, and snowshoeing.
5. The snowshoe race covers 75 miles, whereas the bike race (is, was) twice as long.
6. Monique Cole never (races, had raced) until she entered the Iditasport bike race in 1995.
7. The bike race (has become, will become) an obsession for Cole, who has been living in Hawaii.
8. She even (moves, moved) to Colorado, where she trained in the mountains.
9. During the race, she (is pushing, pushed) herself hard and rode the last 60 miles in 19 hours without a break.
10. The winner (has completed, completed) the race only 2 hours sooner than Cole did.

5. Active and Passive Voice (links to exercise on p. 145)

➡ **1.** In 1986, the Russians launched the first section of the space station *Mir*.

2. Years later, Gene Roddenberry created another space station in *Star Trek: Deep Space Nine*.

Rewrite each sentence, changing the verb from the passive voice to the active voice. Change other words as necessary.

1. The International Space Station (ISS) is considered by scientists to be the starting point for future space travel.

2. Space colonies on our moon and on Mars will someday be established by astronauts.

3. In the meantime, the ISS is being built by people from 16 countries.

4. Work on tools and facilities has been done by engineers and designers.

5. Seventy-five space walks to put the station together have been scheduled by NASA.

6. For these walks, special space suits are being made by scientists.

7. An astronaut will be protected from extreme temperatures by the space suit.

8. Because the space gloves are bulky, special tools have been developed by technicians for use by the astronauts.

9. Eventually, the ISS will be lived in by six astronauts.

10. Everything will be recycled by them in order to cut down on the supplies they will need from our planet.

6. The Mood of a Verb (links to exercise on p. 147)

➡ **1.** subjunctive   **2.** indicative

For each numbered item, identify the underlined verb as indicative, subjunctive, or imperative mood.

Dear Ms. I. Knowitall,

(1) You have no idea how hard it <u>is</u> to be a teenager today. **(2)** I wish I <u>were</u> living in the 1800s. **(3)** The principal says, "<u>Wear</u> a uniform," and "Don't arrive at school wearing T-shirts with slogans." **(4)** At the same time, my friends <u>tell</u> me to get tattoos like theirs. **(5)** All of them want me to be like they are, but I just <u>want</u> to be myself. What should I do?

Independent in Idaho

7. Commonly Confused Verbs (links to exercise on p. 149)

➡ **1.** sit   **2.** teaching

Choose the correct verb from the pair shown in parentheses.

1. The lookout (rose, raised) the spyglass and couldn't believe his eyes.
2. (Laying, Lying) beyond the sand dunes was a lagoon filled with hundreds of whales.
3. The captain of the whaling ship couldn't (let, leave) the whales in peace.
4. As he (sat, set) down his spyglass, he ordered the ship to proceed.
5. When the sailors entered the lagoon, they (lay, laid) their lives on the line.

7 Subject-Verb Agreement

1. Agreement in Number (links to exercise A, p. 159)

➡ **1.** The play's setting is a farmhouse in the early 1900s.
   4. Her motive remains a mystery, however.

Rewrite the incorrect sentences so that the verbs agree with the subjects. If a sentence contains no error, write *Correct.*

1. Since the late 1980s, forensic scientists has used a remarkable technique to help solve crimes.
2. The technique is called DNA fingerprinting.
3. DNA "fingerprints" is not the same as the prints made by a person's fingertips.
4. Technicians use cells from a drop of blood, a strand of hair, or another part of the body to develop a DNA fingerprint.
5. The initials DNA stands for deoxyribonucleic acid.
6. This chemical is found in the nucleus of every human cell, and it is the key to each individual's genetic code.
7. Like the fingerprinting long used by police in crime detection, DNA testing have been used to establish a link between a suspect and a crime scene.
8. Some people has been cleared of crimes thanks to DNA fingerprinting.
9. Scientists even uses DNA analysis to help with historical research.
10. For example, one scientist were able to determine that a woman who had for many years claimed to be Anastasia, the

daughter of the last tsar and tsarina of Russia, was not in fact related to the royal family.

2. Words Between Subject and Verb (links to exercise A, p. 161)

➜ **3.** are **5.** join

Correct the subject-verb agreement errors in the sentences below by writing the correct verb forms on a separate sheet of paper. If a sentence contains no error, write *Correct.*

1. The real-life cases of Di Renjie has served as inspiration for detective novels featuring Judge Dee.
2. Di, a Chinese government official, lived during the seventh century A.D.
3. Historical records from the distant past reveals his remarkable detective skills.
4. Robert van Gulik, the creator of the Judge Dee stories, were an avid student of Chinese history.
5. Gulik's portrayal of Judge Dee and his adventures are both entertaining and informative.

3. Indefinite-Pronoun Subjects (links to exercise A, p. 163)

➜ **2.** involves **5.** points

Correct the subject-verb agreement errors in the sentences below by writing the correct verb on a separate sheet of paper. If a sentence contains no error, write *Correct.*

1. Most of Agatha Christie's murder mysteries feature a detective who investigates and solves a crime.
2. In this story, someone invite ten people to a rocky, isolated island.
3. Nobody in the group, it turns out, know why this mysterious person has brought the ten strangers together.
4. All seems to have terrible secrets in their past, however.
5. After dinner on the first night, each are accused of murder by a voice on a phonograph record.
6. Shortly afterward, several of the characters watch as one guest dies of poisoning.
7. Another are found dead the next day.
8. Everyone are terrified when one more murder takes place; eventually, only two people are left on the island.
9. Both now know who the murderer is.
10. Few guesses the surprising twist before it is revealed at the end of the story.

4. Compound Subjects (links to exercise A, p. 165)

→ **1.** have   **3.** has

Write the verb form that agrees with the subject of each sentence.

1. Chester Himes and his detective novels featuring Grave Digger Jones and Coffin Ed Johnson (has, have) paved the way for other African-American detective writers.
2. Neither the detectives nor their creators (is, are) dull or predictable.
3. Marti MacAlister and Blanche White (is, are) two fictional female African-American detectives.
4. Eleanor Taylor Bland and Barbara Neely, the authors who created them, (knows, know) how to tell exciting stories.
5. Problems at home and pressure from colleagues often (causes, cause) stress for MacAlister, the mother of two and the only African-American female detective in her department.
6. Her toughness and intelligence (help, helps) her succeed.
7. Neither her complicated personal life nor her difficult and dangerous cases (overwhelm, overwhelms) her.
8. Intellect and resourcefulness (enables, enable) Blanche White to solve crimes that baffle others.
9. Blanche's job as a cook and housekeeper and her work as an amateur sleuth (expose, exposes) her to all sorts of people and problems.
10. Either the unusual plots or the exploration of social issues within Bland's books (is, are) bound to capture your interest, whether or not you are a devoted reader of mysteries.

5. Other Problem Subjects (links to exercise A, p. 168)

→ **1.** begins   **4.** is

Write the verb form that agrees with the subject of each sentence.

1. "Art and Authenticity" (is, are) an article you might enjoy if you are interested in the subject of art forgery.
2. *The Art of the Faker* also (provides, provide) a wealth of information on this topic.
3. News of forgeries occasionally (makes, make) headlines.
4. The majority of art forgers (fakes, fake) works of art.

5. These days, 10 million dollars (is, are) not an unheard-of price for a painting by a famous artist.
6. Of course, the majority of art forgeries (duplicates, duplicate) the most valuable works.
7. To fight forgery and theft, the staff of a modern museum (spends, spend) a great deal of time, energy, and money on security.
8. Sometimes, two-thirds of a budget (goes, go) toward such security-related expenditures as insurance and the salaries of security personnel.
9. "Famous Forgeries and Fabulous Fakes" (is, are) the title of a lecture series that the university art museum is currently sponsoring.
10. The audience (seems, seem) fascinated by stories of notorious forgeries.

6. Agreement Problems in Sentences (links to exercise A, p. 170)

➜ 2. criminals, appear   3. example, is

Write the subject of each sentence. Then write the verb form that agrees with the subject.

1. From books and television shows (comes, come) stories of criminals who make incredibly stupid mistakes.
2. There (is, are) many dumb crooks out there, according to these sources.
3. Here, for your amusement, (is, are) two of their stories.
4. Into a pen holding several homing pigeons (sneaks, sneak) one unthinking thief.
5. There (is, are) a dealer in town who is willing to buy the birds.
6. (Does, Do) this man and the thief have any brains?
7. Back to their home (flies, fly) the pigeons the very next day!
8. (Is, Are) a thief who leaves obvious clues behind any smarter?
9. Inside one burglarized office, for example, (was, were) a speeding ticket belonging to the burglar, a recently fired employee.
10. (Do, Does) it surprise you to learn that someone would actually use a speeding ticket to prop open the door during a burglary?

8 Using Pronouns

2. Nominative and Objective Cases (links to exercise A, p. 183)

➡ **2.** they **5.** him

Choose the correct form from the pronouns in parentheses.

1. Though most people watch television, (they, them) may not know how a television show is put together.
2. When my friend and (I, me) went to see a show being taped, we learned a lot about how a TV show works.
3. Before the show, we saw workers scurrying around and learned that it is (them, they) who put the scenery, props, and lights in place.
4. We talked to one worker who told us that (she, her) and other technicians were responsible for controlling the lights.
5. (She, Her) explained that just one televised scene may require as many as 20 different lighting instruments.
6. (Us, We) and the others in the audience watched as microphones and cameras were put in place.
7. We saw a man rushing off to the side of the filming area and learned that (he, him) and others worked behind the scenes, in the control room.
8. The director seemed to be everywhere at once; the one responsible for coordinating everyone and everything on the show is (she, her).
9. Before the taping began, makeup was applied to each performer so that (he or she, him or her) would look natural on camera.
10. After a show is taped, the tape is reviewed by the director, corrected by editors, and stored until the time you and (me, I) will see it on our screens.

3. The Possessive Case (links to exercise A, p. 186)

➡ **2.** their, our

Write the possessive pronouns in the following sentences.

1. Residents of the state of Washington are proud of its natural beauty—the rugged mountains, stately evergreen forests, and sparkling lakes and rivers.
2. No one can blame the residents for their boasting.
3. If you like to hike, fish, or ski, you should consider going to Washington for your vacation.
4. Because we live in Washington, many opportunities for

recreation are ours all year long.

5. A recent visitor to Washington expressed her curiosity about Washington's motto, *Alki,* which is an Indian word for "by and by."

6. When settlers landed at Alki Point—now Seattle—they called it "New York Alki" because they hoped that "by and by" their town would be the New York of the West Coast.

7. The people of Stampede Pass, Washington, claim the record for the snowiest town in the United States as theirs; the average yearly snowfall there is 431.9 inches.

8. A favorite fact of mine is that Washington's Grand Coulee Dam is built with enough concrete to pave a four-lane highway from Seattle to New York!

9. What is your favorite fact about Washington?

10. Everyone has a favorite sight, and mine is the snowy slopes of Mount Rainier as seen from an airplane.

4. Using *Who* and *Whom* (links to exercise A, p. 189)

➡ **1.** who **3.** whom

Choose the correct pronoun in parentheses.

1. (Who, Whom) doesn't know at least something about circuses?

2. Few people know much about the remarkable man for (who, whom) the most famous circus is named.

3. P. T. Barnum's life would interest (whoever, whomever) has seen a circus.

4. Barnum, (who, whom) was from Connecticut, moved to New York City when he was in his early 20s.

5. In 1841, his American Museum began drawing many people, (who, whom) came to see such attractions as Jumbo the giant elephant and a mermaid (fake, of course).

6. The museum was successful, but it could be seen only by (whoever, whomever) could travel to New York.

7. (Whom, Who) had Barnum failed to reach?

8. He was sure that if his show could travel, it would attract those (who, whom) were unable to get to New York.

9. In 1871, Barnum took off on a railroad tour, bringing his show within reach of (whoever, whomever) lived in towns along the route.

10. Now the circus comes to many towns, thanks to Barnum, without (who, whom) the show might never have gone on the road.

5. Pronoun-Antecedent Agreement (links to exercise A, p. 192)

→ **1.** their **2.** his

Choose the correct pronoun in parentheses.

1. Mount Everest divides Tibet from Nepal, with Nepal situated on (their, its) south side.
2. Mount Everest was formed about 60 million years ago, but until May 29, 1953, no one had ever climbed to (his, its) highest point.
3. Sir Edmund Hillary and Tenzing Norgay became the first men to do so when (they, he) reached the summit on that date.
4. Hillary, a beekeeper from Auckland, New Zealand, and Tenzing, the son of a farming family from Nepal, first met when (he, they) joined an expedition to climb Everest.
5. When the men began the expedition, (it, they) all dreamed of being the first to reach the summit.
6. Other members turned back, but neither Hillary nor Tenzing wanted to give up (his, their) dream.
7. Either Hillary or Norgay put (his, their) foot on the summit first, but neither would say who did so.
8. Hillary and other climbers have written books about (his, their) experiences conquering the world's highest monutain.
9. Jon Krakauer describes the natural beauty of Mount Everest in (its, his) book *Into Thin Air.*
10. The mountain was named for Sir George Everest in 1865, but (its, his) name in Nepal is Sagarmatha, which means "ocean mother," while in Tibet it is called Chomolungma, or "mother goddess of the universe."

6. Indefinite Pronouns as Antecedents (links to exercise A, p. 195)

→ **1.** their **3.** their

Choose the correct word or words in parentheses.

1. Everyone who values freedom should pay (their, his or her) respects to Harriet Tubman, a onetime slave who became an American hero.
2. In the years before the Civil War, many who escaped slavery owed (his or her, their) freedom to Tubman.
3. Each of the people who traveled on the Underground Railroad was willing to risk (their, his or her) life for the sake of freedom.

4. Several of the people who were abolitionists risked (his or her, their) lives to help slaves reach the north and freedom.
5. After Tubman made her own escape, she joined forces with some of the abolitionists, working with (them, him or her) to liberate others.
6. Each of the 18 trips she made along the Underground Railroad had (its, their) dangers.
7. Most of the journey was fraught with peril up until (their, its) end.
8. Of the more than 300 slaves Tubman guided along the Underground Railroad, no one lost (his or her, their) life or was recaptured.
9. Both of Tubman's parents, whom Tubman helped escape in 1857, owed (his or her, their) freedom to their daughter.
10. Abolition and women's rights were critical issues to Tubman, and both took (its, their) share of her time and energy.

7. Pronoun Reference Problems (links to exercise A, p. 198)

→ 1. Before Xena became a heroine, she honed her warrior skills, but her human skills were lacking.
2. She paid the price for leaving her army by going through the gauntlet.

Rewrite the following sentences to correct instances of indefinite, general, and ambiguous pronoun reference. (There may be more than one way to rewrite a sentence.)

1. In stories and songs, you get the idea that pirates were dashing, elegant characters.
2. Pirates were desperate men who turned to a life of robbery on the high seas, which paints a less romantic picture than the stories.
3. However, as our history book explains, they often chose the outlaw's life because of the cruel and unfair treatment they received working as honest seamen.
4. A rough form of democracy allowed them to choose their own captains and set up rules.
5. In one nonfiction book, it says that pirates set up free colonies of their own, such as Libertatia on the island of Madagascar.
6. The pirates of Libertatia held all the goods in a shared treasury, which they had stolen.
7. Some pirates became national heroes and patriots, which is the subject of an interesting book I read.

8. In the book, they tell how Sir Henry Morgan became commander of English forces in Jamaica and how Jean Laffite helped American forces in the War of 1812.
9. Sir Frances Drake committed acts of piracy. That surprises people who know him only as a famous explorer and navigator.
10. Not only men became pirates; Anne Bonney and Mary Read were pirates along with Captain Kidd and Blackbeard, who were women.

8. Other Pronoun Problems (links to exercise A, p. 201)

➡ **3.** him

Choose the correct pronoun in parentheses.

1. (Us, We) students were interested in finding out the origins of the English names for the days of the week.
2. A trip to the library helped (us, we) researchers find out that four of the seven days are named for characters in Norse mythology.
3. That Wednesday was named for Odin, ruler of the Norse gods, was a surprise to (we, us) students.
4. Tuesday is named for Tyr, a son of Odin, though a less well-known character than (him, he).
5. Thursday was named for Thor, the god of thunder, so two days were named after Odin's sons, (he, him) and Tyr.
6. Friday was named for Frigg, the wife of Odin; when their son Balder died, no one was sadder than (her, she).
7. It was (she, her), Frigg, who was goddess of marriage.
8. If you read about gods in Greek mythology, you may conclude that Norse gods were not as powerful as (they, them).
9. In fact, Balder, (him, he) who was most beloved of all the gods, was killed in one story.
10. Although no one believes in the Norse gods anymore, (we, us) students still like to read stories about them.

9 Using Modifiers

1. Using Adjectives and Adverbs (links to exercise A, p. 212)

→ **1.** *superstitious:* adjective; *still:* adverb
   2. *some:* adjective; *accidentally:* adverb

On a separate sheet of paper, write each italicized word in these sentences, indicating whether it is used as an adjective or an adverb.

1. Youngsters gather *eagerly* around the *respected* elder.
2. For *three* days, they have waited to hear about the *great* thunderbird.
3. The elder speaks so softly that the children can *barely* hear.
4. *Outside,* a storm rages, and everyone is startled by a *deafening* thunderclap.
5. The *patient Sioux* elder smiles *knowingly* and continues the story.
6. The thunderbird must be sitting in its *mountain* tipi and giving *its* approval.
7. The thunderbird has huge, *powerful* wings and an *extremely sharp* beak.
8. The *loudly* rumbling thunder is made by the flapping of the thunderbird's *gigantic* wings.
9. It wears *enormous* robes made of *dark* clouds.
10. It may seem *mysterious,* but the *thunder* being is the guardian of truth.

2. Problems with Modifiers (links to exercise A, p. 216)

→ **3.** badly   **5.** has

For each sentence, write the correct choice of the words in parentheses.

1. While in a department store, a woman (sudden, suddenly) became very sick.
2. She hadn't been doing (anything, nothing) except trying on a fur coat.
3. The doctor examined her (good, well) and found tiny punctures.
4. He (could, couldn't) hardly believe what he was seeing.
5. Her wounds (strong, strongly) indicated that she was a snake-bite victim.
6. Later the store found a coral snake trapped in the sleeve of (that, that there) fur coat.

7. You may have heard a story like (this, this here) one before.
8. It is one of (them, those) urban myths that seems to have an element of truth.
9. It (has, hasn't) never been disputed that coral snakes are poisonous and strike quickly.
10. A story about a deadly snake in a coat sleeve seems (possible, possibly).

3. Using Comparisons (links to exercise A, p. 219)

➡ **2.** best   **4.** colder

For each sentence, write the correct comparative or superlative form.

1. Many squabbles break out among wild horses, but the (fiercer, fiercest) battles are between stallions.
2. The dominant stallion has been the (more victorious, most victorious) one in battle.
3. In the herd, survival of the (fittest, more fit) is the law.
4. In the competition between two stallions, often only the (stronger, strongest) one survives.
5. When a stallion senses a battle, its instincts become (most acute, more acute).
6. Since the dominant stallion has (greater, greatest) strength than a young stallion, the contest is uneven.
7. But a fight to the death against an equal is the (more challenging, most challenging) contest of all for a stallion.
8. A stallion must fight (better, more well) than his challenger.
9. The (less, least) sign of hesitation could cost him his life.
10. His senses are heightened as his challenger comes (closest, closer).

4. Problems with Comparisons (links to exercise on p. 221)

➡ **1.** the scariest film
   2. than any other actor

Correct the illogical or double comparisons in these sentences. If a sentence contains no error, write *Correct*.

1. Can a teenage girl turn into one of the most deadliest monsters?
2. At first Nancy, the newest student at a school for girls, seems no different from any student.

3. Miss Branding, the chemistry teacher, is much more kinder to her than the other teachers are.
4. In truth, she uses Nancy in the most evilest experiment.
5. In her possession is an amulet that is more powerful than any charm.
6. She uses it to put Nancy in a hypnotic trance, which grows more deeper.
7. While under the spell, Nancy is transformed into a vampire, but later she has no memory of even her most worst deeds.
8. Unlike any vampire, Nancy isn't affected by sunlight.
9. She also sleeps in the same kind of bed as everyone in the dormitory.
10. Yet, like other vampires, she dies when a stake is driven through her heart—the most surest way to stop a vampire.

10 Capitalization

1. People and Cultures (links to exercise A, p. 232)

➡ **2.** Ms. Malaika Fisher   **3.** religion

Identify and rewrite the words that contain capitalization errors in the following sentences.

1. My Uncle believes that few people have equaled benjamin Franklin.
2. He was one of the most famous and respected americans of his day.
3. While still in his teens, Franklin wrote a number of newspaper articles under the pen name mrs. silence Dogood.
4. He was famous for scientific research, and his writings on electricity were translated into french and other european languages.
5. During the American Revolution, the United States sought support from France and received it after the defeat of British forces under general Burgoyne at Saratoga.
6. Franklin was chosen to be a Diplomat who would represent the United States in Paris.
7. During his time in Paris, Franklin was an effective negotiator and very popular with the french people.

8. Franklin's son also achieved a position of importance, becoming Governor of the colony of New Jersey.
9. However, governor Franklin sided with the British during the American Revolution and eventually was forced to flee to England.
10. Some of Franklin's best-known writing appeared in his popular series of books called *Poor Richard's Almanack,* which i may read someday.

2. First Words and Titles (links to exercise A, p. 235)

➡ **1.** Each   **2.** *Gettysburg*

Identify and rewrite the words that contain capitalization errors in the following sentences.

1. "Who can tell me," asked the teacher, "The author of these lines?"
2. "Shall I compare thee to a summer's day? thou art more lovely and more temperate."
3. "I'll tell you," she said. "they were written by William Shakespeare, who may have been the greatest writer of all time."
4. We learned that Shakespeare is especially famous for his plays, such as *the tempest.*
5. There are many movie versions of Shakespearean plays, including a new one of *Romeo And Juliet.*
6. I read a review of that movie in *The Los Angeles times.*
7. I wrote a fan letter to the director of the movie; "Dear sir," it began.
8. I closed the letter by writing "Sincerely Yours," and signed my name.
9. Did you know that the musical *West side Story* is based on that play?
10. We'll read the play this year in school, and we'll also read a novel by Charles Dickens, *the Pickwick Papers.*

3. Places and Transportation (links to exercise A, p. 238)

➡ **1.** Liberal, Kansas; United States of America
  4. Buckinghamshire

For each sentence, write correctly the words that contain capitalization errors. If a sentence is correct, write *Correct.*

1. The Eiffel tower is one of the most remarkable buildings in the world.
2. Its designer, Alexandre Gustave Eiffel, also designed the framework for the statue of Liberty.
3. In addition, he was responsible for the design of the locks of the Panama canal.
4. The Eiffel Tower stands in the heart of paris, france.
5. At 984 feet, it was the world's tallest building until 1930, when the Chrysler building topped it.
6. It is located just South of the Seine river.
7. It is probably the most widely recognized monument in Europe.
8. It may be the best-known structure in the western hemisphere.
9. Tourists can get to it by using the municipal subway, called the Metro.
10. This monument is among the most popular tourist attractions in the City.

4. Organizations and Other Subjects (links to exercise A, p. 241)

➡ **1.** April, Purdue University, Bug Bowl   **2.** Correct

For each sentence, write correctly the words that contain capitalization errors. If a sentence is correct, write *Correct.*

1. If you like dogs, you might be interested in an organization called basset hound rescue.
2. The organization looks for caring owners for homeless basset hounds and publicizes its efforts with special events called basset waddles.
3. For example, in Milford, Ohio, the Ohio branch of the organization participates in the Frontier Day parade.
4. In 1999, the Parade took place on Thursday, June 3.
5. In Williamsport, Maryland, the Great Basset ramble began at 11:00 a.m., and more than 100 floppy-eared bassets were present.
6. None of these dogs are apt to win the American Kennel Club Best-of-Breed Award, but many people love them anyway.
7. During the Summer of 1999, Ellicott Creek park in Buffalo, New York, was the setting for the Basset picnic.

8. Carolina Basset Hound rescue, or cbhr for short, raises money and collects dog food at its annual events.
9. Dogs and human beings have been living together since the Stone Age.
10. Someday you might want to contribute a few cans of Happy Snappy dog food to feed a hungry basset hound.

11 Punctuation

1. Periods and Other End Marks (links to exercise A, p. 251)

➡ 1. Can a child learn to play chess at three years of age?
2. Bobby Fischer, the first American to win the world championship, learned the moves of chess at the age of six.

Write these sentences, inserting periods, question marks, and exclamation points as needed.

1. The TV sports announcer said, "The game of squash has been played since the 1700s"
2. Do some research to see if you can find out what squash used to be called
3. You should be able to find out that it was called racquets
4. Do you already know that squash is played with a long-handled racquet and a small ball inside a fully enclosed court
5. Squash was first played by prisoners in London's Fleet Prison, where they bounced the ball off the prison courtyard walls
6. Do you think it's odd that the next group of people to begin playing squash was the British upper class
7. From the prison yard to the elite clubs of the upper class— that's quite a jump
8. A list of sports similar to squash would look like this:
   1 racquetball
   2 jai alai
9. Racquetball was invented in 1949 in Greenwich, Conn, by an American, Joe Sobek
10. Jai alai, which is popular in Mexico and other Spanish-speaking countries, is played on a much larger court and with a 3-ft-long "basket" strapped to each player's arm

2. Commas in Sentence Parts (links to exercise on p. 254)

➡ **1.** yo-yo, brain-squasher **2.** invention

Write the words that should be followed by a comma.

1. Cricket the game that has been a part of village life throughout England for centuries may have begun as early as the 13th century.
2. In fact it is believed to have developed from a game in which country boys bowled a rock at a tree stump or at the gate of a sheep pen.
3. The original bat probably was a long heavy tree branch resembling a hockey stick.
4. Today cricket is played with a straight wooden bat.
5. At first the cricket wicket had two stumps or upright poles; later a third stump was added.
6. In the 1800s in England the modern style of overarm bowling gained popularity.
7. Throwing quickly a bowler can send the ball at a very high speed.
8. Yes cricket has long been popular with women as well as men.
9. For about 100 years cricket has been enjoyed as an international sport by countries that were once colonized by the British.
10. In the history of international cricket there have been only two tied matches: first in 1960 when Australia played the West Indies; second in 1986 when India played Australia.

3. More Commas (links to exercise A, p. 257)

➡ **1.** Scottsdale, Arizona **2.** Correct

Write each word that should be followed by a comma. If no commas are needed in a sentence, write *Correct.*

1. My teacher said "The bow and arrow are believed to have been invented by prehistoric people."
2. By the 900s the Turks had developed a more advanced bow and by the 1100s the crossbow was used extensively in Europe.
3. Although there is evidence that recreational archery was practiced by the ancient Egyptians and Greeks, the bow and arrow were used primarily for hunting and warfare until the late 1500s.
4. In England, archery societies came into being in the 16th and 17th centuries and archery was practiced as a sport by both royalty and the general public.

5. In 1844 the Grand National Archery Society held its first meeting in York England.
6. The first American archery organization founded in 1828, was the United Bowmen of Philadelphia.
7. The National Archery Association, which held its first national tournament in the year of its founding, was established in 1879.
8. The number of people involved in the sport of archery grew tremendously after 1930 and today more than 10 million Americans participate in archery.
9. The world championships which take place every two years began in 1931.
10. Archery contests which can take place at both indoor and outdoor ranges are also part of the Olympic Games.

4. Semicolons and Colons (links to exercise on p. 259)

➜ 1. Greece;

Write each word that should be followed by a semicolon or colon. If a sentence is correct, write *Correct.*

1. Roman ruins excavated in London provided early evidence of ice-skating: leather soles and blades made of animal bones, which date back to 50 B.C.
2. It is believed that the Scandinavian people used ice skates for transportation as early as A.D. 1100 however, the blades of their ice skates were not made of metal, either.
3. Their skate blades were made from shank or rib bones from the following animals: reindeer, oxen, and elk.
4. Ice-skating for recreation is believed to have begun in the 1100s in England prior to that ice skates were used only as a means of transportation.
5. Metal blades were the next breakthrough in skate technology iron blades came first, in 1250, followed by steel blades on wooden soles in about 1400.
6. The first all-steel skates were developed around 1850 by E. W. Bushnell these skates were lighter and stronger than iron skates.
7. The development of the all-steel skate was a turning point for ice-skating: skating clubs opened as the popularity of ice skating increased.
8. Around 1870 an American ballet dancer named Jackson Haines introduced the idea of blending dance movements with ice-skating he is responsible for introducing this approach in Europe as well.

9. The year 1892 was very important in the history of ice-skating the International Skating Union was founded, and the first international speed-skating and figure-skating competitions were held.
10. Both figure skating and speed skating have been included in the Winter Olympics since 1924 however, women were not included in the speed-skating competition until 1960.

5. Quotation Marks (links to exercise A, p. 262)

➡ 1. "Whoever wants to know the heart and mind of America," one famous educator wrote, "had better learn baseball."
2. "Most young Americans learn about this game, and they delight in stories about legendary players like Babe Ruth and Joe DiMaggio," said my teacher, Mr. Richards.

Write the following sentences, inserting quotation marks and commas where necessary. If the sentence is correct, write *Correct.*

1. Has anyone ever had a coach who was crazy about using motivational quotations? Mindy asked her friends.
2. Mark answered, My football coach used to quote Vince Lombardi and say, Coaches who can outline plays on a blackboard are a dime a dozen. The ones who win get inside their players and motivate.
3. Michael Jordan was my basketball coach's favorite, said Sarah.
4. She continued, He used to tell us how Michael once said, You have to expect things of yourself before you can do them.
5. My wrestling coach liked to quote Muhammad Ali, added Joe.
6. Coach told us that Muhammad Ali said, It's a lack of faith that makes people afraid of meeting challenges, and I believed in myself, which is pretty similar to what Michael Jordan said, quipped Joe.
7. Some coaches use motivational quotes to get you to work better together as a team, Karl said.
8. He continued, My baseball coach liked to quote Babe Ruth, who reportedly said, The way a team plays together as a whole determines its success. You may have the greatest bunch of individual stars in the world, but if they don't play together, the club won't be worth a dime.
9. When my tennis coach wants us to watch videos, added Ryan, he even quotes the skier Jean-Claude Killy, who said, The best and fastest way to learn a sport is to watch and imitate a champion.
10. Mindy couldn't help but laugh as she said, Well, now I don't feel so strange about my coach using quotations!

6. Other Punctuation (links to exercise on p. 267)

➜ **1.** (heavenly bodies that move in large elliptical orbits about the sun)

2. a comet's characteristics

Proofread the following sentences for punctuation errors, inserting hyphens, apostrophes, dashes, and parentheses where necessary. If a sentence is correct, write *Correct.*

1. The roller skate may have been invented by the Belgian inventor and musical-instrument maker Joseph Merlin in the 1760s.

2. However, in 1863, James Plimpton of Medford, Massachusetts, designed the first practical four wheel skate.

3. Plimptons skate caused quite a stir both at home and abroad.

4. It led to the first great roller skating craze to spread over the United States and western Europe.

5. Many rinks most of them used for recreation were built at this time.

6. The late 1900s saw a change in the materials used to construct roller skate wheels.

7. In the mid-1970s, the traditional wooden or metal wheels gave way to lightweight polyurethane wheels. Some still prefer the old metal wheels.

8. Skaters wishes for wheels that were quieter than wooden or metal wheels and that would allow them to move more smoothly were granted with the invention of the polyurethane wheel.

9. During the 1980s, skates with in line wheels gained popularity.

10. In this type of skate, a single row of wheels is used in place of the standard four wheeled rectangular design.

7. Italics (links to exercise A, p. 269)

➜ **1.** *marathon*

Write these sentences, underlining words that should be italicized. Also, indicate which words, if any, are incorrectly italicized. If a sentence is correct, write *Correct*.

1. Rodeo is a sport that involves a series of contests and exhibitions derived from the skills of cowboys and cowgirls of the *Old West.*
2. The word rodeo also refers to a rodeo contest.
3. Although mainly confined to the United States, Canada, and Mexico, *rodeos* are also held in Australia.
4. Rodeos came into being when cowhands got together at the end of cattle-drives and competed for various unofficial titles (best roper, best bull rider, best bucking horse rider, *etc.*).
5. A *paid spectator rodeo* was first held in Denver, Colorado, in 1887.
6. The five main rodeo events are steer wrestling, bareback bronc riding, saddle bronc riding, calf roping, and bull riding.
7. Steer wrestling is also known as *bulldogging.*
8. A bronc, also known as a bronco or bucking bronco, is an unbroken range horse.
9. *Barrel racing,* in which a saddle horse races around a series of barrels, is a women's event at most rodeos.
10. An interesting book to read in order to learn more about rodeos is American Rodeo: From Buffalo Bill to Big Business by Kristine Fredriksson.

Guidelines for Spelling

Forming Plural Nouns

To form the plural of most nouns, just add **-s.**

> **prizes**   **dreams**   **circles**   **stations**

For most singular nouns ending in **o,** add **-s.**

> **solos**   **halos**   **studios**   **photos**   **pianos**

For a few nouns ending in **o,** add **-es.**

> **heroes**   **tomatoes**   **potatoes**   **echoes**

When the singular noun ends in **s, sh, ch, x,** or **z,** add **-es.**

> **waitresses**   **brushes**   **ditches**   **axes**   **buzzes**

When a singular noun ends in **y** with a consonant before it, change the **y** to **i** and add **-es.**

> **army—armies**   **candy—candies**   **baby—babies**
> **diary—diaries**   **ferry—ferries**   **conspiracy—conspiracies**

When a vowel **(a, e, i, o, u)** comes before the **y,** just add **-s.**

> **boys—boys**   **way—ways**   **array—arrays**
> **alloy—alloys**   **weekday—weekdays**   **jockey—jockeys**

For most nouns ending in **f** or **fe,** change the **f** to **v** and add **-es** or **-s.** Since there is no rule, you must memorize such words.

> **life—lives**   **calf—calves**   **knife—knives**
> **thief—thieves**   **shelf—shelves**   **loaf—loaves**

For some nouns ending in **f,** add **-s** to make the plural.

> **roofs**   **chiefs**   **reefs**   **beliefs**

Some nouns have the same form for both singular and plural.

> **deer**   **sheep**   **moose**   **salmon**   **trout**

For some nouns, the plural is formed in a special way.

> **man—men**   **goose—geese**   **ox—oxen**
> **woman—women**   **mouse—mice**   **child—children**

For a compound noun written as one word, form the plural by changing the last word in the compound to its plural form.

> **stepchild—stepchildren**   **firefly—fireflies**

If a compound noun is written as a hyphenated word or as two separate words, change the most important word to the plural form.

> **brother-in-law—brothers-in-law**   **life jacket—life jackets**

Forming Possessives

If a noun is singular, add **'s.**

    mother—my mother's car   Ross—Ross's desk

Exception: the **s** after the apostrophe is dropped after *Jesus'*, *Moses'*, and certain names in classical mythology (*Zeus'*). These possessive forms, therefore, can be pronounced easily.

If a noun is plural and ends with **s,** just add an apostrophe.

    parents—my parents' car   the Santinis—the Santinis' house

If a noun is plural but does not end in **s,** add **'s.**

    people—the people's choice   women—the women's coats

Spelling Rules

Words Ending in a Silent *e*

Before adding a suffix beginning with a vowel to a word ending in a silent **e,** drop the **e** (with some exceptions).

    amaze + -ing = amazing   love + -able = lovable
    create + -ed = created   nerve + -ous = nervous

Exceptions: *change + -able = changeable; courage + -ous = courageous*

When adding a suffix beginning with a consonant to a word ending in a silent **e,** keep the **e** (with some exceptions).

    late + -ly = lately   spite + -ful = spiteful
    noise + -less = noiseless   state + -ment = statement

Exceptions include *truly, argument, ninth, wholly,* and *awful.*

When a suffix beginning with **a** or **o** is added to a word with a final silent **e,** the final **e** is usually retained if it is preceded by a soft **c** or a soft **g.**

    bridge + -able = bridgeable   peace + -able = peaceable
    outrage + -ous = outrageous advantage + -ous = advantageous

When a suffix beginning with a vowel is added to a word ending in **ee** or **oe,** the final **e** is retained.

    agree + -ing = agreeing   free + -ing = freeing
    hoe + -ing = hoeing   see + -ing = seeing

Words Ending in *y*

Before adding a suffix to a word that ends in **y** preceded by a consonant, change the **y** to **i.**

easy + -est = easiest   crazy + -est = craziest
silly + -ness = silliness   marry + -age = marriage

Exceptions include *dryness, shyness,* and *slyness.*

However, when you add **-ing,** the **y** does not change.

empty + -ed = emptied   but   empty + -ing = emptying

When adding a suffix to a word that ends in **y** preceded by a vowel, do not change the **y** to **i.**

play + -er = player   employ + -ed = employed
coy + -ness = coyness   pay + -able = payable

Exceptions include *daily* and *gaily.*

Words Ending in a Consonant

In one-syllable words that end in one consonant preceded by one vowel, double the final consonant before adding a suffix beginning with a vowel, such as **-ed** or **-ing.** These are sometimes called 1+1+1 words.

dip + -ed = dipped   set + -ing = setting
slim + -est = slimmest   fit + -er = fitter

The rule does not apply to words of one syllable that end in a consonant preceded by two vowels.

feel + -ing = feeling   peel + -ed = peeled
reap + -ed = reaped   loot + -ed = looted

In words of more than one syllable, double the final consonant (1) if the word ends with one consonant preceded by one vowel or (2) if the word is accented on the last syllable.

be•gin´   per•mit´   re•fer´

In the following examples, note that when the suffix is added, the accent remains on the same syllable.

be•gin´ + -ing = be•gin´ ning = beginning
per•mit´ + -ed = per•mit´ ted = permitted

In the following examples, the accent does not remain on the same syllable; thus, the final consonant is not doubled.

re•fer´ + -ence   = ref´ er•ence = reference
con•fer´ + -ence = con´ fer•ence = conference

Prefixes and Suffixes

When adding a prefix to a word, do not change the spelling of the base word. When a prefix creates a double letter, keep both letters.

dis- + approve = disapprove   re- + build = rebuild
ir- + regular = irregular   mis- + spell = misspell
anti- + trust = antitrust   il- + logical = illogical

When adding **-ly** to a word ending in **l,** keep both **l**'s. When adding **-ness** to a word ending in **n,** keep both **n**'s.

careful + -ly = carefully   sudden + -ness = suddenness
final + -ly = finally   thin + -ness = thinness

Special Spelling Problems

Only one English word ends in **-sede:** *supersede.* Three words end in **-ceed:** *exceed, proceed,* and *succeed.* All other verbs ending in the "seed" sound are spelled with **-cede.**

concede   precede   recede   secede

In a word in which **ie** or **ei** is used to represent the long **e** sound, use **ei** after **c** and **ie** in all other cases (with some exceptions).

| *i* before *e:* | thief | relieve | piece | field | grieve | pier |
| except after *c:* | conceit | perceive | ceiling | receive | receipt |

Exceptions: *either, neither, weird, leisure, seize*

Commonly Misspelled Words

abbreviate
accidentally
achievement
amateur
analyze
anonymous
answer
apologize
appearance
appreciate
appropriate
argument
associate
awkward
beginning
believe
bicycle
brief
bulletin
bureau
business
calendar
campaign
candidate
certain
changeable
characteristic
column
committee
courageous
courteous
criticize
curiosity
decision
definitely
dependent
description
desirable
despair
desperate

development
dictionary
different
disappear
disappoint
discipline
dissatisfied
efficient
eighth
eligible
eliminate
embarrass
enthusiastic
especially
exaggerate
exceed
existence
experience
familiar
fascinating
February
financial
foreign
fourth
fragile
generally
government
grammar
guarantee
guard
height
humorous
immediately
independent
indispensable
irritable
judgment
knowledge
laboratory
license

lightning
literature
loneliness
marriage
mathematics
minimum
mischievous
mortgage
necessary
nickel
ninety
noticeable
nuclear
nuisance
obstacle
occasionally
occurrence
opinion
opportunity
outrageous
parallel
particularly
permanent
permissible
persuade
pleasant
pneumonia
possess
possibility
prejudice
privilege
probably
psychology
pursue
realize
receipt
receive
recognize
recommend
reference

rehearse
repetition
restaurant
rhythm
ridiculous
sandwich
schedule
scissors
seize
separate
sergeant
similar
sincerely
sophomore
souvenir
specifically
strategy
success
surprise
syllable
sympathy
symptom
temperature
thorough
throughout
tomorrow
traffic
tragedy
transferred
truly
Tuesday
twelfth
undoubtedly
unnecessary
usable
vacuum
vicinity
village
weird
yield

Commonly Confused Words

Good writers master words that are easy to misuse and misspell. Study the following words, noting how their meanings differ.

accept, except | *Accept* means "to agree to" or "to receive willingly." *Except* usually means "not including."
Did the teacher *accept* your report?
Everyone smiled for the photographer *except* Jody.

adapt, adopt | *Adapt* means "to make apt or suitable" or "to adjust." *Adopt* means "to opt or choose as one's own" or "to accept."
The writer *adapted* the play for the screen.
After years of living in Japan, she had *adopted* its culture.

advice, advise | *Advice* is a noun that means "counsel given to someone." *Advise* is a verb that means "to give counsel."
Jim should take some of his own *advice*.
The mechanic *advised* me to get new brakes for my car.

affect, effect | *Affect* means "to move or influence" or "to pretend to have." *Effect* as a verb means "to bring about." As a noun, *effect* means "the result of an action."
The news from South Africa *affected* him deeply.
The band's singer *affects* a British accent.
The students tried to *effect* a change in school policy.
What *effect* did the acidic soil produce in the plants?

all ready, already | *All ready* means "all are ready" or "completely prepared." *Already* means "previously."
The students were *all ready* for the field trip.
We had *already* pitched our tent before it started raining.

all right | *All right* is the correct spelling. *Alright* is nonstandard and should not be used.

a lot | *A lot* may be used in informal writing. *Alot* is incorrect.

altogether, all together | *Altogether* means "completely." *All together* means "as a group."
The news story is *altogether* false.
Let's sing a song *all together*.

anywhere, **nowhere,** **somewhere,** **anyway**	are all correct. *Anywheres, nowheres, somewheres,* and *anyways* are incorrect. **I don't see geometry mentioned *anywhere.*** ***Somewhere* in this book is a map of ancient Sumer.** ***Anyway,* this street map is out of date.**
between, among	are prepositions. *Between* refers to two people or things. The object of *between* is never singular. *Among* refers to a group of three or more. **Texas lies *between* Louisiana and New Mexico.** **What are the differences *among* the four candidates?**
borrow, lend	*Borrow* means "to receive something on loan." *Lend* means "to give out temporarily." **He *borrowed* five dollars from his sister.** **Please *lend* me your book.**
bring, take	*Bring* refers to movement toward or with. *Take* refers to movement away from. **I'll *bring* you a glass of water.** **Would you please *take* these apples to Pam and John?**
can, may	*Can* means "to be able" or "to have the power to." *May* means "to have permission to." *May* can also mean "possibly will." **Vegetables *can* grow nicely without pesticides.** **We *may* not use pesticides on our community garden.** **Pesticides *may* not be necessary, anyway.**
capital, capitol, **Capitol**	*Capital* means "excellent," "most serious," or "most important." It also means "seat of government." A *capitol* is a "building in which a state legislature meets." The *Capitol* is "the building in Washington, D.C., in which the U.S. Congress meets." **Proper nouns begin with *capital* letters.** **Is Madison the *capital* of Wisconsin?** **Protesters rallied at the state *capitol.*** **A subway connects the Senate and the House in *the Capitol.***
choose, chose	*Choose* is a verb that means "to decide or prefer." *Chose* is the past-tense form of *choose.* **He had to *choose* between art and band.** **She *chose* to write for the school newspaper.**

desert, **dessert**	*Desert* (des´ ert) means "a dry, sandy, barren region." *Desert* (de sert´) means "to abandon." A *dessert* (des sert´) is a sweet, such as cake. **The Sahara in North Africa is the world's largest *desert*.** **The night guard did not *desert* his post.** **Alison's favorite *dessert* is chocolate cake.**
different from	is used to compare dissimilar items. *Different than* is nonstandard. **The hot sauce is very *different from* the yogurt sauce.**
differ from, **differ with**	*Differ from* means "to be dissimilar to." *Differ with* means "to disagree with." **The racing bike *differs* greatly *from* the mountain bike.** **I *differ with* her as to the meaning of Hamlet's speech.**
farther, further	*Farther* refers to distance. *Further* refers to something additional. **We traveled 200 miles *farther* that afternoon.** **This idea needs *further* discussion.**
fewer, less	*Fewer* refers to numbers of things that can be counted. *Less* refers to amount, degree, or value. ***Fewer* than ten students camped out.** **We made *less* money this year on the walkathon than last year.**
good, well	*Good* is always an adjective. *Well* is usually an adverb that modifies an action verb. *Well* can also be an adjective meaning "in good health." **Dana felt *good* when she finished painting her room.** **Angela ran *well* in yesterday's race.** **I felt *well* when I left my house.**
imply, infer	*Imply* means "to suggest something in an indirect way." *Infer* means "to come to a conclusion based on something that has been read or heard." **Josh *implied* that he would be taking the bus.** **From what you said, I *inferred* that the book would be difficult.**
its, it's	*Its* is a possessive pronoun. *It's* is a contraction of *it is* or *it has*. **Sanibel Island is known for *its* beautiful beaches.** ***It's* great weather for a picnic.**

kind of, sort of	Neither of these two expressions should be followed by the word *a*. **What *kind of* horse is Scout?** **What *sorts of* animals live in swamps?** The use of these two expressions as adverbs, as in "It's kind of hot today," is informal.
lay, lie	*Lay* is a verb that means "to place." It takes a direct object. *Lie* is a verb that means "to be in a certain place." *Lie* and its past form *lay* never take direct objects. **The carpenter will *lay* the planks on the bench.** **My cat likes to *lie* under the bed.**
lead, led	*Lead* can be a noun that means "a heavy metal" or a verb that means "to show the way." *Led* is the past-tense form of the verb. ***Lead* is used in nuclear reactors.** **Raul always *leads* his team onto the field.** **She *led* the class as president of the student council.**
learn, teach	*Learn* means "to gain knowledge." *Teach* means "to instruct." **Enrique is *learning* about black holes in space.** **Marva *teaches* astronomy at a college in the city.**
leave, let	*Leave* means "to go away from." *Leave* can be transitive or intransitive. *Let* is usually used with another verb. It means "to allow to." **Don't *leave* the refrigerator open.** **She *leaves* for Scotland tomorrow.** **The Cyclops wouldn't *let* Odysseus' men *leave* the cave.**
like	as a conjunction before a clause is incorrect. Use *as* or *as if*. **Ramon talked *as if* he had a cold.**
loan, lone	*Loan* refers to "something given for temporary use." *Lone* refers to "the condition of being by oneself, alone." **I gave that shirt to Max as a gift, not a *loan*.** **The *lone* plant in our yard turned out to be a weed.**
lose, loose	*Lose* means "to mislay or suffer the loss of." *Loose* means "free" or "not fastened." **That tire will *lose* air unless you patch it.** **My little brother has three *loose* teeth.**

majority refers to more than half of a group of things or people that can be counted. It is incorrect to use *majority* in referring to time or distance, as in "The majority of our time there was wasted."

Most of our time there was wasted.

The *majority* of the students study a foreign language.

most, almost *Most* can be a pronoun, an adjective, or an adverb, but it should never be used in place of *almost,* an adverb that means "nearly."

Most of the students enjoy writing in their journals. (pronoun)

Most mammals give birth to live young. (adjective)

You missed the *most* exciting part of the trip. (adverb)

Almost every mammal gives live birth. (adverb)

of is incorrectly used in a phrase such as *could of.* Examples of correct wordings are *could have, should have,* and *must have.*

I *must have* missed the phone call.

If you had played, we *would have* won.

principal, *Principal* means "of chief or central importance" or
principle refers to the head of a school. *Principle* means "a basic truth, standard, or rule of behavior."

Lack of customers is the *principal* reason for closing the store.

The *principal* of our school awarded the trophy.

One of my *principles* is to be honest with others.

quiet, quite *Quiet* refers to "freedom from noise or disturbance." *Quite* means "truly" or "almost completely."

Observers must be *quiet* during the recording session.

We were *quite* worried about the results of the test.

raise, rise *Raise* means "to lift" or "to cause to go up." It takes a direct object. *Rise* means "to go upward." It does not take a direct object.

The maintenance workers *raise* the flag each morning.

The city's population is expected to *rise* steadily.

real, really *Real* is an adjective meaning "actual" or "true." *Really* is an adverb meaning "in reality" or "in fact."

Real skill comes from concentration and practice.

She doesn't *really* know all the facts.

seldom	should not be followed by *ever,* as in "We seldom ever run more than a mile." *Seldom, rarely, very seldom,* and *hardly ever* all are correct. **I *seldom* hear traditional jazz.**
set, sit	*Set* means "to place" and takes a direct object. *Sit* means "to occupy a seat or a place" and does not take a direct object. **He *set* the box down outside the shed.** **We *sit* in the last row of the upper balcony.**
stationary, stationery	*Stationary* means "fixed" or "unmoving." *Stationery* means "fine paper for writing letters." **The wheel pivots, but the seat is *stationary.*** **Rex wrote on special *stationery* imprinted with his name.**
than, then	*Than* is used to introduce the second part of a comparison. *Then* means "next in order." **Ramon is stronger *than* Mark.** **Cut the grass and *then* trim the hedges.**
their, there, they're	*Their* means "belonging to them." *There* means "in that place." *They're* is a contraction of *they are.* **All the campers returned to *their* cabins.** **I keep my card collection *there* in those folders.** **Lisa and Beth run daily; *they're* on the track team.**
way	refers to distance. *Ways* is nonstandard and should not be used in writing. **The subway was a long *way* from the stadium.**
whose, who's	*Whose* is the possessive form of *who. Who's* is a contraction of *who is* or *who has.* ***Whose* parents will drive us to the movies?** ***Who's* going to the recycling center?**
your, you're	*Your* is the possessive form of *you. You're* is a contraction of *you are.* **What was *your* record in the 50-yard dash?** ***You're* one of the winners of the essay contest.**

SPELLING

Index

in signaling abrupt change of
thought, 266
Dates
apostrophes to show missing
numbers in, 265
commas in, 256, 270
Days, capitalization of, 240
Declarative sentences, 45, 63
punctuation for, 250
Definite articles, 17
Demonstrative pronouns, 11
as adjectives, 210
Dependent clauses, 92
Details
adding, with phrases, 84–85
adding supporting, 294
Diagramming, 54–56, 80–83
adjective clauses, 105
adverb clauses, 105
appositive phrases, 81
complex sentences, 105–106
compound-complex sentences, 107
compound sentences, 104
compound subjects, 54
compound verbs, 54
direct objects, 56
gerund phrases, 82
indirect objects, 56
infinitive phrases, 82–83
noun clauses, 106
participial phrases, 81
predicate adjectives, 55
predicate nominatives, 55
prepositional phrases, 80
simple sentences, 104
simple subjects, 54
simple verbs, 54
subject complements, 55
subjects, 54
verbs, 54
Direct address, nouns of, commas to
set off, 253
Directions, capitalization of, 236–237
Direct objects, 52, 62
as complements, 52
diagramming, 56
gerund phrases as, 74
noun clauses as, 98
with transitive verbs, 14
capitalizing first word of, 233
Divided quotations, 260

capitalization in, 233, 260
quotation marks for, 260
Double comparisons, 220
Double negatives, 214–215

E

Ellipses, 268
Elliptical causes, 200
Emphatic form of verb, 134
End marks, 250–251. *See also*
Exclamation points; Periods;
Question marks
with ellipsis points, 268
Essays.
quotation marks to enclose titles of,
262
Essential appositive, 69
Essential clauses, 94, 95
Ethnic groups, capitalization of, 231
Exclamation points
with exclamatory sentences, 45, 63,
251
with imperative sentences, 45, 63
with strong interjection, 29, 251
with parenthetical information, 266
with quotation marks, 261
Exclamatory sentences, 45, 63, 251

F

Family relationships, capitalization of,
231, 246
Figurative language, 297
first, using commas after, 252
First words, capitalization of, 233, 246
Foreign phrases, italics to set off, 268
Foreign words, italics to set off, 268
Fractions, use of hyphens in, 264
Future perfect progressive tense,
139, 154
Future perfect tense, 135, 139
Future progressive tense, 139, 154
Future progressive verbs, 134
Future tenses, 134, 135, 139

G

Gender, pronoun-antecedent agreement
in, 191
Gender-free language, 191

RESOURCES

INDEX

apostrophes to show omission of, 265

O

Object
  direct, 52, 62
  indirect, 52, 62
Objective case, 180, 182, 187, 206
Object of a preposition, 23–24
  gerund phrases as, 74
Objects of verbs, 52–53. *See also* Direct Objects; Indirect Objects
Organizations, capitalizing names of, 239
Outlines
  capitalizing first words of entries in, 234
  periods after numbers or letters in, 250

P

Paragraphs
  improving, 298–299
Parentheses, to set off material that is loosely related to sentence or paragraph in which it occurs, 266
Participial phrases, 71, 88
  dangling, 72, 78
  diagramming, 81
  misplaced, 72
  placement of, 287
Participles, 71
  past, 71
  present, 71
  use of, as adjectives, 210
Parts of letter, capitalization of, 234
Parts of speech. *See* Adjectives; Adverbs; Conjunctions; Interjections; Nouns; Prepositions; Pronouns; Verbs
Passive voice, 144–145, 289
  changing active voice to, 144
Past participles, 71, 130, 286
Past perfect progressive tense, 138
Past perfect tense, 135, 138
Past progressive tense, 138
Past progressive verbs, 135
Past tenses, 134, 138
Periods

after each number or letter in outline or list, 250
after initials, 250
after most abbreviations, 250
with declarative sentences, 63, 250
with imperative sentences, 63, 250
quotation marks with, 261
with sentences containing indirect questions, 250
Person, pronoun-antecedent agreement in, 191
Personal pronouns, 9, 180, 185
  nominative case of, 180, 181
  objective case of, 180, 182
Personal titles, capitalization of, 230
Phrases, 64–89, 117
  adding detail with, 84–85
  appositive, 69, 88
  checklist for, 89
  dangling, 72, 78
  diagramming, 80–83
  as fragments, 117
  gerund, 74–75, 88
  infinitive, 76–77, 88
  misplaced, 72, 78
  participial, 71–72, 88
  placement of, 78–79
  prepositional, 23–24, 66–67, 88
  verb, 15
Place names, commas in, 256
Planes, capitalizing names of, 237
Plays. *See also* Dramatic scenes
  capitalizing important words in titles of, 234
  italics to set off titles of, 269, 275
Plural indefinite pronouns, 162
Plural nouns, 6
  spelling, 341
Poems
  capitalizing first word of, 233
  capitalizing important words in titles of, 234
  italics for titles of, book-length, 269, 275
  quotation marks to enclose titles of, 262, 275
Positive form of modifier, 217
Possessive case, 180, 185–186, 187, 206
Possessive nouns, 7
  apostrophes in, 265

Q

INDEX

R

raise, rise, 148
References
    ambiguous, 197
    general, 196
    indefinite, 196
Reflexive pronouns, 11
Regular verbs, 130
Relative adverbs, 94
Relative pronouns, 12, 94
    to introduce noun clauses, 98
Religious terms, capitalization of, 231
rise, raise, 148
Run-on sentences, 101, 120–121
    fixing, 126, 127, 279

S

Scene, setting, with modifiers, 222–223
School subjects, capitalization of, 240
Science reports, 122–123
second, using commas after, 252
Semicolons
    before conjunctive adverb, 258
    in forming compound sentences,
        101, 112, 258
    quotation marks with, 261
    in series, 258
Sentence fragments, 38, 93, 116–118
    correcting, 126, 278
Sentences
    beginning with *here* and *there,* 47
    capitalizing first word of, 233
    checklist for editing, 63
    complete, 36, 92
    complex, 102, 112, 113
    compound, 101, 108, 112, 113
    compound-complex, 102, 108, 112,
        113
    declarative, 45, 63, 250
    diagramming, 54–56
    exclamatory, 45, 63
    imperative, 45, 48, 63, 250
    improving weak, 290
    interrogative, 45, 48, 63
    inverted, 47, 63, 169
    placement of subjects in, 47–48
    predicate in, 38, 41, 62
    relative pronouns in combining, 12
    run-on, 101, 120, 126, 127, 279

    simple, 101, 108, 112, 113
    structure of, 108–109
    subject in, 38, 41, 62
    subjects in inverted, 63
    and subject-verb agreement, 169
    varying beginnings of, 292
    varying structure of, 293
    in vivid writing, 108–109
Series
    commas in, 252
    semicolons in, 258
set, sit, 148
Short stories,
    capitalizing important words in titles
        of, 234
    quotation marks to enclose titles of,
        262, 275
Simple predicates, 38, 62
Simple sentences, 101, 112, 113
    diagramming, 54–56, 104
Simple subjects, 38, 62
    diagramming, 54
Simple verbs, diagramming, 54
Singular indefinite pronouns, 162
Singular nouns, 6
sit, set, 148
Slang, avoiding, 295
Songs, quotation marks to enclose
    titles of, 262, 275
Special events, capitalization of, 240
Spelling, 341–345
    commonly misspelled words, 345
    plural nouns, 341
    possessives, 342
    prefixes and suffixes and, 344
    words ending in consonants, 343
    words ending in *y,* 343
    words ending with silent *e,* 342
    words ending with the "seed"
        sound, 344
Stores, capitalization of names, 239
Subject complements, 50
    diagramming, 55
Subjects, 38, 62
    complete, 41
    diagramming, 54
    gerund phrases as, 74
    in inverted sentences, 63
    placement of, in sentences, 47–48
    simple, 38–39, 62
    words between verb and, and

subject-verb agreement, 160
Subject-verb agreement, 156–177,
    280–281
    and amounts, 167, 176
    and collective nouns, 166, 176
    and compound subjects, 164, 176
    fixing, 280–281
    and indefinite pronoun, 162, 176
    and inverted sentences, 169, 177
    and nouns ending in s, 166, 176
    in number, 158
    and predicate nominatives, 169, 177
    for sentences beginning with here or
        there, 47, 169–170, 177
    and time, 167, 176
    and titles, 167, 176
    and words between subject and
        verb, 160, 176
Subjunctive mood, 146
Subordinate clauses, 92, 113
    combining, in creating complete
        sentences, 92
    in forming complex sentences, 102
    in forming compound-complex
        sentences, 102
    as fragments, 118
    relative pronouns to introduce, 12
    to vary sentence structure, 109
    who and whom to introduce, 188
Subordinating conjunctions, 26–27
    to introduce adverb clause, 96
    to introduce noun clauses, 98
Suffixes,
    spelling words with, 344
Superlative form of modifiers, 217

T

teach, learn, 148
Television
    capitalization of titles of shows, 234
    italics for titles of shows, 269, 275
    quotation marks for titles of shows,
        262
that
    as demonstrative pronoun, 11
    in introducing essential clause, 95
there, sentences beginning with, 47
this, as demonstrative pronoun, 11
those, as demonstrative pronoun, 11
Time

abbreviations for, 240
and subject-verb agreement, 167
Titles of written works
    capitalizing important words in, 234,
        246
    italics for, 275
    quotations marks for, 275
    and subject-verb agreement, 167
Transitive verbs, 14

U

Underlining. See Italics
Universe, bodies of, capitalizing, 237

V

Verbals
    gerund phrases, 74
    infinitive phrases, 76
    participial phrases, 71
Verb phrases, 15
Verbs, 14–16, 128–155
    action, 14, 16, 35
    auxiliary, 15, 286
    commonly confused, 148–149
    compound, 43
    conjugation of, 134, 135
    definition of, 14
    diagramming, 54
    helping, 15, 286
    intransitive, 14
    irregular, 131, 286
    linking, 14–15, 35
    mood of, 146–147
    objects of, 52–53
    principal parts of, 130–132
    regular, 130
    transitive, 14
    words between subject and, and
        subject-verb agreement, 160
Verb tenses, 134–143
    in describing events, 150–151
    emphatic form, 134
    fixing, 286
    future, 134, 139
    future perfect, 135, 139
    future perfect progressive, 135, 139
    future progressive, 139
    past, 134, 138
    past perfect, 135, 138

RESOURCES

Acknowledgments

For Literature and Text

Susan Bergholz Literary Services: Excerpt from *How the Garcia Girls Lost Their Accents* by Julia Alvarez. Copyright © 1991 by Julia Alvarez. Published by Plume, an imprint of The Penguin Group (USA). Originally published in hardcover by Algonquin Books of Chapel Hill. Reprinted by permission of Susan Bergholz Literary Services, New York. All rights reserved.

Brandt & Hochman Literary Agents: Excerpt from "The Most Dangerous Game" by Richard Connell. Copyright © 1924 by Richard Connell. Copyright renewed © 1952 by Louise Fox Connell. Reprinted by permission of Brandt & Hochman Literary Agents, Inc.

James Hurst: Excerpt from "The Scarlet Ibis" by James Hurst. Copyright © 1960 by The Atlantic Monthly and renewed 1988 by James Hurst. Reprinted by permission of James Hurst.

Men's Fitness: Excerpt from "Marathon Man" by Michael Konik, *Men's Fitness,* October 1998. Copyright © 1998 by Men's Fitness. Reprinted by permission of Men's Fitness. All rights reserved.

Putnam Berkley: "Two Kinds," from *The Joy Luck Club* by Amy Tan. Copyright © 1989 by Amy Tan. Reprinted by permission of Putnam Berkley, a division of Penguin Group (USA) Inc.

Reader's Digest: Excerpt from "Tales Out of School" contributed by Liz Bassett, *Reader's Digest,* November 1998. Copyright © 1998 by the Reader's Digest Association, Inc. Used by permission of Reader's Digest.

University of New Mexico Press: Excerpt from "The Great Taos Bank Robbery," from *The Great Taos Bank Robbery and Other Indian Country Affairs* by Tony Hillerman. Copyright © 1973 by Anthony G. Hillerman. Reprinted by permission of the University of New Mexico Press. All rights reserved.

University of Pittsburgh Press: Excerpt from "The Bass, the River, and Sheila Mant," from *The Man Who Loved Levittown* by W. D. Wetherell. Copyright © 1985 by W. D. Wetherell. Reprinted by permission of the University of Pittsburgh Press.

Art Credits

TABLE OF CONTENTS   v top Illustration by Daniel Guidera; **bottom** © Copyright Getty Images; **vi, vii, viii** Illustrations by Daniel Guidera; **ix** © Jim Cummins/Getty Images; **x** Illustration by Daniel Guidera; **xi** © Copyright Getty Images; **xii** Corbis/Charles O'Rear; **xiii, 1** Illustrations by Daniel Guidera.

COVER © Ryan Aldrich/McDougal Littell

CHAPTER 1   2, 3 © Ron Chapple/Getty Images; **4 background** © Corbis/Henry Diltz; **top** © Getty Images; **6** Photo courtesy of the Chicago Symphony Orchestra; **18** © Getty Images; **19** Copyright 1997, Brooke McEldowney. Distributed by the Los Angeles Times Syndicate. Reprinted by permission; **21 background** © Getty Images; **foreground** *Ludwig van Beethoven* (1819), Josef Karl Stieler. © The Art Archive/Corbis; **25** © Corbis/Robert Holmes; **30** © Getty Images; **31** Photo by Sharon Hoogstraten.

CHAPTER 2   **36 background** © Getty Images; **40** Calvin and Hobbes © 1989 Watterson. Dist. by Universal Press Syndicate. Reprinted with permission. All rights reserved; **42** © 1995 Dan McCoy/The Stock Market; **46** IN THE BLEACHERS © 1996 Steve Moore. Reprinted with permission of UNIVERSAL PRESS SYNDICATE. All rights reserved; **57** © Tribune Media Services, Inc. All rights reserved. Reprinted with permission; **58** © Getty Images.

CHAPTER 3   **64** © Getty Images; **72** © Tribune Media Services, Inc. All rights reserved. Reprinted with permission; **84** Photo by Sharon Hoogstraten; **86** AP/Wide World Photos; **88 left, right** © Getty Images.

CHAPTER 4   **90** AP/Wide World Photos; **92** Farkas family. From a private collection; **100** Foxtrot © 1995 Bill Amend. Reprinted with permission of Universal Press Syndicate. All rights reserved; **108 background** © H. Armstrong Roberts; **foreground** © L.L.T. Rhodes/Animals Animals.

CHAPTER 5   **114 background** © Burke: Triolo/FoodPix/PNI; **foreground** Photo by Sharon Hoogstraten; **117** © Getty Images; **122 center** Photo by Sharon Hoogstraten; **top right** © 1997 Peter Menzel; **123** © 1998 Peter Menzel.

CHAPTER 6   **128 background** Detail of *The Road to Oregon* (1933), William Henry Dethief Koerner. 26 1/8″ x 40 1/8″. Buffalo Bill Historical Center, Cody, Wyoming. 6922.1. Gift of Ruth Koerner Oliver. © The Art Archive; **foreground** © Getty Images; **137, 138, 139** © Luiz C. Marigo/Peter Arnold, Inc.; **141** © Tribune Media Services, Inc. All rights reserved. Reprinted with permission; **145** NASA; **148 background** © F. Stuart Westmorland/AllStock/PNI; **foreground** © Getty Images; **150 foreground** Illustration by Nobee Kanayama © 1997 McDougal Littell Inc.

CHAPTER 7   **156** Tabletop by Sharon Hoogstraten; **171** © 1999 Zits Partnership. Reprinted with special permission of King Features Syndicate; **172** Photo by Sharon Hoogstraten.

CHAPTER 8   **178 top left** Photofest; **top right** © Frank Connor/Photofest; **182** © Getty Images; **184** Tournament in King Arthur's court. MS Douce 383, fol. 16r. The Bodleian Library, Oxford, England; **186** Photograph © Courtney Milne; **192** Corbis/Lindsay Hebberd; **194** Corbis/Hulton-Deutsch Collection.

CHAPTER 9   **208** © Getty Images; **212** Calvin and Hobbes © 1986 Watterson. Dist. by Universal Press Syndicate. Reprinted with permission. All rights reserved; **218** © Getty Images; **222 background** Photo by Sharon Hoogstraten; **foreground** © Getty Images; **223** © Corbis/Bettmann; **226** © 1992 Thaves. Reprinted with permission.

CHAPTER 10   **228** AP/Wide World Photos; **232 background** © SuperStock; **233** AP/Wide World Photos; **237** Culver Pictures; **240–243** © Getty Images.

CHAPTER 11   **256 center left** © Terry E. Eiler/Stock, Boston/PNI, **bottom** Peanuts reprinted by permission of United Feature Syndicate, Inc.; **261** © Jim Cummins/Getty Images; **268** © Christopher Morris/Black Star/PNI; **270** © Getty Images; **271 bottom right, bottom left** © 1998–1999 EyeWire, Inc. All rights reserved; **bottom center** © Getty Images.

The editors have made every effort to trace the ownership of all copyrighted material found in this book and to make full acknowledgment for its use. Omissions brought to our attention will be corrected in a subsequent edition.